Mortal Men, Immortal Warriors

Mortal Men, Immortal Warriors

Books may be purchased in quantity and/or special sales by contacting the publisher, Writer's Guild Publishing House, by email at wg.aubg@gmail.com.

Published by: Writer's Guild Publishing House; Blagoevgrad, Bulgaria

Interior Design by: Diana Elagina

Cover Design by: Steven London

Editing by: Ivaylo Urdev; Xenia Cotlearova

Creative Consultant: Steven London

ISBN: 9781980971467

10 9 8 7 6 5 4 3 2 1

1. Anthology 2. Military History 3. War 4. Afghanistan 5. United States Army

First Edition

This book is dedicated to the Warriors, their families, and the Afghan people. May we all find the balance between what we left behind and what we brought back.

Table of Contents

History builds its foundation upon the backs of warriors by eternalizing mortal men in mythical proportions. During the height of the Roman Empire, following military conquests, the public often focused on the victorious General at the forefront of victory marches. Very few noticed the slave who would whisper into the commander's ear *"Memento mori"* The meaning of those words served as a reminder to even the greatest leaders and soldiers of their own mortality. This served as a means of keeping egos in check between the hubris of triumph and the reality that captured the losses incurred in attaining such victories.

In modern conflict, very little has changed in respect to the philosophy behind war. Empires rise. Soldiers fall. Life continues. But a divide between citizens and soldiers exists and has widened to the point that we tend to take for granted the necessity of heroes in our lives. This book helps bridge that divide and provide an alternative to understanding war outside the scopes of news media or history books.

The stories, interviews, photographs and other aspects of this book only scratch the surface of fully showcasing the feats of the Warriors in Afghanistan. Just as their predecessors, these men, their families, and the Afghan people who supported their efforts bore an incredible burden throughout nearly seven continuous years of fighting alongside each other – on both the battlefield and home fronts. The war in Afghanistan still looms on since its inception in 2001, long after the Warriors were called home in 2011. Words alone cannot serve the justice required to enshrine these men and their actions and experiences.

It is with that knowledge that I am honored to present to you, the reader, a humbled attempt at preserving their legacy for generations to come. Not all of us came home - whether physically, mentally, or spiritually. Some men died fighting alongside their brothers while others lost personal battles to their demons after returning to "normalcy". This book is my gift to my fellow Warriors: past, present, and future – that you may be immortalized through written account and never forgotten.

Noli Me Tangere

Steven London
SGT (RET), US Army

HISTORY OF THE 1ST BATTALION, 4TH INFANTRY LINEAGE

[BRIAN HAMMOND]

18 December 2009

The 1st Battalion, 4th Infantry has served in the defense of the United States for over two hundred years. The Battalion traces its lineage to the original Fourth United States Infantry, which was organized as the Infantry of the Fourth Sub-Legion on September 4, 1792 - only four years after the adoption of the Federal Constitution. The Infantry of the Fourth Sub-Legion fought at Miami Rapids in 1794. In 1796 it redesignated into the Fourth Regiment of the Infantry. The Regiment existed for ten years, as a youthful country experimented with building a military force to serve its needs. Due to a reduction in the Army the regiment disbanded in 1802.

In 1861, the Fourth Infantry moved to Washington D.C., to become part of the garrison in defense of the capitol, during the Civil War. The Regiment's first engagement of the Civil War took place between April and May 1862 during the Siege of Yorktown. The Fourth witnessed Lee's surrender at Appomattox. The former Lieutenant U.S. Grant, then commanding the Armies of the Union, never forgot the Fourth Infantry with which he had served in Mexico and the many Indian Wars. As recognition of its valor during the Civil War, he named the Fourth Infantry as the guard unit at his headquarters for Lee's surrender.

The Fourth Infantry boasts many accolades for bravery. On July 2, 1901, 2nd Lieutenant Allen J. Greer of the 4th Infantry was near Majada, Laguna Province, Philippine Islands, when he charged alone into an insurgent outpost with his pistol, killing one, wounding two, and capturing three insurgents with their rifles and equipment. For his courageous act, 2nd Lieutenant Greer received the Medal of Honor. On November 23, 1901, 1" LT. Louis J. Van Schaick, pursued a band of insurgents, near Nasugbu, Batangas, Philippine Islands, where he first emerged from a canyon to the sight of a column of insurgents. Fearing the insurgents might turn, he dispatched his men as they emerged one by one from the canyon, galloped forward and closed in on the insurgents. His actions threw the insurgents into confusion until the arrival of others from his detachment. For his actions, 1st Lieutenant Van Schaick received the Medal of Honor.

In 1902, the Regiment returned to San Francisco, having circled the globe. The Regiment returned to the Philippines for another tour from 1903 until 1906. In October 1906 the Regiment moved to Wyoming in time to stop the Ute uprising - its last campaign against hostile Indians. In 1908, the Regiment received orders to the Philippines for a third time and remained there until 1910.

In 1917, the United States entered World War I. On October 1, 1917, the Fourth became assigned to 3rd Division. Stationed at Fort Brown, Texas, the Regiment recruited and trained up to strength and on the first anniversary of the United States' entry into the war, left for France. The Fourth Infantry disembarked at Brest, France in 1918 and participated in the defensive actions of Aisne, Chateau-Thierry, Champagne Marne, and in the Aisne-Warne, St. Michiel, Meusse-Argonne offensives. The entire Regiment earned the French Croix de Guerre for their actions. Having lost eighty percent of its men, under constant and grueling fire during thirty days on the line, the 60th Infantry replaced and relieved the Regiment.

On October 7, 1918, near Cunel, France, PFC John L. Barkley, Company K, 4th Infantry took up an observation post half a kilometer from the German line. On his own initiative he repaired a captured enemy machine gun and mounted it onto a disabled French tank near his post. Shortly afterward, when the enemy launched a counterattack against US forces, PFC Barkley entered the tank and waited under the hostile barrage until the enemy line was abreast of him. He then opened fire, completely breaking up the counterattack and killing and wounding a large number of the enemy. Five minutes later an enemy 77-millimeter gun opened fire on the tank pointblank. One shell struck the drive wheel of the tank, but he nevertheless remained inside the tank and after the barrage ceased PFC Barkley broke up a second enemy counterattack. His actions enabled US forces to gain and hold Hill 25. PFC Barkley received the Medal of Honor for his actions.

On November 9, 1918, the Fourth received orders to move on a moment's notice. The men knew they were to take part in the final drive to encircle Metz, in the event the Germans did not accept terms of the proposed armistice. The Fourth made preparations for departure on the morning of November 11th, when French villagers heralded the end of the war; shouts of *"Viva la Americus"*-*"Viva les Allies"*-*"Fini la Cuerre"* echoed through the air following the German surrender. The Fourth Infantry served as part of the Army of Occupation in France until 1919.

After returning to the United States, the Fourth Infantry moved to Camp Pike, Arkansas, and then to Camp Lewis, Washington, the site of which contained part of the tribal grounds of Chief Leschi, the Regiment's enemy in 1855-56. In June of 1922, the Regimental headquarters, headquarters and service companies and 2nd Battalion of the Regiment relocated to Fort George Wright, Washington, while the other two Battalions occupied Fort Missoula, Montana and Fort Lawton, Washington. On February 19, 1925, the unit earned permission to wear the red-green-red patch. The Fourth Infantry became the only US Army unit to wear a non-metal unit crest.

The 1st Battalion, 4th Infantry pioneered military development of the Strategic Alaskan territory. The rest of the regiment arrived shortly after and started clearing ground for what is now Fort Richardson. It became the first organization of such size to arrive in Alaska. The Fourth formed the nucleus for the Alaskan Defense command to deter a Japanese invasion of Alaska. The Japanese began to build up forces on the southern-most Alaskan Islands and the Fourth fought its first major battle of the war, the Battle of Attu, on the Japanese-held Island. On May 8, 1943, soldiers of the Fourth climbed over the sides of their transport ships to land on Massacre Bay. Major John D. O'Reilly, Commander of the Battalion, who later received a battlefield promotion to Lieutenant Colonel for outstanding leadership, reported to Major General Landrem. Carrying extra rations and ammunition, the troops marched directly into a battle sector and engaged the enemy less than 24 hours after they landed. On Attu Island, the First Battalion fought the Japanese at altitudes of 2000 feet on snow-covered mountains. Moving north along the high west ridge of Chichagof Valley on May 21, 1943, the Battalion came up against strong enemy opposition from machine gun and sniper positions. Later that day, the Battalion moved along the ridge to a point where it established visual contact with other American forces that had proceeded inland from the Holtz Bay area, on the opposite side of the Island.

After five straight days of strong enemy opposition, the First Battalion pulled to the rear to rest and prepare for their next mission. After a day's rest, the First Battalion received the task of clearing entrenched Japanese defenders from the high peaks of Fish Hook Ridge. Covered only by mortar and machine gun fire, troops of Company A scaled steep cliffs while facing heavy enemy fire. The spectacle fascinated observers watching the action from a distance. Small groups of clearly visible soldiers slowly inched their way up to the enemy-held peaks. One observer later stated that the scene resembled a Hollywood adventure movie rather than reality. On May 27, 1943, with many wounded or killed soldiers, the Battalion finally secured a portion of a high rock on the northeast end of the ridge which provided them a commanding position overlooking the main ridge running east toward the Chichagof Valley.

The fighting continued into the night and by 1900 hours on the next day, the Fourth Infantry's battle-weary troops had accomplished their mission. Company A received the Presidential Unit Citation (PUC) for its heroism during the attack on the peaks. The next day, the American invasion force engaged and defeated 1,000 Japanese in a suicide counter-attack near Sarana Valley. The Fourth resumed the task of combing the area of Chichagof Valley by active patrolling, hunting out and capturing or killing Japanese stragglers. This turned out to be the last engagement with the Japanese for the regiment. The Japanese had been driven from Alaska's Aleutian Islands, and the Fourth Infantry had added another battle streamer to the 29 already on its colors (no other unit in the Army could boast so many). But the Fourth paid a high price with approximately five officers and sixty enlisted men killed during the conflict.

In the fall of 1943 the Fourth returned to the United States and after consolidating the Regiment at Fort Lewis, Washington, it moved in early 1944 to Fort Benning, Georgia, where it served as demonstration troops for the Infantry School. On November 1, 1945, the Fourth Infantry took assignment to the 25th Infantry Division and saw two years of occupation duty in Japan. The unit inactivated on January 31, 1947, at Osaka, Japan, returned to the United States and concluded its assignment to the 25th Division on February 1, 1947.

In May 1983, the First Battalion of the Fourth Infantry began to reorganize to the Division 86 concept in the Army of Excellence program by President Ronald Reagan, guarding the Pershing Missiles sites in Germany. This caused the Battalion to expand to four rifle companies, an anti-armor company and a very large Headquarters and Headquarters company.

In May 1984, the First Battalion of the Fourth Infantry transitioned to the Bradley Infantry Fighting Vehicle. The unit completed its transition in August 1984. In the late 1980's the US government again initiated reduction of the armed forces and listed the First Battalion, Fourth Infantry for inactivation. The inactivation took place on December 16, 1987, and relieved the Fourth Infantry from assignment to the 3d Infantry Division.

On November 16, 1990, the 1st Battalion, 4th Infantry reactivated in Hohenfels, Germany, under the 7th Army Training Command to serve as a permanent OPFOR, Motorized Rifle Regiment Opposing Force. The Combat Maneuver Training Complex activated in 1986, but the training units had to supply their own opposing forces. In Hohenfels, the 1-4 IN fully developed and trained in OPFOR tactics to support Brigade and Battalion-level maneuvers using electronic systems to monitor and record every movement and battle action in near-real time for an unbiased assessment of the task forces' performance. Take-home data packages served home station reviews and subsequent training in weak areas.

In 1998, the US Army realized in its strategic assessment that the old OPFOR tactics based off of Cold War/Warsaw Pact doctrine no longer held relevance. The Army deemed that future threat would come from disenfranchised minorities, power struggles in a global community and technological proliferation ideology. On September 11, 2001, the Army's 1998 assessment became a reality with the terrorist attacks on the United States. Army Chief of Staff, Gen. Eric K. Shinseki, authorized the immediate training of the new and still unfinished OPFOR doctrine. This new doctrine of Contemporary Operational Environments (COE) highlights a wider spectrum of operations, increased unpredictability, and more complexity, driving BLUEFOR training objectives.

OPFOR missions include: conduct an attack, conduct a defense, and conduct insurgent operations. OPFOR capabilities include: organic anti-tank fires, area and zone reconnaissance, employment of combat security outposts, air-mobile operations, deliberate and hasty breaches, insurgent cell replication, complex ambushes, and IED attacks. The Battalion includes tankers as well as infantrymen, along with various other MOS fields in a normal battalion-sized organization. 1-4 Infantry's fame is well known throughout USAREUR as THE unit to beat.

The battalion has trained units deploying to Bosnia, Kosovo, Iraq, and Afghanistan during High Intensity Conflict Rotations, and Mission Readiness Exercises. Additionally, the Battalion has deployed forces to other countries to take part in training exercises to include the training of security forces for the 2004 Summer Olympics in Athens, Greece.

AN OVERVIEW OF 1-4 INFANTRY'S AFGHANISTAN DEPLOYMENTS

[MARVIN WIDEMAN JR.]

In August 2004, the Battalion deployed Company A to Afghanistan in support of Operation Enduring Freedom. Team Apache earned the Meritorious Unit Commendation (MUC) for its outstanding performance of duty as the only US force in the International Security Assistance Force from August to December 2004.

The MUC citation reads:

During the period of 31 August to 12 December 2004, Company A, 1st Battalion, 4th Infantry distinguished themselves while in support of the International Security Assistance Force operations led by the North Atlantic Treaty Organization in Afghanistan. They provided superb support to coalition forces supporting a safe and successful Afghanistan National Presidential Election. Throughout the operation the company performed as a lethal, responsive, and relevant combat force directly responsible for supporting security and stabilization forces in theater. Their ability to respond to crisis was superb. Company A, 1st Battalion, 4th Infantry's efforts reflect great credit upon themselves, the North Atlantic Treaty Organization, and the United States Army.

In August 2005 the Battalion deployed Company D to Afghanistan in support of Operation Enduring Freedom. Team Dragon worked as a force protection company for the newly formed Afghanistan elections. Team Dragon received the Joint Meritorious Unit Commendation for its outstanding performance of duty. After a successful mission most of Team Dragon returned November 2006.

Starting in July 2006 and ending in January 2011, the 1st Battalion, 4th Infantry relieved its sister battalion in Zabul Province, Afghanistan, as part of ISAF's [1] assumption of responsibility for the province. As part of TF [2] Zabul, nominally under Romanian command, 1-4 Infantry maintained a reinforced infantry company in the mountainous northern regions of the province, responsible for all combat operations in that area.

---

[1] ISAF: International Assistance Force
[2] TF: Task Force

The Battalion rotated companies every 7 to 8 months, starting with C Company, followed in turn by B, A, and D companies.

In July 2006, Cherokee Company of the 1st Battalion, 4th Infantry Regiment deployed to the Zabul District of Afghanistan. This deployment started the Battalion's rotational commitment in support of OEF [3] and NATO ISAF missions. TF Warrior retained responsibility for 13 forward operating bases (FOB) and combat outposts (COP). C/1-4 assumed responsibility for COPs Mizan, Baylough, and Lane in Northern Zabul, leaving the Romanian Infantry to patrol Highway 1. The headquarters for the Romanian-American (RO-AM) Battle Group (BG) would remain at FOB Lagman in the Qalat District. In order to maintain a direct link between the Romanian and American forces, a field grade officer from 1-4 IN held the position of deputy RO-AM BG Commander. Through the work of the Deputy Commander, the efforts of Romanian forces and U.S. forces synchronized to effectively achieve the NATO mission in Afghanistan. This deployment marked the beginning of the 1-4 IN continuous deployments to Zabul Province.

During this period, the Battalion lost its first Soldier in combat since World War II. On 30 October 2006, CPL Isaiah Calloway, 23, of Jacksonville FL, made the ultimate sacrifice when his unit came into small-arms contact with enemy forces in the Marah Valley. His platoon, along with U.S. Special Forces and Afghan Army elements, conducted counter-insurgency operations when they came under extreme hostile enemy fire in a narrow mountain pass. CPL Calloway immediately returned fire, engaging several insurgents before being fatally wounded. The resulting firefight and Close Air Support strikes left up to 70 enemy personnel dead. After seven months of combat operations, Team Cherokee redeployed to Hohenfels, Germany in late 2007.

Beginning in 2010, the 1st Battalion, 4th Infantry Regiment became the longest continuously deployed unit in the Army. The Battalion established its mission through 2010 with the following directive:

1st Battalion, 4th Infantry Regiment conducts Full Spectrum combat operations in the COE to provide realistic joint and combined arms training conditions that develop USAREUR training units for success on current and future battlefields. On order, deploy forces to conduct combat operations in support of the Global War on Terror.

---

[3] OEF: Operation Enduring Freedom

In pursuit of this mission, 1-4 IN began 2010 with Team Apache deployed to Zabul Province, Afghanistan, with all other Companies actively performing in the Opposing Forces (OPFOR) role for the Joint Multinational Readiness Center (JMRC).

On 26 March 2010, the 1st Battalion, 4th Infantry Regiment welcomed home Team Apache, who over the course of their deployment, successfully constructed 3 fully functional Combat Outposts (COP) along Highway 1 and assisted their Romanian allies in maintaining freedom of movement along Highway 1. On March 1, 2010, Team Dragon deployed to Zabul Province, Afghanistan replacing Team Apache. 1-4 IN continued its role as the longest continuously deployed battalion in the Army. Team Dragon began combined operations with Afghan National Security Forces (ANSF), focusing on the population, in order to increase the operational capability of the ANSF and to defeat Taliban forces operating in their area of operations (AO). Over their 7 month deployment, Team Dragon organized and controlled a combined U.S., Romanian, and Afghan Tactical Operations Center (TOC). This TOC further facilitated the growth of a strong partnership between the Armies of Romania and the United States and served to further train the ANSF in TOC operations, thus increasing their operational capability as a standalone force.

In addition, Team Dragon conducted daily combined patrols and frequent meetings with the local political and tribal leadership in order to discuss security issues and develop plans for the improvement of the local area for the future of Afghanistan. Acting as the main effort, Team Dragon executed Operation (OPN) Kwandi Dukan, OPN Tor Asp, OPN Watchdog, and OPN Mountain Shape, each conducted as joint operations. Taking the lead on these operations, Team Dragon partnered with the Combined Joint Special Operations Task Force (CJSOTF) and served as the Supporting Effort on OPN Mountain Shark, OPN Sea Serpent, and OPN Sea Serpent II, each with the mission of capturing provincial and regional High Value Individuals (HVI).

Team Dragon worked under the operational control of the Romanian-American (RO-AM) Battle Group and partnered with the 3rd Kandak of the Afghan National Army as well as the local Afghan police and intelligence units. As a result of this focus on the combined operations, Team Dragon not only achieved their mission, but also facilitated the improvement of NATO and Afghan partners. Operating out of the Shajoy District of Zabul Province, Team Dragon assisted the Romanians

8

and the Provincial Reconstruction Team (PRT) in multiple projects to improve the Afghan infrastructure and security. This included the completion of 3 underground irrigation canal renovation projects and the establishment of a commerce support program staffed with 350 Afghan security personnel who provided additional security to the bazaar.

In the Summer of 2010, as Team Dragon prepared to redeploy to Hohenfels, Germany, General Ham, the United States Army Europe (USAREUR) Commanding General, decided to end 1-4 IN's commitment as a deployed force in support of the International Security Assistance Force (ISAF) in Afghanistan. 1-4 IN held responsibility for one more Company rotation, supported by Team Cherokee. In keeping with GEN Ham's order, Team Dragon shifted operational responsibility of its AO to the 2nd Stryker Cavalry Regiment (2SCR). As part of this effort, Team Dragon transferred COP Baylough, the site of heavy fighting and the most remote of 1-4 IN's Combat Outposts. Equally critical, Team Dragon signed over all property and executed a battle handover with the leadership of 2SCR, ensuring a smooth transition of responsibility. Finally, Team Dragon reconsolidated into a small area of responsibility (AOR) in preparation for the final deployment in of 1-4 IN's nearly 7-year commitment to the mission of Operation Enduring Freedom.

Team Dragon returned to Hohenfels, Germany on 23 September 2010, having completed a successful tour of duty in Afghanistan. Team Dragon suffered casualties resulting in 17 soldiers wounded in action (WIA) and three soldiers killed in action (KIA). Additionally, two soldiers from Team Dragon received the Army Commendation Medal with Valor Device for their actions during combat.

On 30 August 2010, Team Cherokee began their third deployment to Afghanistan. This would be the final Company to deploy from 1-4 IN in support of the NATO ISAF mission in Afghanistan. Team Cherokee occupied and completed the construction of 2 COPs that Team Dragon had initiated concerning COP Bullard and COP Al Masak in the Shajoy District of Zabul Province. Within the Shajoy District, Team Cherokee, partnering with the 5th Special Forces Group, the 812th Romanian Infantry Battalion, and ANSF, conducted village stability operations in an effort to secure the local area and develop constructive relationships with the local populous. Team Cherokee completed its primary mission to successfully close out the 1-4 IN mission in Afghanistan. Their success marked the end of a five-year commitment to the ISAF NATO mission and ended the deployment of the longest continuously deployed unit in the United States Army. Team Cherokee returned to Hohenfels in early January 2011. Over the course of their deployment, Team Cherokee suffered casualties which resulted in four soldiers WIA. Cherokee Company's redeployment back to Hohenfels, Germany, marked a close to the final deployment of 1st Battalion, 4th Infantry Regiment in the Global War on Terrorism.

Having completed its mission in Afghanistan, the 1st Battalion, 4th Infantry Regiment renewed its current mission as follows:

The 1st Battalion, 4th Infantry Regiment conducts Full Spectrum Operations (FSO) at JMRC and on ETCs replicating the Operational Environment IOT provide realistic joint and combined arms training conditions that develop USAREUR, NATO, and other partnered units for success on current and future battlefields. All companies at 1-4 IN are currently working to support this mission and to support all units who travel to JMRC for their mission readiness training.

Through the years the 4th Infantry, through a tradition of bravery and courage has served its country well, and today the 1st Battalion, 4th Infantry stands proud and ready as USAREUR's **"MEN IN BLACK!"**... **WARRIORS!**

JON WRIGHT [2004]

I first arrived to Hohenfels, Germany, in October of 2003. I had been assigned to Alpha Company 1-4 IN [4]. As soon as I showed up to the Company my squad leader introduced himself and asked me if I looked forward to deploying. I said yes and then he responded with, "*Well, too bad because this is a non-deployable unit.*" At 19 years old and with Iraq going on I was crushed to be unable to deploy. But that would change. Nine months later we deployed to Afghanistan and started working out of Camp Julien in Kabul – a camp which the Canadians ran. I remember landing in Afghanistan and then riding out to Camp Julien. That intense experience filled my nerves. The insane traffic in Kabul forced me to think "*Wow. We're going to die right there in this traffic jam.*" We arrived at Camp Julien and completed our normal weeklong in-processing of classes on ROE [5] and customs before we could roll out the gate. The time during the week seemed to stretch indefinitely just because I wanted to get out and go on patrols.

This deployment showed it uniqueness in many ways. We became the first soldiers from 1-4 IN to deploy since World War II, the first American forces to work with NATO [6], and we were tasked to help with security for the very first presidential election in Afghanistan. ISAF [7] included NATO troops working together. The awesomeness of this deployment became one of the many reasons why I stayed in the Army for almost ten years.

At 20 years old (then) I thought "*Wow. This is it. I am here in combat ready to kick some ass.*" Well that didn't exactly happen. We conducted patrols, over-watches, and provided security for the polling trucks during the elections. I really enjoyed the patrols we led outside of the city; I thought that this was my chance to see some shit. This deployment didn't compare to the other ones that I would later go on, where you could say I was in the shit. No this was a five month deployment.

The worst thing that happened to my Company occurred when my squad leader SSG [8] M. had been shot in the leg on an ambush that had been set in place for us. This happened on Halloween in 2004. A suicide grenade

---

[4] IN: Infantry
[5] ROE: Rules of Engagement
[6] NATO: North Atlantic Treaty Organization
[7] ISAF: International Security Assistance Force
[8] SSG: Army rank of Staff Sergeant

attack occurred in downtown Kabul earlier in the day on what we called Chicken Street. We carried out the task to a patrol the area. We dismounted three guys at a time and moved the gun truck two or three blocks ahead and then rotated once the three guys got to the truck. My squad leader, another soldier (SPC [9] E.), the terp [10] and myself moved second in this rotation. I still remember SSG M. talking to us about the Gulf War and his first firefight; he said his asshole puckered up real quick.

The first team came to us and we moved out of the truck and began our push. As soon as the trucks left and we moved, we were immediately ambushed with small arms fire. SSG M. went down with a gunshot wound to his ankle. A ditch full of shit right next to us provided us cover and the capability to return fire. We called for our truck to come back and take SSG M. to nearest camp we could get to. During this time I was thinking *that's it, it sure wasn't like the movies*. Movies capture only a sliver of the realities of combat. In real life people get hurt. We finished the rest of the deployment with no further incidents. We conducted patrols and more security over-watch for the elections until December when we redeployed back to Germany.

Overall this deployment provided its own moments of boredom. We played a lot of spades, exercised a lot, and talked a lot of shit to each other. But this deployment would help make decision on staying in the Army. There is an *esprit de corps* that you learn when serving alongside your military brothers in arms. And it is a bond that is difficult to break. I would later go on to do two more deployments: one to Iraq, and another to Afghanistan. These deployments didn't compare to my first one with 1-4 IN, and my last one to Afghanistan was really tough. My time with 1-4 IN helped shape and prepare me for future combat deployments.

---

[9] SPC: Army rank of Specialist
[10] Terp: interpreter

TOM AMBROSETTI [2005]

MONDAY 01 AUG - THURSDAY 04 AUG 2005

We have been up at the Rhein Ordnance Barracks for what seems like forever now, even though this is our fourth day here. I guess it was asking too much to leave on the day they told us we would – the 31st.

I think by the time we reached the loading area on Monday, I was hyped to go. I haven't really found it easy to motivate myself about this whole thing. Perhaps it's because I'm thinking too much, yet again. If I continue to read too much into this whole thing, it'll be a miserable trip. So I'll have to put aside all my thoughts on the "War on Terror" for now and take each day as it comes, focusing on the small picture that concerns me as opposed to the big picture which doesn't.

The past few days haven't been entirely without their highlights. It's funny how you learn to appreciate the little stuff in this job. We went to Chili's up at Ramstein Air Base last night and had a dinner that for the moment served to make me forget where we were going and how it might be. The flyboys [11] sure have it nice up there, big PX [12], pretty base, and a Chili's bar and grill! I am wondering if I joined the right service. I stopped by the Kathi Wohlfahrt store on base. Brought back a lot of memories from winters in Germany.

Of course a year ago, I never saw this coming. A year ago I was leaving Fort Lewis to go home on leave for a couple weeks before taking an exciting cross country trip to Fort Knox. I knew I was going OPFOR, and in Germany, so hell, I never expected to deploy.

Summer is normally a great time, and I couldn't have asked for a better one last summer; I had managed good times in Tacoma, seeing the family for two weeks, buying a new Mustang, and taking a cross-country trip. That was the immediate prelude to my time at Knox, and ultimately Germany, which I find I will recall throughout this deployment. We are still here at the Deployment Center, nothing more than a warehouse with bunks, waiting to catch our flight. 17:00 tonight, they're saying; I'll believe it when we're on the ground in Kabul. Well, the time is coming for a daily

---

[11] Flyboys: nickname for Air Force personnel
[12] PX: Post Exchange, a military shopping center

trip to the mess hall. Get my last good cooking for ninety days, I guess. Hopefully, my next entry will find me in Afghanistan.

My buddy R., Outlaw Platoon Leader, told me something over a few beers one night. It was something he had read in a book, but couldn't remember where. It is something that I think changed my apprehension of leaving and made me almost look forward to it.

"Every great story, Tom, is about one of four things: a journey, a battle, a sacrifice or a homecoming. Sometimes all four."

I guess this is our story.

FRIDAY 05 AUG 2005

Well, we arrived in Kabul early this morning, in time to see the sun rising over the surrounding mountains. The trip on the C-17 was nice and both SGT D. and myself got to step up to the cockpit in the middle of the night and watch them fly. I am still convinced the flyboys have the better life. It was like a whole different world, up there so close to the stars, flying miles above different countries – so separate from the mundane problems of the world below. After they dropped us and our vehicles off, they prepped the flight and took off again on their separate path, with stories to tell of their own adventures barely tangent to the ones upon which we were about to embark.

Kabul itself is nothing more than an impoverished shithole. I think it is really the land that God forgot. No rain in the recent months has left the area a big dust pit, with trash lining the streets, and the kids herding goats in and out of traffic. Shops are built out of boxcar-like metal storage containers and mud huts with ambitious names such as Mahmed Construction Company (which in itself was composed of only a few dilapidated caterpillars and dozers).

The people are a timeless people, it seems. They wear turbans and their robes still; I am sure behaving much the same as they did a hundred some odd years ago when the Brits colonized here. The introduction of automobiles here has simply added to the bizarre mayhem on the streets.

Camp Phoenix is located only a short distance away from the Kabul Airport. We made the ten-minute trip and took in the scenery. The radio crackled, but SSG S. was on it this morning, giving me an opportunity to observe this new culture. We arrived at Phoenix and I was instantly amazed by the distribution of the coalition among allied nations. Our immediate neighbors are composed of a British Gurkha unit, our Romanian higher unit and the French "Quartier Lafayette", which has a sign displaying the US and French flags together, each building being named after a battle in the Revolutionary War, in which they helped us. The Slavic nations have a presence too, as well as the ever-slipshod Italian Army.

We made it to a bazaar this afternoon where I managed to haggle a deal on a Mazar-E-Sharif carpet and a hand-woven bed-set, not to mention two miniature hookahs which adorn my hooch and a postcard of some Afghani statue (a "free gift" from a cunning nine- year-old entrepreneur) which I don't quite recognize. The carpet was a 25 minute session in itself. The eleven-year-old with peach-fuzz on his upper lip saw me eyeing the damn thing and immediately pounced on me.

"Hello my friend."

He had the confident air of a seasoned salesman, and would have done well in any half-ass used car lot back home.

"Hi."

"For you, seventy dollar. Special deal."

I shook my head and started to leave.

"Sorry, too much." My curt reply.

To this he reacted by deftly slipping in front of me and blocking my path.

"Okay, meester, sixty-fife dollar."

I had about seventy in my wallet but I wasn't about to buy the thing for that much.

I shook my head again and tried to get past him. He looked around and pulled a little pocket calculator out. I could tell it was getting serious, he didn't want nearby vendors to hear his compromise.

"You put what you pay." He insisted.

I punched in $35.

He erased it and came back with $60.

"Can't do it." I apologized.

15

"Wait! Wait! No business all day. I need profit."

He punched in $50.

I came back with $45.

His reply was $49.

We finally settled on whatever I had in my wallet, so I pulled out $44 and he accepted. After he inspected the $20 bills he handed one back.

"No good." He pointed to a slight tear in the corner. *"They will not take in Kabul."*

I insisted he take it or no sale, and after calling over to his fellow vendors and having a rapid-fire discourse in their native tongue, he took the twenty. I offered my thanks but he put his hands up, making a disgusted and disappointed look.

"You go now, here take carpet; just go now."

I gladly did.

Well, we meet our interpreter tomorrow. Also, we have a couple missions running in the morning and R. should be getting in country. The overall company mission is leaning more towards peacekeeping, which is fine for me, but some of the more aggressive types aren't taking it so well. We shall see.

SATURDAY 06 AUG05

Today was the first of many boring days. I slept well last night only to wake at 0630 to what looked like a hot afternoon. This place is the land of perpetual afternoons, since, no matter what time of day it is, the shadows are long and the sun is hot.

We met our interpreter around 1030. A kind of slight guy who looks like he can carry his own, named xxxxx. His English is really good, having learned, he told me, in Pakistan. He's seen service with Marines and SF guys, so hopefully he'll get into the groove ok.

R. came in today. It was good to see him finally here, I realized as I stepped in the door of the TOC (Tactical Operations Center) for the 20:00 meeting. He and I went for an O'Doul's in the mess hall after, then checked out the Karaoke night at the PX. Like a whole other world, it seemed. What it most reminded me of was the shadows in the Allegory

16

of the Cave. The non-alcoholic beer and the karaoke in uniform served simply as weak reflections of another life being lived on the other side of the world.

Nothing much else happened today. Worked on the vehicles a little and pretty much tried to stay cool.

There is a growing stench here, most noticeably when around the locals, but I think it is in the dust here too. I can't place my finger on it, but it smells like a combination of feces, earth and, oddly, falafel. Well, the hour is getting late and I need to get some rack time [13]. The sand, as ever, still blows outside.

MONDAY 08 AUG 2005

While we were driving around today I realized more how utterly hopeless this country seems. I looked at the children as we drove by and wondered where their opportunities would come from; will NATO, the UN and the Coalition really sort all this out for these people? Are the Afghans content with this life they live? Do they even know there is more? Or are the children I see playing in the dirt on the roadside today going to end up living in the same squalor in the years to come? Will this new Afghan government work or will it fail?

These people seem so utterly helpless that I have pity for them, yet still, reason tells me that we owe these people nothing. It is the good will of a few nations that is at work here, and how many of our actions are actually sparked by goodwill? How many ulterior motives are there, that we don't realize? How much has the government, if at all, exploited the good will of the American Soldier? It has in past wars. These are doubts that I still have, and I wonder if they will leave me as time goes on.

I think the nights here are my favorite time, at least in base camp. It is quieter and the stars are beautiful. A crescent moon has been lingering early in the night over the peaks to the west, and underneath it, the reddish hue of the still fading day. Over in Quartier Lafayette, the French are playing cards, and a few Romanians are enjoying an evening smoke on the other side of the HESCO barriers.

Well, it is getting late and our HMMWVs are leaving at 0515ish in the morning. It'll be another lovely day in the Sand Box.

---

[13] Rack time: sleep

WEDNESDAY 10AUG 2005

Yesterday we patrolled Kabul and the outlying areas with a German platoon. Kabul is an interesting city with a variety of culture. More modern dress and culture can be noted in the areas around the embassy and the universities, while the more traditional dress is still prominent in other areas. Basically, it is a dirty city, but rich in history and bustling with life.

Market Street is a hodge-podge of traffic and bicycles darting in and out of the street. Near the university, the women have more western attire. There was one who caught my eye as we made our way through the traffic. She had dark hair and eyes, with pretty features; there was something alluring in an exotic way about her. She smiled at me, but I was wearing sunglasses so I don't think I looked very receptive to smiles.

We patrolled a short way outside Kabul, driving through refugee and nomadic camps. Everywhere we went, the kids would flock to the vehicles, expecting candy, ballpoint pens (which they have a fascination with) and other stuff. We finished the day at the German camp where we received a brief from some of the German staff, regarding recent operations and a threat brief. The area they named as a potential hot spot was a place called Sarobi, to the east.

Today we patrolled to Sarobi. All in all, it was about an eleven-hour drive, hair-raising at times, through mountain trails filled with traffic. We stopped at several locations, potential observation posts (OP's) and surveyed the area. We ended up visiting an Afghan National Army (ANA) post and the Major had lunch with them while we relaxed by the surprisingly pristine river that flowed from the dam. Also, I spent the day with the Germans in a "Dingo", one of their heavy armored vehicles. After the initial queasiness from the smooth suspension, it turned out to be a good ride and an effective vehicle.

I found out today that one of my buddies from Knox and Lewis was injured in an IED attack in Iraq. It was a strange feeling. He and I were never close friends, but it was a weird feeling nonetheless.

We work with the Norwegians tomorrow. Early morning.

SUNDAY 14AUG 2005

Yesterday and the day before, we patrolled with the Italians, who fall under the Norwegians in the sector to the west. We got a good look at the AOO (Area of Operations), and it actually rained a little while we were in Lalander Valley. The rain was welcome as it had been at least three months since the last rain.

The Italians are great guys to work with and I really enjoyed it. They were laid back and hospitable, not to mention that their work day revolves around getting espresso every hour or so. My kind of work ethic. We passed a lot of cemeteries on the patrol and noticed the varying sizes of green flags on graves. We were informed that the green flag represented someone who had been a great soldier. I suppose the bigger the flag the greater the hero.

Today the Royal Gurkhas, the British unit, gave us some briefings and we went to see their AOO. They were clearly experts on this type of warfare, considering the British experience in North Ireland. After the 18th of the month, it gets busier, as we pick up our individual patrols, instead of having NATO escort us around on area familiarization.

There were apparently shots fired about three kilometers down the road from us this afternoon. MEDEVAC choppers came rushing in to get one of the National Guard guys evacuated after he was hit by small arms fire. Word has it the .50cal on top of the truck jammed and he couldn't get any shots off. I think it stems more from the lax attitude that Task Force Phoenix is taking, essentially discouraging any return fires in case of attack. Returning fire and engaging the enemy is what we have trained on since I got the platoon in May. To break that habit now will be tough.

I feel I am getting acclimated to this place. I went for about a three mile run mid-afternoon, and it was probably not less than 100 degrees outside. It was good for the tan I guess.

We work with the French for the next two days. I am sure it will be tiresome; they aren't the best at briefings.

MONDAY 15 AUG 2005

I was right about the French briefings. They were torture. But the French are pretty squared away guys. The first comment the French Major had when he saw all the Americans coming into his office was that it looked like D-Day. I think that, as much as Americans dislike the French (most out of ignorance and prejudice), we are two nations with more in common than most nations. We ate with the officers in their Officers' Mess, which looked like a miniature of the British one from "The Far Pavilions". We have more patrolling with them tomorrow.

Some shots were fired tonight as SFC W. (my Platoon Sergeant) and I were talking outside our huts. Apparently a few guys decided to take a few potshots at the guard tower right next to us. I thought 1LT L. (Bulldog Platoon Leader) was going to flip. He had all his gear on and was ready for a fight. We more or less waved the incident off and let the guards handle it.

After our briefing tonight I was walking back to my hooch and heard the call to prayer in town. The sky was clear and a half moon shined brightly. I sat and listened to the somber tones and it was a weird feeling. Maybe the same that the Crusaders had while looking at the same moon or the British the night before Khyber Pass. It was an eerie, solemn sound. And it was a lonely, anonymous voice, calling the masses to come together at the day's end.

THURSDAY 18 AUG 2005

We patrolled with the French up to Bagram the other day. It was pretty scenic, especially from the hatch of the French recon vehicle. Up near Bagram, the quality of living is a little better, which I attribute to the presence of water. There is significantly more flowing water than Kabul, and as a result, more greenery.

As we were leaving Kabul International Airport (KIA), I saw one of the most beautiful and inspiring things I've seen in a long time. We were driving parallel to the airstrip, about fifty meters away when two Norwegian F-16's roared by and took off. The sound was deafening but I was in the perfect spot to watch as they streaked down the airstrip, one after the other, and banked tightly before disappearing over the mountains. It made me wonder about how life is for the flyboys. Their kind of war is a digital war, push button, far away from the people they are defending or fighting. For us, motorized infantry, five kilometers through Kabul is a lot of traffic; for the flyboy, it's a blink of an eye. For us, shooting someone is personal; for the flyboy, it's the push of a button. Who has the better life? Who learns more from the human folly of war? The combat arms of the Army, the grunts, the tread-heads - we're the warriors. Yet where are our laurels when we walk on base or into a bar back home? No one says "*There is a tanker.*" or "*He was an infantryman.*"

What they see is the flyboy and his cocky swagger, as people whisper among themselves "*He's a fighter pilot.*" No, we are the ones who hold the line, who patrol tiresomely, who endure the grit and shit of this pitiful, broken cesspool. We are the ones who put the fear of IEDs aside each day as we leave the wire. We are the ones who clean our pistols and rifles personally, knowing that with them we will kill our enemy. We are the ones who sweat and curse under the hot sun. Despite the fact that they provide support from above, it is us, not the flyboys, who see the weariness on the face of this country in the eyes of its children. The moon is growing fuller each night, and if the wind is in the right direction, the call to prayer can be heard quite clearly in the moonlight.

I was listening to my music last night as I worked on an operation for Saturday. A song played that reminded me of somewhere distant. And snowfall. How utterly distant that seems. It is approaching high 90's outside and I am sitting here thinking of snow.

SATURDAY 20 AUG 2005

The past couple days we have been fighting our worst enemy... boredom. We conducted a bit of training here at the camp. The evening meetings have become longer, because everyone wants to come up with that great idea, and yet we all end up hemming and hawing forever. The meetings have gotten so bad that I have absolutely no nails left to bite. I hate it. Such a waste of time.

Nothing too crazy happened in Kabul. They're saying a local warlord has a monetary reward for anyone who will put a bomb on a Coalition vehicle. Makes me feel warm and fuzzy. The Canadians fired a couple rounds into a van today for getting too close to them... Those crazy Canucks. And we had a false alarm last night. I didn't hear the alarm going off on camp till one of my soldiers woke me. I told him to go back to sleep. Lucky it was a false alarm.

The moon is beautiful tonight, just before it starts waning again. It is nights like this that I think of many things, people and places. This place offers a lot of time for reflection. They're saying our ninety days hasn't even started yet. Great. Spend the holidays in this compost pile of civilization.

Two thoughts occurred to me tonight as I watched the day's last cigarette burn out. One was, "*I wonder what everyone else is doing right now*". The other was simpler, I guess, but with a harder answer. *"When am I going to see home again?"*

WEDNESDAY 24 AUG 2005

Our ninety days started today, as we are officially attached to ISAF now. The past couple days have been more or less without incident. Just working on the patrol matrices with the squad leaders. I went out with 3rd Squad on patrol last night. We all left the from gate singing Queen's "Bohemian Rhapsody"; I think the National Guard guys who were on gate duty thought we were nuts. But not as nuts as the locals think we are for belting out Elvis' "In the Ghetto" as we drive through the bad side of town... which consequently is pretty much the whole town. We managed to nearly flip a Humvee and ended up getting it stuck in an irrigation ditch in the middle of nowhere. While we were towing it out in the dark, a local farmer appeared with two shovels and offered assistance. He also said that he didn't have much, but if we were hungry, he had some cucumbers we could have. I declined, but thanked him. We shook hands and parted ways. These people can be so kind and generous sometimes, I think it is only a minority who really hate us. Hopefully.

Some of the guys from Bulldog Platoon locked me in the Porto john [14] with a winch strap tonight. It was vaguely humorous. I just escaped and laughed with them, which I am sure they were not expecting. Having a gold bar on one's collar makes one a constant target for pranks. I can only imagine what will happen at my promotion this winter.

SATURDAY 02 SEP 2005

It's September already. We have spent the week trying to sort out our vehicle issues, since some genius with more on his collar than me decided to send us down here with experimental vehicles. As usual, no one quite knows what is going on more than a few days in advance. Be flexible, or as they say, "Semper Gumby".

Two different worlds meet. I look at the people and kids as we drive by. We, in our armored vehicles, suited in body armor and packing a good deal of firepower. We, doing a job that has a light at the end of the tunnel. They, on the donkey carts, in their robes and rags, living a life that they have known, and will, most likely, continue to know. What are we bringing these people? Democracy? Who thinks this democracy will

---

[14] Porto john: outdoor toilet

bring peace and prosperity? Who thinks it will fail miserably? I watch the children and realize that they will live on to witness things that will probably happen after my lifetime. They are trapped in this dusty limbo; we are just visitors, like Dante, guided through this pit. How will we be remembered? What mark will we leave? The things we take for granted everyday: TV, microwaves, McDonald's, sewage systems... these are things that most of these people can just imagine.

I suppose the purpose of this drawn-out digression is to look at my own life, my own choices, and realize that that opportunity was given to me by people in the past who sacrificed. Then I watch the kids here as they fly their kites, barefoot, through trash and sewage and wonder about their children's children. Will the children of Afghanistan in the year 2105 look back, while studying their history and say *"We had our first elected representatives a hundred years ago."* Will they recall how foreign soldiers of democracy, nameless now with time, came and ensured that their great-grandparent's votes, their actual ballots, were escorted under arms to the counting center? Words and places that are commonplace for us here in Kabul, may be history for this nation in following centuries. Will the Afghan youth be able to decide where they want to go and what they want to do in life? Will they form happy memories, as I did, from their university years? What will they give back to the world, these waifish youngsters? And will Afghanistan someday be called to defend democracy for a less fortunate country? Every country has humble roots, Afghanistan is no different. 1LT L. can't stand the kids, [he] considers them annoying. I, however, realize that they are the future.

Well, we are running some night patrols it seems, so I need to go take care of some things. But what I have written are just a fraction of the thoughts that are with me every day.

TUESDAY 06 SEP 2005

Today was slower. We had QRF (Quick Reaction Force) duty. So, it's 01:30 and we are still on a 15 minute NTM (notice to move). Our shift ends at 05:00. More stuff went on at the TOC and I really realize how much of a kiss-ass some lieutenants can be. I, for one, don't use that method. I prefer to go through five pieces of chewing gum in these hour-and-a-half meetings and make it no secret that I am more focused on how fast the clock hands turn than anything being discussed. Some phrases I am sick of hearing are:

"That's a great idea, sir."

"This is why I am glad he's my commander; he comes up with stuff like this!"

"We'll implement it immediately, sir!"

"The colonel will be coming, so we need to square things away."

"Too easy, sir!"

Some phrases I want to say (but what is on my collar keeps me from being taken seriously):

"Sir, your idea is ridiculous. Have you tried this yourself?!"

"Sir, my Soldiers will not do that."

"Sir, he's only a colonel, not God Almighty."

"Sir, you made that change in the plan, not me."

Unfortunately, we don't all have the opportunity to voice our opinions. Never mind the fact that I am one of the officers here, but it seems I don't matter. Even though, every time I see a problem in advance, it always comes up later, resulting in *"Gee, we shoulda seen that one coming."* Oh, but I did tell you weeks ago, you just never listened.

TUESDAY 20 SEP 2005

So, I thought early this morning, sitting on my Humvee and listening to the pre-dawn call to prayer, from the corner in the neighborhood where we had set our OP. So, what kind of officer am I? My soldiers have told me at one point or another that I am the *"most NCO officer [they] have met"*. I take this as a compliment, as it is the NCOs who have the real respect in the Army. I suppose it's not officer-like to be able to cuss with the best of them, to go out and get rowdy on weekends. I suppose it's not officer-like to familiarize with your troops to the point I do. Nor officer-like to have an abiding resentment for the leadership of my company. But these are my men, and I need their trust more than they need my leadership. Our mutual trust is gained both ways by sharing our concerns, our triumphs, our gripes and our praises. By sharing our good times and bad. We are not the best platoon, but our quality lies in the bonds between us. So maybe I am a poor officer, maybe I can't manage for shit, and I am too easy on my guys. Maybe. Or maybe I am just down-to-earth enough, so that when the chips are down, my boys know they have a lieutenant they can rely on.

THURSDAY 20 OCT 2005

It's midnight here and insomnia strikes again. I'm not a bit tired, and I am keeping away from the Nyquil, because it tastes like Absinth or licorice, both of which I hate. So, I decided to walk around post, followed by my shadow, which was present due to the waning moon in the clear sky.

We patrolled a new sector today from 03:00-08:30. I stood on a hilltop with my NCOs and some maps as the sun came up over the not so distant mountains. It was something that I don't think I will be forgetting. Two Blackhawk helicopters flew by and for a moment, we were separated from this sorry place. Everything was a shade of pink as the sun rose higher and that pre-dawn chill, to which we have become accustomed, began to fade. Such beauty in a torn land.

I wondered tonight, as I returned to my hut, what kind of course I am wandering. Three months in the desert has made me miss the ocean. And the green of the mountains back home. Trees here are a rarity, only growing in certain places, and green grass is even rarer. The memory of how the trees in Idaho used to whisper at sunset is replaced by nothing more than dust and rocks. Dust and rocks. I wouldn't say this is exactly hard here, but it isn't a cakewalk.

Perhaps my biggest fear is now that we are so short, something will happen within our last two weeks here. It seems to be an irony the Army repeats. Just Fate. Or your number's up. I personally put the thoughts aside, but when I see my soldiers already making plans for their homecoming, I worry about them and the thoughts resurrect in full force.

I still can't sleep. I think of those many nights in college when I'd sit all night and stare at the numbers on my clock ticking by. A nightcap would cure this. Too bad I don't have anything.

I look back at this deployment and wonder what we, Delta Company, 1-4 Infantry, accomplished. Did we really ensure that this democracy thing will get off the ground for the Afghanis? How secure did we make this place? Has there been no real enemy activity because we did our job, or because we got lucky? Too many questions and no answers.

I suppose I'll try and make myself go to sleep, only to be up in five hours to do the intel summary at the TOC. I promised myself I'd tackle the growing amount of admin work tomorrow. As much as I want to roll with my guys on patrol, I don't think I will tomorrow.

The soft cold has been replaced by a harsher cold over the past couple of days. Perhaps there will be snow in Germany by the time we return. Hard to believe we leave soon. Part of me almost wants to come back here and I have absolutely no clue as to why. I honestly have no clue why.

WEDNESDAY 26 OCT 2005

Well, today I got scared. I was on my way back from breakfast when SSG S. told me I needed to head to the showers; SGT F. had had an accident. SGT F. is my youngest sergeant, having just gotten promoted a couple weeks ago. He is possibly the best Soldier I have, and is a hard worker. He's a good man, and honest, who knows how to balance his friendship with the other soldiers and his new leadership responsibilities. I arrived at the showers in time to see SFC W. and SPC A. carrying F. to the ambulance that had arrived. He had a gash across the back of his head and was slipping in and out of consciousness. He also had temporary memory loss, and couldn't remember who anyone was, or where he was. I walked into the showers as SFC W. explained that F. had a seizure and had fallen. There was blood everywhere inside and it looked like little fragments of F.'s scalp on the floor and shower curtain. The ambulance sped to the clinic, on the other side of post, and I suddenly felt helpless, and not in control. What could we do but wait? It was in the medics' hands now.

I visited him later, and his memory had returned. The pretty medical officer gave me her prognosis. He would have to be evacuated to Bagram, most likely, where they had a CT scan available. During lunch I was informed that he had another seizure, so I rushed to the clinic with SSG B., SPC F. and SPC C. F. was in the process of being medevac'd (medical evacuation by chopper) out to Bagram. One of my soldiers, one of my "kids" was hurt, and nothing I could do but watch. The medical team efficiently loaded him in the ambulance, and we followed it to the helo pad [15], where the chopper would be arriving. SFC W., his uniform still splotchy with blood, and I waited by the ambulance as the Blackhawk made its approach. I watched as the medics loaded him on board. He wasn't just going to Bagram, they were sending him all the way to Landstuhl. Back to Germany for F-. The crew got on the chopper, while SFC W., the three medics and I stood there. In an instant, the pitch of the engine changed, the rotors bit into the air, and it had lifted off. F. [He was] Gone. The medical officer looked at me and reassured me he'd be in good

---

[15] Helo pad: Helicopter landing pad

hands. She was in a joking mood. *How can she be cheerful?* I thought angrily. I just lost a good Soldier.

Another fear hit me as I returned to my hut. If this is my emotional reaction to an accident, what would happen if one or more of my guys got shot? Am I really ready to lose Soldiers? Would I cope? Of course, that's what they trained me for. But then again. We're a family here. We are a family.

SUNDAY 30 OCT 2005

Well, the other night I made my move. I told the guys I'd win the National Guard's Camp Phoenix Halloween costume contest, and I did. I still can't believe I went as a cheerleader. And an ugly one at that. The CO didn't know what to think when I entered his quarters after the contest in a miniskirt and stuffed halter top. The guys got it all on camera. Good for morale I guess.

We started packing up today. Not long now. Little things are changing around here. They put up a light out behind my hut, so it's harder to see the stars at night. Just little things changing. Our last patrol is in two days. I plan to go. I haven't been on patrol in a week, largely due to the redeployment paperwork I have been busy with. I have a slight twinge of regret over this. It may be my last time as a platoon leader to be with my troops in a combat zone. It has been a strange journey, but our return to Germany will usher in different adventures. I look around at my soldiers and wonder what will happen. Each on their own path. Some of us will meet again, many will not.

WEDNESDAY 02 NOV 2005

The last. What exactly do we mean when we say "*last*"? I think there are two types. Predicted and unpredicted finality. Unpredicted is probably the kind where you look back and say "*Oh, that was the last time I was there.*" It's the kind where you don't know it's the last time you do something until you look back at it. Predicted finality is more of the kind where you know in advance that something is the last thing of its sort you'll ever do or see. It's the kind where you sit out at night, thinking, and promise yourself you'll savor every moment of that last occurrence.

Last night was Delta Company's last patrol in Afghanistan. And it was 2nd Platoon that was tasked. And I was there. We dismounted from the vehicles (I was with SSG P.'s squad, in SGT T.'s truck) and walked across the fields in the dark with our NODS on. The CO was behind me. Some distant fireworks had us worried for a few minutes, and we huddled behind a stone wall, scanning the field. We realized it wasn't gunfire, but fireworks celebrating the end of Ramadan.

I listened to every sound. The crackle of the radio in the truck. The guys joking back and forth to keep awake. I watched the town as we passed through. This was the last. A few more days and we would literally become history. We sat on an OP with the Kabul City Police for a bit, in their hut at the top of a hill. [Our interpreter] Rashid was there and we talked with the guys for a good half hour. I thought back to Mr. A. I had told him I would visit his marble factory when it was finished. It occurred to me that I had never had the time. I wish I could have seen how it looked.

We came back in the gate and the commander shook our hands.

"White Elements, this is 6." I called over the radio. *"We just completed our last patrol in Afghanistan. Congratulations and good job."* And that was that. The last was over.

I walked to the coffee shop that night and got my nightly cup of Earl Grey tea, and a muffin, since I had missed dinner. Behind the hut, I sat under the stars, alone, and recounted in my mind all the events of the deployment. Maybe I was meant to find peace in a war-torn third-world country. I don't know. Whether I was meant to or not, I think I have.

I thought about earlier that day when I had gone to the barber shop. In the chair, I looked at the attractive gal from Kyrgyzstan who has done my hair nearly every week for the past three months. I told her it was my last haircut, and I thought I saw a funny look in her normally cheerful blue eyes. She took 20 minutes to do a flattop that should've taken 10 minutes. Our version of goodbye was my tipping her, saying thanks and leaving, getting a simple, pretty smile in return.

How can you hate a place so much, yet feel attached to it? I had felt this way before about The Citadel and Charleston. I spent every day for nearly a year regretting it, then one morning I woke up and realized there was no place I loved more. Charleston had stolen my heart, as it had done to so many others before me. The last time I saw The Citadel was on a thundering, rainy day through the rear window of a cab. I had watched long after the cold, white parapets had disappeared. I wouldn't say Kabul has had that effect by a long shot, but it has intrigued me, and I feel there is a lot of unfinished business here. Also, the simplicity, the closeness with my soldiers. Something I won't experience again once I make Captain.

THURSDAY 03 NOV 2005

Tonight is the last night in Kabul it seems. I had gone with R. for our final walk across post to the coffee shop, where I got my usual Earl Grey. R. and I talked a bit; his application for the Ranger Regiment was turned down, all the slots had been filled. He's considering Special Forces, but he can't decide if he wants to do that or focus on a career path that would give him more time to raise a family in the future. I know which I would choose.

So now I am having trouble going to sleep. The heartburn is gone, yet my mind is teeming with thoughts regarding the life to which I am about to return.

"How long will it be till you miss this place?" R. had asked me and the XO at dinner.

"Two days in Germany." I said, recalling the prediction 1LT B. had made, seemingly forever ago.

Orion [16] stared down at me tonight, as I had one last session of quiet nighttime thought under the desert sky. Earlier in the evening I had heard the call to prayer celebrating the end of Ramadan. It'll be odd not hearing that sound anymore.

xxxxx gave his farewells with watery eyes today. I think he too had become attached to the platoon. He hopes to go to America someday; funny how that seems to be his dream, and yet so many Americans take it for granted.

So tomorrow we run a large convoy to Bagram. As Brigadier General Taber (one of the generals here) put it the other day, it will be an odyssey returning home. So it will be, but hopefully not too much of one. Bagram, Kyrgyzstan, Germany, a bus to Hohenfels, then released home. Then the part I dread. The part where I open the door to my apartment and am greeted by that heavy silence that seems to be ingrained in the place. The emptiness. Eventually names of places will fade from memory; Pol-i-charki, Bagrami, Jalalabad Road, Sarobi, Chicken Street Market, will all fade. Then faces. And soon it will be as with any other memory, and will

---

[16] Orion: the constellation

be stirred up with the weather is just so, or I hear certain sounds. Next my boys will begin leaving. Each on their own path to rendezvous with their respective destinies. And they too will inevitably fade from memory, as will I from theirs.

And it is late and I am thinking way too deeply on this matter. 0500 call tomorrow and it's past midnight.

MONDAY 07NOV 2005

We have been in Bagram for going on three days now. Bagram Air Field is an interesting place, seemingly a poor imitation of civilization. The roads are good paved roads on base, the first I've seen in months. Also, there are European street signs and much more westernized traffic. There are more people here. And the base is much larger than Camp Phoenix. The air is oddly clearer even though it is at a lesser altitude than Kabul's mile high. The airfield is not too far from the tent where we are all staying.

MONDAY 14 NOV 2005

The past few days have been a whirlwind. We left Bagram on the 8th or so – I can't really recall. But we flew out in the evening on a flight to Manas, Kyrgyzstan, and landed later that night.

Coming off the C-130, we could already sense an improvement, as the air was a good deal fresher and it had that smell of recent rain. And there were trees. More trees than we had seen our whole time in Afghanistan. We downloaded our gear at the small Air Force Base and headed to the mess hall. Definite improvement. The flyboys know how to live well. Soft serve ice-cream and, even better, blueberry pie. It beat the cream pie at Camp Phoenix. After, XO [17], R. and I went to the coffee shop and had late night drinks. I looked around the shop as I drank my Earl Grey and noticed the murals on the walls. The murals portrayed lush, green valleys in the mountains and small, hide covered huts near a stream. The designs and clothing of the people in the murals looked very similar to Native American. The only problems with the mural were the U.S. fighter planes that had been painted in above the mountains.

The people of Kyrgyzstan seemed interesting. The men looked mostly oriental or Russian. But the women were a mix between an almost Native American look and Eastern European/Russian, and have a strange

---

[17] XO: executive officer

beauty about them. The place in general had the aura of a frontier outpost, and I found myself wanting to lose my uniform, throw on a fur coat and local garb and explore eastward, towards the Himalayas and wherever Shangri La was last reputed to be. After two days in Manas, we left on a late afternoon flight. To be honest, I didn't want to leave Kyrgyzstan; although I hadn't even gotten to know the place, it seemed interesting enough, and it intrigued me. I had this sudden desire to go somewhere where one of the greater powers in the world had not yet become involved, somewhere where Americans have not been heard of, somewhere where there is simplicity and original culture without the mark of Westernism. Perhaps it is like that in the mountains south of China, where we were for only a couple days. Perhaps. Something tells me I will never find out.

Anyhow. We arrived in Germany shortly after sunset. I stood out on the runway and watched the moon rise. The Battalion Commander and Command Sergeant Major were shaking everyone's hands as they came off the plane. We had some gear inspections and then bussed to Hohenfels, only stopping once or twice. The adjustment was beginning already. We stopped in a McDonalds and I looked around at my first glimpse of Western civilized life in a good three months. Aside from the uniforms, we didn't really stand out here. Something to get used to. No roadside bombs to consider, no need to examine every person head-to-toe as you drive by.

We made Hohenfels by midnight on Veterans' Day. Veterans' Day, I thought, as we stood out in formation, before being sent home, couldn't have picked a better day. The wives looked for their husbands in the formation as we received a brief welcome home speech. The midnight air was chilly, but fresh, and I watched the men from the VFW hand out their poppies to everyone. I had received a poppy as I came off the bus, a little bewildered from the massive activity. I had displayed it on my pocket, like some strange boutonnière. The Colonel released the formation and the Soldiers made a dash to their waiting wives and sweethearts. The activity, excitement and mere thought of being back left me in a bit of a daze, I must admit. I just wandered off the field slowly. I watched my men hug their wives and girlfriends. R. was right. Coming home was harder than leaving. I felt my left breast pocket for my St. Christopher medal. It was there. I looked for someone I knew in this sudden field of strangers. Faces I hadn't seen in months, many whom I didn't know and who didn't know me.

Walking inside, I helped out the XO and 1LT N. with the arms room inventory. We finished everything by about 03:00. Time to go home and try to sleep. We had to come in for re-integration training the following afternoon.

Later that night [next day], R. came by and we went to Regensburg to enjoy the nightlife. It was strange, being among throngs of people and no longer standing out. I got so used to being the center of attention when we rolled through Kabul that it was nice not having all eyes on us. A refreshing sort of anonymity. I ended up meeting a local tour guide who I still swear was a dead ringer for Shania Twain and we danced all night. Again... strange. Relaxing. Not watching one's back. I made it back to my house sometime the next morning and fell asleep, only to be quickly awakened by a reverberating boom. For only a split moment, in my dark bedroom, I reached for my boots, pants, and helmet. None were there. I heard the other aircraft fly over and recalled that military jets often broke the sound barrier in the Hohenfels area. With a sigh of relief and a good laugh at myself, I went back to sleep.

It was a Sunday morning. I woke again an hour later and got ready for work that afternoon. I opened the bathroom window and heard a sound that I had not heard in three months. No longer the prayer call to which I had become accustomed. No, I heard a bright chorus as was only fitting for a Sunday morning in the village. I heard church bells.

MONDAY 21 NOV 2005

This is the last entry. We have been home for over a week now, and this may seem more like an epilogue than an entry.

Today is my first day back in the green Battle Dress Uniform. No more desert uniforms. I am currently in my office, as the snow continues to fall outside, trying to relearn MS Outlook and Form Flow (the Army's document filler). I wonder what's happening in Kabul right now... lunch time, probably cooler out. Patrols getting ready to mount up and roll out.

It is odd. I fought the snow this morning to come to work. Right when my car got warm, I arrived at work. Go figure. Life's little ironies. The apartment is quieter than ever, and I really try to spend as little time in it as I can. It's not a bad apartment at all, I just need to get used to living alone again.

I was tidying up the place last night when D. came by. He and his wife were making dinner and wanted me to come over. I went and enjoyed a great home-cooked meal. After, D. and I went out on the balcony overlooking what were, in the summer, rolling wheat fields. Now everything had the blanket of the first snow on it. The snow fell, D. sipped his schnapps (which I avoid ever since one night when German hospitality and multiple rounds of schnapps got the better of me) and we chatted. It was almost like I hadn't left.

So how does one end a log of ninety-plus days? A narrative, not really of war, but of a new lieutenant and his soldiers. It was a short deployment, and our company saw very little combat, yet we influenced a nation's future, a people's future. How does one end a final entry?

When I was a kid, I read in school about Louis the Sun King of France, and how he would sit every day under a tree and have his people come to him with their problems and concerns. That image, that anecdote, made a lasting impression on my philosophy of leadership. No leader is ever too good for his or her people, whether in charge of a nation or merely thirty soldiers.

I wonder what exactly we did downrange. It occurs to me now, as I sit at my desk, that the change will be visible in twenty or so years. The inspirations for this sudden thought are a few memories that came to mind. The little barefoot girl whom I gave a piece of chewing gum to one day, and the astonished look I received from her when she first tasted it. The kids on the hill above the Green Zone who were flying kites, their clothes and faces dirty, sandals worn through, but smiling nonetheless. The 12-year-old kid who learned six languages from soldiers of different nationalities; we all agreed he'd be going places someday. Mr. A., hard at work with his employees, building what might be part of a new commercial zone in a few years, in East Kabul. It brings a smile to my face, and I realize that Ghost Platoon, my platoon, did not work in vain. Following those thoughts, I find that I have nothing left to say.

THURSDAY 25 MAY 2017 – Afterthoughts

I'm sitting in my home right now, having just read my musings from a portion of my Lieutenancy. I would go on to serve another eight years in the Army, with a tour to Iraq and another Germany tour, before continuing to serve my nation as a civilian.

I still think about my boys, all of whom are men now. They were men then. They were men when they volunteered to take up arms in service of their nation and do what so few have for their country. I stay in touch with many. SPC C. reminds me every so often of my cheerleader outfit, sending me pictures which are sure to haunt me the rest of my days. SGT T. checks in from time to time, the last time I visited with him was at a Green Beans coffee shop in Baghdad some years ago. SSG P. has gone far in the Army, as I knew he would. SGT F. recovered well, and is a senior NCO. R. is married with children now. I see the XO frequently, as he lives nearby. He is still grouchy, but he no longer has 5988s [18] to worry about, so he manages a smile more often. Most of my men are well; many have had their struggles, as have I. The burden we assume for the Republic when we take up arms for her wears upon us in many ways.

At least one of my Soldiers is gone. SGT G. left this world sometime after we redeployed. He is buried in Montana, and a few years ago, while driving south of his hometown, it occurred to me to visit his resting place. I didn't. The once gutsy LT couldn't bring himself to do it yet. I'm not sure why, but perhaps I think that somehow we are still out there patrolling that dusty pit, in all our youthful vigor, thinking not of the future. I will pay my respects at some point to that eager young man, who for all his brash enthusiasm, held so much promise given a few more years in the NCO corps.

I became the man I wanted to be in many ways. I married, have three children, and have spent Christmas Eves past building their bicycles, as I daydreamed I might when I was in Kabul. I have often enjoyed a book by the fire with my wife. Some military memorabilia adorns one corner of our modest townhome, but for the most part, children's art hangs upon the walls.

It was a short deployment all-in-all, and some moments were not captured in my journal (after all, I was sending these home to my folks and didn't want my mom too worried). It was a short deployment early in what has become our nation's longest war. I have many thoughts still, many of my skeptical observations have been tempered with age, but one thing remains. To me, the United States Soldier is as timeless, if not more so, than the Roman Legionary of old. Despite our changes in uniform and equipment, as I observe the new Soldiers of today and reminisce upon my Soldiers of before, I see that they display that indomitable spirit that will make them, make us, an icon in history.

---

[18] 5988: Maintenance paperwork

At my desk, from which I can see Washington D.C., a small picture hangs. It's us. White Tank. On a sunny afternoon in Kabul. We are all there, in one perfect moment, smiling in the sun.

I'm proud of my Soldiers, regardless of where they are now. I'm proud of 2nd Platoon. Being their Platoon leader for fourteen months is one of the greatest things I've gotten to do.

-White Six, Out.

CASSIDY DAUBY [2006/2007]

2nd PLT/C Co/ 1-4 IN REG

WEDNESDAY 04OCT – SUNDAY 08 OCT 2006

During the 2006/2007 deployment, 2nd (MadDawg) Platoon of Cherokee Company ran missions out of FOB LANE, near the village of Deh Afghanan on the Arghandab River in Zabul Province. Deh Afghanan is located about 20 miles downriver from what was then the district capital of Sayagaz, where an element of Afghan National Police (ANP) and the district leader stayed. The district leadership had switched out a couple of times, with the previous group being Hazaras [19], from the central region of the country. Traditionally shunned and persecuted as a race of slaves by the Pashtuns, they were extremely motivated to find and kill Taliban. Unfortunately, by mid-September, they [Hazaras] had come under attack from all sides and were driven from the base. On the night of the attack, 2nd PLT [20] and Cherokee Company's higher headquarters, the 2nd Romanian Infantry Battalion, called to ask what support we could provide. We determined the conditions to be too adverse to make the movement, which usually took between four to eight hours during periods of darkness. We departed the next day, and, along the way, received a media report from the provincial government, that the district leader and his ANP element had abandoned their post, stolen government weapons, and gone on the run. Having a distinctly racist edge to it, the report was likely a way of throwing the blame on the "corrupt" Hazaras and an attempt to minimize the efforts of the local Taliban. I found this to be an ineffective public affairs move for personal reasons.

By early October, a new group of ANP had arrived at FOB LANE to take over at Sayagaz. They were not Hazaras, so they would theoretically have more support from the provincial government. 2nd PLT organized a patrol to Sayagaz to install the new leadership and to show them around. We departed FOB LANE on 4 October 2006, driving up the Arghandab River as much as possible, and alternating which side of the river we drove on, when the riverbed provided an unhospitable route.

Upon our arrival in Sayagaz, the facilities now remained in worse condition than we had left them a few weeks earlier. When the previous

---

[19] Hazaras: ethnic group native to the region of Hazarajat in Afghanistan
[20] PLT: platoon

ANP contingent left, the Taliban had blown up their old building, but left the new, under-construction, ANP headquarters across the road intact. This time, even the new one had been mostly destroyed. The ANP began moving in to the remnants of the old compound and organizing themselves, while we pulled security and patrolled the local roads. This went on through 5 October [2006].

On the morning of 6 October, we took up our security positions around the ANP base when SSG A. called from his checkpoint to say he needed an interpreter. A truck full of injured men had just arrived and they looked like they needed medical attention. Our interpreter xxxxx, Doc S. and a couple of other Soldiers joined 2nd Squad to assist. It turns out they had been victims of an IED along the Arghandab, by the village of Eraqi. They claimed their truck was full of people, including children, when it exploded. The explosion killed three children and they were being buried in the village that morning. Doc and the others rendered what aid they could, before sending them on their way to the hospital in Shajoy, which is the nearest city along Highway 1. We informed the ANP of the situation and put together a patrol to visit Eraqi. There were two roads, one along which the truck had just come, and the one along which we had arrived in Sayagaz. We chose the one that had just been driven by the civilians, the road which wound behind the mountain to the southwest of our position to the village.

Our patrol arrived at the village and set up a security perimeter on the high ground, overlooking the riverbed. We dismounted all but the necessary vehicle crews, and approached the mass of people who had gathered on the North side of the village. Everybody was crying and wailing over three wooden bedframes with blanket-wrapped bodies on them. xxxxx, the ANP chief, and I approached a group of men who emerged from the crowd and we gave them our condolences for their losses. They explained that the children had been riding in the truck the night before, when it hit an IED just over the bank from the village in the riverbed. The truck had been destroyed, and several of the people who had survived had headed to the hospital. We explained that we had met them, given them aid and sent them along. The villagers thanked us. In the background, xxxxx reported that people were shouting *"Fuck Mullah Omar! Fuck Mullah Omar! "*, referring to the leader of the Taliban and former President of Afghanistan.

We asked where the incident happened exactly, and they said we could just drive to the river and would see it. As the villagers began carrying

37

the beds to the cemetery, we expressed our condolences again, mounted our vehicles and began looking for the site of the explosion.

Once in the riverbed, the patrol headed northeast, back towards Sayagaz. After about 200 meters, we came across the blown up remains of a pickup truck. The site appeared surprisingly clean, since the villagers had apparently already picked up the cargo from the vehicle. What remained, though, showed itself as a nightmare, reminiscent of any deadly, high-speed crash on an interstate. It was hard to imagine how anybody could have survived such devastation. The likely answer is that those who survived had positioned themselves on top of the cargo in the back, and flew into the air instead of being smashed against the inside of the vehicle. The truck rested upside down, about 20 feet from the crater left by the explosion. The timing and placement of the IED indicated that it had been meant for our element's return trip to FOB [21] LANE. We had driven over the spot two days prior, and the insurgents had planted the IED [22] the night after we had passed. On previous patrols, we had usually come and gone over that same road and had typically not stayed more than one night. The fact that the bomb had been meant for us was not missed. A part of me wished that we had hit it, since our armor would have provided more protection than that pickup had provided for the innocents riding in it. On the other hand, it is hard to feel guilty for the actions of bad guys who were trying to kill you. That might be why they say there are no winners in war.

After checking out the pickup truck, our patrol returned to Sayagaz to finish helping the ANP settle in. We continued to do local patrols around the station and maintained checkpoints to check the occasional vehicle that passed by. On or about 8 October, a route clearance package finally arrived from Qalat, via Highway 1, passing through Shajoy. They had hit an IED halfway between Shajoy and Sayagaz, and had been delayed a day. We received instructions to help escort them down the Arghandab to FOB LANE, from where the RCP [23] would return to Qalat. We had initially intended to stay with the ANP a while longer, but found it difficult to argue with instructions to return "home" behind a mine clearer. Throughout the long, excruciating trip, we did find and clear a couple of mines that had been placed in the road at some point. In the following weeks and months, our patrols took 2nd PLT to other parts of

---

[21] FOB: Forward Operating Base
[22] IED: Improvised Explosive Device
[23] RCP: Route Clearance Patrol

the district and province, leaving us unable to support the ANP as much as we should have. Their logistics and reinforcement from the provincial government lacked support and their outpost eventually closed, moving the district headquarters to Bagh, a village with a bazaar not far from FOB LANE. This effectively ceded the 15 miles of the Arghandab between Sayagaz and Bagh to the Taliban, who emboldened their positions by this advance, to say the least. As Bravo Company and others followed on at FOB LANE, they had to deal with an enemy who was accustomed to winning. The saga told by others in this book paint a picture of what that was like.

BOYD JOHANSEN [2006]

The way I found out that there was even a possibility of receiving a bonus for signing up, happened after I had already signed my life away and my father asked me because, *"A son of a friend of mine said..."* Maybe the explanation doesn't serve it justice, but that is how I like to describe why I enlisted. Because I wanted to. I wanted to feel that sense of duty and accomplishment. I wanted to push myself and I wanted to see things that weren't possible otherwise.

The point always comes when you are asked where your "dream" duty station would be. I know everyone goes through it and it probably makes no difference on where they send you, but if you want to see Europe, what better place to pick than Germany. Right at the center of it all. So that is where I headed to in late January 2006.

It didn't take long and 1-4 IN began picking guys to deploy. Since only a platoon of scouts remained and half a dozen were on their way out, either by PCS [24] or ETS [25], it made room for us newbies. They [1-4IN] took a squad and attached them to an infantry platoon and then spread a few of us out throughout the rest of the company. I felt a little betrayed at the time that I had to be one of the only ones on his own, and not in and around the scouts. Those guys became closer and closer and prepared to deploy together, while I had to be stuck with a bunch of infantrymen. Once I finished all the shit that you have to put up with being the new guy, including being hogtied and set on the CQ [26] desk, I decided this was the place for me. I wanted nothing else. Those guys then became my brothers. And it helped that a couple new guys arrived, so the pressure of being the only new soldier began to leave my mind. After a few months of training and hellish ruck marches, I succeeded in getting into the best shape of my life and didn't have a problem carrying an 80 extra pounds. Which was good, because carrying shit up mountains sucks.

We arrived in country and everyone basically went their separate ways. Each platoon had its own FOB. We loaded into our new trucks and headed out to Mizan. Driving along that desolate Highway 1 is when you know shit's real. Things I never had imagined. The way people live. The dirt, the wind, the heat. It sucked. Within a week of waiting to get everything signed over, we encountered our first dust storm. As if we

---

[24] PCS: Permanent Change of Station
[25] ETS: Expiration of Term of Service
[26] CQ: Charge of Quarters

weren't dirty enough already. If you could make it half a day staying clean after showering, you were doing good.

Once we signed everything over and the FOB was ours we could start patrols and missions. We also started our routine of guard duties and other chores around the FOB which included: filling water cans for showering and laundry (from the nearby river), burning shit and trash, and improving our place of residence. Everything correlated with which tower your squad manned that day. That meant we could shower and do laundry every few days, but that at some point we had to do the nasty shit as well. And on the days we weren't in the tower, we were usually on a patrol or mission.

Until it actually happens, you can never really imagine what it will feel like to know that your life could end with that next bullet that flies towards you. The snap that comes with the round barreling its way by your head is nothing that can be described, but something you have to experience to truly understand. For me, I understood it one afternoon/evening on guard duty. Until that moment, we as a platoon hadn't really seen much, but then again, we hadn't been there so long. Because of that, we had a rather "relaxed" duty standard. Of course we had all of our equipment right by our side as we pulled duty, but we didn't have to be wearing it. So there I was, calling TOC[27] with our little handheld as I am ducking down trying to get my plate carrier and k-pot [28] on my body.

As I get back up, I am seeing small dust clouds coming off the side of the guard tower where the rounds are impacting as well as hearing that damn snap as one passes by my head. Of course my initial instinct to return fire with my SAW [29] stayed ingrained within me as second nature, but when the contact comes from the opposite direction you're supposed to be scanning, your platoon sergeant may yell at you and say; *"What the puck are you doing?!?! Scan your sector!!!"* (Being from the Philippines, there is no "F" when [he] says a certain word). Another battle [30] came up as reinforcement and we could only stay low and scan out into the small "shopping district" of Mizan as the mortars began their fire mission and the rest of the platoon, not pulling guard, fired hell towards the general direction of those assholes on the mountain. Most attacks came around

---

[27] TOC: Tactical Operations Center
[28] K-pot: Kevlar helmet
[29] SAW: Squad Automatic Weapon
[30] Battle: a nickname for fellow soldiers

dusk, so the enemy could escape with the cover of darkness. Since they had nothing in the form of night vision, besides the moon, it was hard for them to perform a successful attack at night. Though, I must say, they knew their surroundings perfectly and could navigate, most of the time, better than we could *with* NODs [31].

That is the moment that I believe stands out the most in both of my deployments. It may not have been as intense as others, but it sticks with me as the first of those experiences. Patrols and missions came with even more risk as we faced exposure to everything and everyone trying to kill us in every way possible. Another patrol that stands out because of what I found at the time to be a little comedic.

We received small arms contact from a mountain range in the vicinity. We reacted to contact and ended up leaving the vehicles to make our way up to a compound that sat on a small hilltop, for better protection and eyes on. Right before we get out of the truck, my team leader asks: "*Jojo, you ready?*"

Me: "*Hell no!!*"

TL [32]: "*Good, let's go!*"

What a smartass, I thought. *And, you motherfucker, I am not leaving this damn comfortable, safe, non-exhausting seat that I am in right now.* So, of course I get out and we run up to the first set of trees. In between breaths:

TL: "*You ready?!*"

Me: "*Hell no!*"

TL: "*Good, let's go!*"

Me: "*Fuck!*"

As we made it to the other side of a riverbed, I plop my SAW-bearing ass down, take a breath and just waited for my TL. Same damn story. The next 50 to 100 meters we ran through a small orchard with those small dust clouds appearing at our feet. "*Those assholes are coming a little too close*" I thought. And it wasn't like the pomegranate trees' 6" of girth is going to give much protection. Finally after what seemed an eternity of bounding through trees, a riverbed, and an orchard, we made it to the compound. I

---

[31] NODs: night vision goggles
[32] TL: Team Leader

laid down, which was so nice, set my SAW up and returned fire to the little specks on the mountain side. When they returned fire, I just took cover behind the building and saw the round make their marks where I had been laying. It seemed then, out of nowhere, an ANA soldier came up with no mind to what was going on, stood where I had previously laid, and at this moment I was formally introduced to the term "spray and pray [33]." After a few minutes of running from cover to cover, our trucks found their way up and laid some serious waste to anyone who thought they might have a chance. Before I knew it, we withdrew back into the safety of our trucks and finished our patrol. Thinking back on it later, had we detained two men on a motorcycle we had stopped just minutes before, we may have been able to avert that particular confrontation. I know it's like saying *"What if we'd have done that?"* but when radio chatter comes just minutes after a stop like that, it makes a person wonder.

Situations like that make it even easier to have no trust in anyone else except for those whom you have come to call brother and trust with your life as they trust you with theirs. There is no better feeling of comradery then that between you and the men you have trained with, lived, and fought alongside especially in the austere conditions that we served.

I deployed two times, with two separate Companies. The second time I deployed to Baylough attached to C Co. I faced many times where I thought *"What the hell..."* We had one squad with trucks which was not ours. We conducted our patrols on foot across terrain that most people like to call mountainous.

One particular mission with an integrated patrol took us on about a 20km round trip. During the Company-level operation our squad had been tasked to provide over-watch to make sure nobody would make their way up a specific valley and take us by surprise. We stayed perched in our position after a nice couple hour rock climb during a nice sunny afternoon, peaceful night and long morning until our very fast descent and ruck across a very wide-open area where we met up with the trucks to make our exfil [34]. Mind you, all we had were rucksacks that weighed around a light 75 pounds or so in addition to a full battle load. At one point, an ANA soldier, providing over-watch from an adjacent mountain top, had decided we looked like enemies and somehow he did not expect anyone in our position. We realized this as we looked over to see said ANA soldier pointing an RPG in our direction after just missing with an

---

[33] Spray and Pray: a term used to describe firing a weapon without aiming
[34] Exfil: military term for exiting

AK round. Five minutes later, when the situation cleared and neutralized, we picked the round that had impacted just above one of the heads of our soldiers out of a nearby rock. The mission proved interesting to say the least and made me even more cautious of the Afghan Army and [Afghan] police. There is only a certain amount of trust, if that's what you want to call it, which can be given.

Outside of basic training, I never really worked as my MOS [35] described, but instead as an infantryman, as many scouts in the 1-4 IN Battalion did. Had I stayed in longer and been stationed elsewhere, as other battles know, it would have been a different story. Once I was able to ETS and make it back to civilian life, there was a huge rope, it seemed, that was trying to pull me back in. Battles that were still in made it even harder to not reenlist, though my wife made it slightly easier. As the years have gone on, it has become possible to take the memories as they are and know that it could never be the same without the men that I had enjoyed all those missions with, at home and on the battlefield.

---

[35] MOS: Military Occupational Specialty

DAVID SCHWARTZ [2006/2007]

First Contact, FOB Baylough 2006-2007, Cherokee Company deployment.

On a dismounted patrol to one of the outlying villages near FOB Baylough, the soldiers of 3rd squad [Death Row platoon] engaged in our first enemy contact. We patrolled down a dirt road just leaving a small village. The area of farm land and orchards contained skinny little trees all over and small rock walls divided some of the farm land. We conducted our patrol right before sundown. I moved in the rear of the formation with my m249 machine gun when we heard a lot of gunfire in front of us coming from beyond the orchard area up where our Afghan allied soldiers were ahead of our squad. I remember stopping for about two seconds and thinking *"Are they shooting at us?"* Then the quick realization hit me that were are actually in a gunfight.

I quickly took cover inside a hole to my right alongside the road. I looked over at the road I had previously walked on and I witnessed our two-man M240B machine gun team take off running straight down the road toward the enemy gunfire. Another guy in my squad and I took cover in the hole for a few seconds when we heard our team leader yelling at us: *"Bound up!"* We waited a few more seconds and I gazed over the edge of the hole to make sure we were safe to run forward. Then both of us ran approximately 100 meters as fast as we could to the edge of another orchard.

I could see the rest of the squad was already there. Our squad leader decided we would get "on line" and assault through the orchard. We lined up on the edge of the orchard, maintaining a straight line but keeping good distance between us. We assaulted through the orchard. The whole time I waited for someone to start firing at us and kept hunched over and low to the ground with my machine gun pointed forward. Once the squad got through to the edge of the orchard we could see a large open area in front of us. We set up the m240B in a trench facing toward that open area. The Afghan Army squad was already in this area and was firing RPG's into the hillside from where the enemy fire had been coming. My team leader started firing the m203 grenade launcher attached to his m16. Then the M240B machine gun fired a Z pattern into the enemy position. After the M240B started firing the enemy didn't fire back. A lull in the battle occurred.

However, we had an Afghan Army soldier that would not stop firing his RPG. He was standing right in front of me shooting as I was in the prone providing rear security for the squad. The back blast from the RPG hit me. Our squad leader yelled at another guy in my squad, telling him to stop the Afghan soldier's firing. We kept yelling "*Stop!*" to the Afghan soldier and I remember him looking over and saying "*Yes.*", loading another grenade and firing. He shot off a couple more before he finally ceased fire.

A tunnel with water flowing through it ran close to our position at the edge of the orchard. I think it might have been part of an underground well system. One soldier said he could hear something sloshing around in the water. Someone else asked the squad leader if we should send a couple guys in to clear it. Our squad leader decided to frag the hole with a grenade instead. Our squad RTO [36] threw a fragmentation grenade in and we covered our ears. And waited and waited and waited..... No boom. It must have been a dud because it never went off. He threw another grenade in the hole and this time it exploded.

Now darkness set in and we waited for a while with our NVG's on (night vision goggles). The LT on our patrol with us radioed for some IR illumination rounds from the mortar team at the FOB (IR: illumination lights up the area like a flare, but only visible when wearing night vision). No one saw anything and no return fire came from the enemy, but we heard the sound of an engine to the rear of our position. While providing rear security for our squad, I likely became the first one to see the Afghan guy on a motorcycle riding down the road we had come from earlier. We stopped him and searched him. We found a flashlight and some mirrors (most likely used to signal his buddies who shot at us). We detained the guy on the motorcycle and zip cuffed him. Then my squad leader had me use my machine gun on the motorcycle. I shot about ten rounds into it before it hit the gas tank and lit on fire.

After that, 3rd squad walked back to FOB Baylough.

---

[36] RTO: radio transmission operator

MARCEL GREEN [2007]

On February 7, 2007, about six miles northwest of FOB Mizan, we conducted a patrol comprising of Special Forces and 3rd Platoon, B Company, 1-4 Infantry to set up a trap across a known Taliban infiltration route. Our lieutenant detected about 40 Taliban in the area. He pinpointed them inside a saddle in a peanut-shaped mountain and immediately reacted by maneuvering our vehicle and another [vehicle] around the side. Our movement alerted the Taliban to our position and they acted like the cowards they are. In rapid succession the Taliban then fired five deadly RPG rounds at our vehicle. Throughout the barrage of incoming RPG rounds, I just kept firing my weapon. BOOM. An explosion blew off three of my fingers. The incoming round blasted open all four doors of our vehicle and propelled our driver PFC Z. from the truck like a rocket. One round knocked our LT unconscious and our medic in the vehicle, PFC M., suffered a severe concussion and shrapnel wounds to his hands. Meanwhile, our Humvee took its position on a crest moving towards the enemy, but without Z. to hit the brakes it rolled into a gully.

DAVID KUHN [2008]

For our final mission before heading back to Germany we decided to go to the wonderful Challackor Valley [insert sarcasm]. I remember setting up for the night a few miles from the entrance into the valley. Everyone remained eager and wondered what tomorrow would bring us.

Just before the sun broke over the horizon we pushed forward. As we headed into the mouth of the valley we had *Flight of the Valkyries* playing in our headsets. We only thought it fitting for that song to be on while on our last mission to a place like that.

The first set of compounds we encountered contained an eerie silence. The trucks in the rear took up their positions on the high ground with our mortar section taking up their spot as well. Everything remained quiet while our trucks rolled into their positions. Not a soul in sight. As we started to push up to the other set of compounds near the river, it started.

A call flooded the radio net. One of the back trucks watched as an RPG hit right behind them. We then started taking fire from every angle of the surrounding mountain. Being up in the front with the ODA [37] and the MTT team's truck, we started performing beautiful music with our .50 cal. machine guns.

Next thing I knew, I heard my LT tell me he lost communication with the ODA team located about 150 meters to our right. He then proceeded to tell me that he planned to run over there and link up with them to make sure everything continued all good on their end. As I started to give him the best cover fire he could ask for I heard a loud smack on the front of the truck. BAM. The driver proceeded to tell me we took a RPK round to the passenger windshield. This is where the lieutenant would have been sitting while commanding the vehicle.

Trying to keep the bullets down range at other targets I heard another smack on the windshield. BAM. Thinking I saw where it came from I traversed the .50 cal. to the wood line about 180 degrees to my 12 o'clock position. As I performed a quick scan I heard a loud CRACK as an enemy round passed my head. At that point I was pissed. I started slinging rounds into the wood line where I thought that bastard fired from.

Next thing I know I observed a man on a motorcycle with a rifle slung across his back dart out of the wood line behind the trees traveling fast

---

[37] ODA: Operational Detachment Alpha; Special Forces

down the road. As I sent my first burst down range I watched the dirt kick up about 10 feet behind him. I continued on with firing my weapon. I sent another burst down range, this time much closer but not on target. As I slung the next rounds headed his way all I could think of is "*FUCK YOU!*"

Next thing I know, the man and his bike hit the ground. By that time I began to run extremely low on ammo and our mortar team moved in to take up the spot where the MTT team has positioned itself because their .50 cal. Became inoperative. At this point ODA had called in an airstrike and the big guns headed our way.

As we consolidated our ammo we heard the fixed wing aircraft coming in as it laid a nice size bomb on the compound in front of us. We finally reestablished communications with ODA and the time to figure out if we were going to keep pushing or call it a win and head back had arrived. When the LT asked me what I wanted to do the only words which came out of my mouth were "*fuck it*". After a brief deliberation we decided we needed to turn around and head on back.

One hell of a mission.

BARRY LESNICK [2008]

We woke up like normal with the intent to head out to Kandahar and I was pretty excited. It was Black Friday and we had just come off a mission running mortars to support SF [38]. As a group, we were all pretty excited to go to Kandahar (especially when you compared the size of Kandahar to where we were living in Afghanistan). No one had any bad feeling – it was just another run up HWY 1 to get there (Kandahar) quick. We put the guns on the truck and that is the last thing I remember due to the brain injuries I sustained from that day. From that point on, I gathered first-hand accounts from my team members.

We were about 10km outside of Qalat City on a stretch of HWY 1. Our first truck's remote IED interception system started blinking. Before we really knew what had happened, the second truck (the one I was in), approached a wadi and as we drove over it, the IED ignited. The IED had been packed with approximately 1000 lb. of fertilizer to boost its power. The immediate contact with the IED launched my body out of the gunner's hatch from on top of my MRAP vehicle. The mechanic in the vehicle behind me slammed on his vehicle's brakes to avoid the IED crater and brought it (his vehicle) to a dead stop. He witnessed me fly over the dust cloud created by the IED while being simultaneously thrown about 50 meters up and out towards Taliban fighters shooting at me.

At the same time, one of my team members, A. was ejected out of the passenger's side of the vehicle through an opening where the door no longer existed. He was very badly injured (internal injuries: punctured lung, broken wrist, and brain injuries) as he crawled around covered in vehicle fluids. Covered in gasoline, he shouted our names to learn our statuses. Our driver, P., was still in his driver's seat at this point and not much was known about his injuries at that time. He (P.) told us not to worry about him because he couldn't feel anything.

Through all the commotion, I had hit the ground far away from my vehicle and soldiers. I attempted to stand up. Our mechanic, SGT R. had already called the 9-line [39] and ran to my position alongside Doc W. and S. (all of them from the first and last two vehicles). S. provided supporting fire by literally jumping on top of me to secure my position. The three of them dragged me about 50 meters away and uphill so that they could assess my injuries under more suitable cover. Everyone who had

---

[38] SF: Special Forces
[39] 9-line: medical evacuation radio call

sustained injuries laid out on litters, under constant enemy fire, while awaiting medevac. As soon as the firefight died down and the helicopters landed, I was strapped in with A. and they (medics) put me to sleep.

We were taken to Kandahar for emergency surgery to stabilize us. Once stabilized, I was then flown to Bagram for more emergency surgery. Once stabilized again, I was sent for minor surgery to Landstuhl, Germany where I stayed until my continued transfer to Walter Reed in Washington, DC. After more surgery, I woke up.

I found out that P. was two doors down from me and within three days, I had learned that he was quadriplegic with numerous broken bones. His mom came and broke down to me about her sadness that he would never get "better". About a week later, A. showed up in the psych ward where I visited him for his first 72 hours. We were later transferred to the Malogne House on Walter Reed campus until recovery in May.

Following all of this, I came home to a family who treated me like a criminal recently released from prison. I was pushed away and secluded from family that was within 20 miles of me. I battled with addiction and alcohol for a few years. After I decided to stop using drugs, I secluded myself in my home. I held it together for about two more years but then everything fell apart and I became suicidal. I attempted suicide three times in my home. I have a failed marriage because of my depression.

The injuries I sustained from Afghanistan include: a shattered femur (left leg) – with a prosthetic core rod and plates, shattered radius and ulna in both arms (requiring full rods plates), wounds from being shot six times in my left leg, and brain injuries – frontal lobe and both temporal lobes. I required total facial reconstruction surgery on my nose, both eye sockets, cheekbones, and jaw. I had to learn to walk again, alone, at Walter Reed. The only family that stayed were my brothers (fellow Soldiers). They were the only ones would truly understand.

I still have a slight speech impediment. Constant pain. Survivor's guilt. The nightmares. It's been ten years already this year and I still think about my guys every day. Every minute. I replay that day in my mind over and over, trying to fix it, but I can't. If only *this* had been different, or *that* had changed, maybe I would have been the one driving. Because of that day, I had to retire and could no longer fight alongside my brothers. This is something that I don't accept easily.

To this day, we have reconnected and I have made sure that we stay in contact so we can be there for each other. It is good to see them doing well in their lives and to be there for those who are not doing so well. I have since moved from a place where I felt no support to a place where I am finding peace. I love you brothers.

JOHN LEE [2009]

I'm always writing or even talking about my experiences in combat. I'm not ashamed about my experiences, other than the faint sense of embarrassment that every adult feels in the back of their mind when recalling the foolishness of youth. I'm proud of them. The trope of the beer-bellied, scruffy old timer waxing poetic about his experiences is well established in Veteran culture and to some extent, I am "that guy". No, what makes me nervous about sharing what I did is that my memory may fail me, maybe I'll take credit for something someone else did or someone that I served with will read this and send an angry email about something that I said that isn't true. I don't aim to hold this essay up to the standards of objective truth; this is written from my memory alone and is as emotionally tinged, as anything else in my life will ever be. I hope that the men that I served with (and I say men, because there were no women at these outposts that we fought at) find these words acceptable, because it is their respect that I hope to earn. Of course I'm also going to tell you a story about a dog, thus avoiding casting any real people in my unobjectively true story.

I was a heavy smoker during my first deployment, and indeed throughout all three deployments I would always have a pack of Camels in my grenade pouch or in one of my pockets. So when I walked out of the chow hall in the afternoon about a month into my first deployment I was easily able to flag down an Afghan Army sergeant carrying a puppy. I proceeded to trade him a pack of American cigarettes for the dog. He was a tiny little thing. The Afghans usually cut short the ears and tails of their dogs, but this one was too young for the knife. He could fit in the palm of my hand or inside an ammo pouch. His big brown eyes and thick black fur instantly hooked me. He shook as I carried him back to my room and I estimated that he was only 4 or 5 weeks old. I was able to scrounge some milk from the chow hall and some bread for those first few weeks, until the puppy food that I ordered from Amazon came in the mail. He slept in the top bunk with me, in a nest of towels that I'd made for him, so he wouldn't fall off. He whined whenever I left my room and after a significant amount of debate I decided to name him Sonic because he looked like a hedgehog.

This was before the fighting season started so I had some free time. I'd sit outside of my concrete and plywood b-hut [40] and he would curl up in my

---

[40] B-hut: temporary housing structure

lap while I read. I was on an anti-war author kick at that time, reading Vonnegut and trying to balance my past life as an art student with my new identity of an infantryman. I cringe reading some of my letters home, full of pseudo-intellectualism and false bravado, the type of idiocy I hope I've grown out of by writing this. But as Sonic grew the weather turned warmer and fighting season started. Sonic grew into a big mangy mutt. I had my first firefight and first close calls soon after acquiring my new friend. I sat on the porch with him and watched Apache gunships kill Taliban in the hills around our outpost as I kept him calm during the noise. I had to lock him in my room when I rolled out on Quick Response Force (QRF) missions when we would often rush to the scene of an Improvised Explosive Device (IED) strike and watch the medics work on what remained of the Afghan Army truck that had rolled over a bomb. Once, we went on an extended patrol that lasted days longer than expected and I remember the burning embarrassment as I got my ass chewed by our mechanics who had remembered I had left Sonic in my room and brought him food and water. After that I let him run free when I was on patrol and he'd happily run up to me as I jumped off my truck.

We started to fight more and more as the summer progressed. I found bullet holes in my truck and I remember exclaiming "*They tried to kill me!*" after hearing an AK round whine past the back of my neck. Some weeks we had firefights every day and we'd come back to our bunks hopped up on adrenalin and bravado, cleaning our weapons and going over the details of the gunfights. Sonic, as insightful as ever, would prance around us as we stumbled exhausted to the showers. He would try and play tug of war with my gear or dirty socks. He also started to pick up on the emotional toll that fighting the Taliban had on us. He picked up on the fact that we didn't particularly like the Afghans. The interpreters were on our side but we didn't trust the Afghan locals that helped cook our food and perform other tasks on the outpost.

Things started to become less fun as the summer drew on and the fighting intensified. A friend from another outpost showed me a bullet hole in his body armor where his plate had stopped it. But a replacement was slow to arrive. The Taliban had ambushed us on a large patrol and instead of overwhelming the enemy with our firepower we rushed out of the kill zone with A-10 Warthogs and Apache gunships providing cover close overhead.

I returned from one of those patrols when Sonic was about six or seven months old and couldn't find him. It wasn't anything that bothered me.

He'd roam around the outpost for hours at a time or hang outside the chow hall hoping for some scraps. The Afghan cooks hated him but we made sure that he was well fed, fat and happy. After taking off my gear and attending our debrief one of our team leaders ran up to me and informed me I needed to talk to the Platoon Sergeant. Sonic had bitten a Special Forces soldier who had been visiting us. As I thought it through it wasn't hard to figure out. Sonic became confused by the beard of the soldier, alien to my regular, clean-shaven Army unit, but worn as a badge of pride by the more elite warriors among us. With a rock in my stomach I heard how Sonic had mistaken him for an Afghan and tried to stop the soldier from entering one of our buildings. Sonic had ripped his pants from boot to crotch much to the amusement of the other soldiers and embarrassment of my leadership. I didn't have much to say to the Platoon Sergeant after I heard - he handed me an M9 pistol and a rope. Sonic was my dog and he was my responsibility.

I borrowed the Gator, a small utility vehicle we used to take trash around our outpost and tied him in the back. He kept slipping out of the rope and collar so I sat him on my lap and we drove to the range just outside the concertina wire and Hesco barriers. When we arrived I sat with him a while and fed him some bacon I'd stolen from chow and we watched the sun set over the Arghandab river. I ran through how I wanted to feel in my mind - the first time I'd indulge in a mental exercise that would eventually become a coping mechanism I was well-versed in. "*You're hard, you don't feel anything; you've killed people and felt nothing; you can kill a dog and feel nothing.*" I painstakingly felt the divide between me and the not quite real memory of my life in the United States. I stood on a great precipice. Stepping over would forever cement me as a soldier, separated from the soft fuzziness of American life. By doing this, I knew I would become hard and survive anything that the war could throw at me. Sonic never usually sat still, but as I had my hand on his back he stared peacefully out at the sunset. The sunsets in Afghanistan were always particularly beautiful. The dust makes them pretty. I sent my mom dozens of pictures of them.

I shot him in the base of his skull, where the spine meets the neck, because the bullet would sever his spinal cord and enter the base of his brain - killing him painlessly. The hardened pull of the trigger didn't cause me to blink as the shot echoed across the valley. He immediately went limp and collapsed into the dust as if his strings had been cut. I stood mute, cautiously dwelling on what I had done - much like probing the edges of a fresh wound to determine the damage. My mind lost focus when Sonic started to shake and convulse on the ground. I panicked, not knowing what to do for a moment. Looking around I stood on his neck and shot him in the head several more times while begging him to go to sleep. It took almost a full minute but he eventually died. I didn't cry. The ground proved too hard for me to dig a proper grave so I dug only a few inches down and piled rocks over his body. I took his collar and the dog tags that I had custom made for him and draped them over a tall rock at his head, unintentionally copying the Afghan cemeteries that dotted the countryside. I called up the Sergeant of the Guard to tell him I was headed back in and as I drove back into the compound he said "*Don't sound so sad Lee.*" I gave the pistol back and went to bed. A week later I logged my first confirmed kill. A month later we took our first casualty.

Now years later, my muscle has turned to fat and I've let my hair grow long. Sonic wouldn't like the beard that I wear now or having to wear a leash. Sometimes at night, with my dog on my chest I think of Sonic and of the shallow grave I buried him in. I wonder if his collar is still there and what that valley looks like now. A couple of years later the Americans would pull out of that valley completely. The decision would be rendered in the ongoing cost benefit analysis that is modern warfare that the valley wasn't worth the blood already spilled. And years later, here I am sharing a story about packing up the outpost and driving out of the valley forever, leaving behind a dead dog and stories that don't mean anything.

JEFF TRAMMEL [2009]

Jeffery Trammell
CPT, IN
The Blue Door Battle

In August of 2009, Alpha Company, 1-4 Infantry, deployed to Zabul Province, Afghanistan. The 1-4 Infantry deployed a Company to this province every six to eight months in support of a Romanian Battalion. Each company would send its three platoons to three separate Combat Outposts (COPs) in Zabul Province. One platoon deployed to COP Mizan in the Mizan District, one platoon to COP Lane in the Arghandab district, and the other platoon to COP Baylough in the Dey Chopan District. I served as the platoon leader (PL) for the platoon that deployed to COP Baylough. On October 6, 2009, a battle ensued in the Dey Chopan district, of Zabul Province, in southern Afghanistan.

The Dey Chopan district consisted of extremely mountainous terrain; the average elevation continued 7000m above sea level. The area had no improved roads and existed in almost total isolation. Only could small pickup trucks and M1151 HMWVVs could maneuver in the area. Nearly 90 percent of the missions we conducted were foot patrols. The area divided into three bowls between the mountain ranges. My platoon occupied the Baylough Bowl. Taliban occupied the Dauvdzay bowl, to the west, which could only be accessed by vehicles. To the north, the Taliban occupied the Larzarb bowl, an area only accessible by foot or through the air. To the south, Route Lion led to COP Lane and COP Lagman, where the Company HQ [41] stayed.

60 kilometers of harsh terrain separated COP Baylough from the Company HQ. The only way to access the COP came by Route Lion or by air. Helicopter flights and air drops existed as the most common way to access and resupply the COP. We augmented our platoon with about 40 Afghan Security Guards (ASG), a squad of Afghan National Army (ANA), and another 40-man department of Afghan National Police (ANP). Our platoon received the mission to retain the ground, build relationships with the locals, and mentor the ANA and ANP. The isolation that our platoon faced made this particular mission unique. We realized how much of the area was shaped by just the platoon.

---

[41] HQ: Headquarters

Before my platoon arrived, 2nd Platoon, Bravo Company, 1-4 Infantry, held responsibility for this area. Its operations had focused on both the west and the north. The Company Commander, Captain Mark Garner, had also coordinated several Company-sized missions to the north and had subdued what his Company could of the northern Larzarb Bowl. The Larzarb Bowl still remained a safe haven for the Taliban, but enemy infiltration from the north was significantly reduced because of Bravo Company's actions. The death of Captain Gardner in July 2009 factored in as another key event. While returning to COP Lane from COP Baylough, an IED claimed the life of Captain Gardner along Route Lion. This event led to Route Lion being classified as BLACK [42], which further isolated COP Baylough and bolstered the morale of an already confident enemy. This also led to a further decline in resources that COP Baylough received, as the COP would only be resourced through the air from that point forward.

I took over this area of operations in August 2009. During the RIP [43], the Platoon Sergeant, Sergeant First Class Stephen Carney, informed me that Dauvdzay remained a hot bed of Taliban activity. He also stated that it was only safe to approach the Larzarb Bowl with a company-sized element. With this information, I decided to focus platoon operations on the Dauvdzay Bowl. In September, we conducted patrols near the Dauvdzay Bowl to develop relationships with the locals and to recon the Dauvdzay area. We also conducted a foot patrol to a village called Chino 1 to identify a route for vehicles, key terrain around the area, and entry points into the bowl. On this patrol, we identified a compound that we called the Blue Door Compound because of a very identifiable blue door in the front of the compound. This compound's location at the entrance of the Dauvdzay Bowl had been identified as a Taliban safe house. After compiling all of this information, I developed a tentative plan for a cordon and search of the Blue Door Compound.

Several weeks before conducting our cordon and search, an ODA [44] team planned to conduct a mission in the Dauvdzay bowl, and we would serve as a Quick Reaction Force (QRF) for this mission. The ODA had setup two OPs [45] on hilltops at the entrance to the Dauvdzay Bowl. We located one OP on our designated Target Reference Point (TRP) 7 and another on our

---

[42] BLACK: a level where travel is severely restricted
[43] RIP: Relief in Place; conducted between incoming/outgoing military units
[44] ODA: Operational Detachment Alpha; Special Forces element
[45] OP: Observation Point

designated TRP 21. An Air Weapons Team (AWT) also supported the ODA by presenting a strong presence throughout the day. Lastly, we positioned ourselves in a hidden security position in five M1151s [46] about halfway between the Dauvdzay entrance and our COP.

The ODA Soldiers wanted to develop information on the area and build relationships with the locals because a supply route for the Taliban ran through the area all the way down to the ODA's specific AO[47]. This mission proved vital to us in terms of shaping our operation. The ODA team came into audio contact with the Taliban, but they never directly engaged by enemy fire. I spoke with the ODA commander and we determined that our strong security posture hindered the Taliban from moving to their positions due to fear of our presence. When the ODA team decided to ex-fil, helicopters picked them up at the entrance to Dauvdzay. The ODA used us to secure the HLZ [48], which enabled us to recon the Blue Door Compound due to the HLZ's location right next to it. Because of this mission, I identified a mounted route to the objective, specific positions for our trucks, and the make-up of the actual compound. I also noticed that the Blue Door Compound formed not just one compound but three separate compounds. Orchards and the rolling terrain obscured the two other compounds.

Once I had all of this information, I developed and issued a completed plan to our platoon's team leaders and above. The task organization for the mission comprised of 2nd and 3rd squads mounted in five M1151s, the entire twelve-man detachment of ANA [49], and a squad of ASG led by a Canadian Sergeant Major who worked with a security firm at the time. He used the call sign Canuck One. We planned to leave before sunrise and reach the objective right at dawn. The main reason for not performing the entire mission at night arose because the ANA and ASG elements had no night vision capabilities or training. The ANA and ASG elements would move dismounted in front of the two mounted squads. The ANA element would be controlled by a dismounted fire team from 3rd Squad.

The order of movement included the ANA element, the ASG element, 3rd Squad, and finally 2nd Squad. I moved in my HQ vehicle between 2nd and 3rd Squads. The Platoon moved along a predetermined unnamed

---

[46] M1151: Model of Humvee
[47] AO: Area of Operations
[48] HLZ: Helicopter Landing Zone
[49] ANA: Afghan National Army

route that used the road as little as possible. This was done in an effort to avoid IEDs as much as possible. The Platoon had one 60mm mortar that would be carried with us and deployed in conventional mode inside the actual compound. The Platoon also had a 120mm mortar located at the COP that would target TRPs as we moved. Once we reached a TRP, the 120mm mortar would switch to the next TRP along the route. We would then establish an Objective Rally Point (ORP) and reaffirm the plan with the ANA element before we reached the compound. We would then move quickly to the last covered and concealed position and, from there, have the ASG [50] element move up to TRP 7 and establish an OP. The vehicles then moved up to the Blue Door Compound and established an outer cordon around all three compounds. Once we established an outer cordon, the ANA element moved up to the compound and established the inner cordon.

I assumed control of the ANA element once it moved up to the cordon, and the fire team that controlled the ANA element stayed in covered and concealed positions to watch over the ex-fil route, while our element conducted the search. The search team, consisted of a fire team, members of the ANA, and myself. Together we searched the compound. Once we finished with our search, the ANA element moved back to the ORP [51], followed by the ASG element, and then the rest of the platoon. I established a complete engagement priority list for all of the elements. Also, all positions received mutually supported fields of fire. The complete plan had been prepared two days before the mission elapsed. That gave us the following day to complete rehearsals and PCI/PCCs [52].

The next day, I awoke to find that the Deputy Task Force Commander, Major Cannata, had arrived to accompany us during the mission. I informed him that we had no seats left in the trucks, and he let me know that wasn't a problem and that he would walk. "*Crap.*" I thought. I remained confident in my ability as a platoon leader, but this was my first big operation. I had developed it and planned it all by myself, and I certainly did not want my boss to be around when I messed it up. Still, Major Cannata taught me very important lessons, and by the end of the mission, he became one of the most respected officers by the Soldiers in the platoon. He empowered all of the leaders rather than trying to take

---

[50] ASG: Afghan Security
[51] ORP: Objective Rally Point
[52] PCI/PCC: Pre-combat Inspection/Pre-combat Checks

over the operation. He assisted us and demonstrated himself an asset that would prove vital later on in the mission.

The day of PCIs and PCCs proved very successful, especially in terms of the vehicles. When we first arrived to the COP, only three of six M1151s operated without faults. Not because the previous unit had not performed maintenance, but rather because the isolation of the COP made it so that we still received parts that the previous unit had ordered half-way through its deployment. This day of preparation allowed us to finally ensure that five vehicles would be operational and stay operational for the entire mission. For rehearsals, we walked through actions on contact thoroughly, but we also emphasized simple things, like getting out of the trucks and ensuring everybody knew where he would sit and on which special team(s) he belonged to. Small things like this proved vital in making us able to quickly react to situations and get into positions. Once I achieved satisfaction with everything, we ended the day early to give everybody enough rest for the next morning.

The night before the mission, I barely slept. Until now in the deployment, we had small engagements with the enemy. During these engagements, the enemy fire missed not by a couple of feet, but by a couple of hundred feet. This operation had the chance to be very different: we faced a high risk of someone getting hurt through the enemy's direct engagement. Now, this is what we all signed up for, but still, when actually faced with this possibility or risk, it played with your nerves, especially for a young Lieutenant. I also believed some of the soldiers to be just as nervous as me, so the next morning I tried to galvanize the platoon during the patrol brief.

The next morning did not start off as I had hoped. The ASG element showed up ready, but the ANA soldiers, slow to rise, delayed our departure until after sunrise. Finally, with everyone prepared, I gave one last patrol brief to ensure that everybody knew the purpose of the mission and how to conduct it. These types of briefs only lasted about five minutes. I told them that if and when we came into contact to respond violently and make sure the enemy knew what a huge mistake they had made. I used this final talk to inspire the men and mask my own nervousness. I often thought speeches like this were corny, but to my surprise, it seemed to have an effect. After its conclusion, the men exuded high motivation and visible excitement to conduct the mission. I still don't know if the men could grasp my nervousness, but if they did, they didn't show any signs.

At 0700 hours, on October 6, 2009, we left COP Baylough and headed to the Blue Door Compound. At first, everything appeared great. Major Cannata had taken over the dismounted fire team that controlled the ANA element. We moved along the route, and as we turned out of the local bazaar, control of the ANA element became difficult. They would often drift off route and the formation would have to be stopped to collect them up. At one point, an ANA soldier ran off after a suspicious person, who turned out to be just an older intoxicated man. These constant ANA soldier missteps slowed the formation, but eventually, we arrived at the ORP with no serious incidents regarding the enemy. When we reached the ORP, a truck-full of Afghans pulled up. At first, we noticed only five personnel in the vehicle, so we decided to stay at the ORP and enroll the personnel in the BATS/HIIDE [53] system. When all of the personnel exited the truck, I was amazed to find out the truck actually contained twenty men, women, and children. My distress grew when another truck of twenty Afghans pulled up. By then, all surprise had been lost due to our slow movement, so I decided to enroll all the men into the system from the ORP.

We over-watched the objective from a hilltop by the ORP. Major Cannata's fire team occupied the over-watch position, and I pushed the ANA forward to the orchards to stop anybody who tried to flee the compound as we approached. While enrolling the Afghans into the system, a man fled the compound and headed north on a motorcycle. The over-watch position fired a warning shot, and the man stopped. The ANA element moved down to question the man, and as it approached, the Taliban began to fire on them from the top of TRP 7. With only about five enemy personnel, the Taliban provided heavy fire and easily routed the ANA soldiers. The ANA element quickly fled to a nearby town, called Chino 1. At this point, I quickly ordered all of the vehicles to load up and told the civilian Afghans to flee to the west. I knew the safest thing for the civilians would be to make as much room between us and them as possible. I then maneuvered the trucks up to the compound by having 3rd Squad move by bounding over-watch. My 2nd Squad trailed 3rd Squad, and I moved with the latter. This drew the weapon fire away from the ANA but placed most of the fire directly onto my vehicle. I took pleasure in knowing that the ANA soldiers, no longer pinned down, found protection, but seeing bullets kick up in front of my vehicle and bounce off of my vehicle didn't exactly make me happy. Still, we easily

---

[53] BATS/HIIDE: military identification database collection systems

repelled the small enemy attack, but we couldn't fix on the enemy's position and destroy them as they broke contact alongside the backside of the hilltop.

Once I had maneuvered our trucks down to the compound, I set them up in their positions. My truck and 3rd Squad's trucks covered the west and the north. My 2nd Squad's trucks covered the south and supported 3rd in the north. Major Cannata's fire team set up about halfway in between the compound and ORP at a release point to over-watch the ex-fil route. The ASG element moved up and cleared TRP 7. Once it cleared TRP 7, it split its forces between TRP 7 and 8. The ASG, on TRP 7, over-watched the Dauvdzay bowl and the ASG, on TRP 8, over-watched to the north to observe the route that fed into the Larzarb Bowl. We positioned our 120mm mortar on TRP 21. Once all friendly elements took their positions, I brought the ANA in to establish an inner cordon around the Blue Door Compound. Once the ANA established its position, I gathered the rest of the platoon search team together, linked up with the ANA, and began to search. During the search, we moved through and examined all of the rooms in the compound, the people in the compound, all fire pits, wells, and basements.

Also at this time, two A-10 Warthogs came on station. I had trouble communicating with them so I turned over control of the A-10s to my 2nd Squad Leader, SSG Matthew Gabbert. I gave SSG Gabbert directions to have the A-10s conduct a show of force within the Dauvdzay bowl and recon potential enemy in-fil routes from the north and west. The A-10s soared on and off station throughout the day. At this point, I felt very good about myself. I had repelled an enemy attack and even though the mission had some hiccups so far, everything moved well and Major Cannata had only good things to say. I thought "*This was great; we are going to find some weapons or drugs and then go home after being in a successful firefight in which the enemy ran away out of fear.*" I didn't realize that Murphy [54] would play a role as the day progressed.

As we started the search, the ANA soldiers brought the man who previously fled into the compound to question him. The man immediately broke down and began to cry. He couldn't have been more than 18 years old. I felt sorry for the man, not because he was crying, but because he was obviously so shaken by what had occurred. After calming

---

[54] Murphy: References Murphy's Law

him down, I talked with him and determined that even if he did work with the Taliban, it was out of complete fear - although he never admitted it. At the end of all of it, we released him because I didn't believe he actively worked for the Taliban and we also had no evidence to detain him. I always thought that that encounter exemplified a good reflection of Army conditioning. Here, we were, almost completely unaffected by the small fire fight that just happened, and here was this man who had been living in this area all of his life visibly shaken and brought to tears by what just happened.

After we released the man, we continued to search the compound. We couldn't find anything in the compound, to include people. This should have been a warning to me, but, to be honest, it didn't look as though anybody had been living there for some time. We decided to move to the next compound a couple meters to the south of the Blue Door Compound. When we entered, there we saw several women, children, and elderly men. There were no military aged men though. Again, I should have started to worry, but my confidence was still brimming from the earlier engagement. We continued to search the compound, and we entered a section that was inhabited by four women. The women cried and huddled together in a corner. I felt extremely bad for scaring these women. We did a quick search and found nothing. The ANA Soldiers, though, unmoved by the crying women, held their suspicions about the section and wanted to perform a more thorough search. They made the women stand up and move away from their corner. When they walked away, a bag of about forty pounds of opium fell from between one of the women's legs. The Afghan soldiers then searched a fireplace and found two more bags of opium buried. They also found an AK-47 buried in the same fire place. We also found shotgun shells, brass casings, and links for a PKM. I was completely amazed and slightly impressed. We had extensively searched the other compounds and rooms, but the Taliban had hidden the illegal materials with the women, knowing that Americans traditionally showed empathy and courtesy towards women. The ANA element took possession of all of the materials, and we prepared to search a third compound further south of the original Blue Door Compound.

At this point in the operation, it was late in the afternoon, and the sun started to set. I knew that if we were going to get the ANA and ASG back safely, we would have to get at least half way home before it became dark. I decided to not search the third compound and begin our ex-fil. As previously mentioned, in the plan, the ANA element would move back first. They would be followed by the ASG element and then the mounted section. Every element understood the plan, but I talked with the ANA squad leader one last time to confirm the plan. I informed him no matter what happened, he was to move his squad back to the ORP. If his squad came under contact, it was to break contact and head back the ORP. I then made him tell me the plan and the contingencies to ensure that he understood what he was exactly supposed to do. Once he did, I sent him back to the ORP, and I went back to my truck. Again, I thought nothing bad could happen. We had already been so successful and everybody knew exactly what he was supposed to do and where to go. Then, the enemy decided to cast their vote on how the day would end.

As the ANA soldiers moved past the mounted formation, they immediately came under fire from an orchard and hilltop to the north. The ASG element began movement down TRP 7 as the ANA Soldiers passed the mounted formation. The A-10s were again on station at this point and now joined by two AH-64 Apaches. At first, this simple engagement seemed as though it would be over quickly with all of the assets available. Then, as the ASG element moved down TRP 7, it came under fire from atop TRP 7. As the ASG element began to come under fire, my truck and the 3rd Squad vehicle to my south came under fire from a small hilltop in the Dauvdzay bowl and a mountaintop just past TRP 21. Then, the ANA soldiers, became routed again and moved back to the village of Chino 1. "*Are you kidding me?*" I thought, "*Don't these guys know that I'm new at this?*" Still, I composed myself and assessed the situation. The ANA Soldiers had run right into friendly fields of fire, and if we didn't suppress TRP 7, the ASG element would not be able to move all the way back to the ORP. Also, the battlefield stretched about 3KM from south to north. I also assessed that between four maneuver squads, two air assets, a 120mm, mortar and a 60mm mortar, I was beyond my span of control.

I first decided to split the battlefield between 3rd Squad and 2nd Squad. I would control 3rd Squad and focus on suppressing the enemy in the south and west. I would also take control of the fixed wing aircraft and retain control of all indirect fires. 2nd Squad would focus on suppressing the north and covering the ASG element as it moved back to the ORP. Major Cannata assumed the most difficult task of rallying the ANA soldiers and moving them back to the ORP.

Next, the actual execution of this plan commenced. The 120mm mortar went cold, because with all of the air assets we had no method of using them; however, we used the 60mm mortar in direct lay. I had the mortar sergeant pull the 60 and put it on direct lay targeted at TRP 7. By this point, the enemy actively engaged all elements. I had always heard that insurgent fighters were poor marksman, but that day proved that notion wrong. The mortar sergeant, SSG Marty Brosset, had difficulty pulling the mortar from his truck because every time he would get to the back of the truck, he would come under heavy fire. Often times, bullets would ricochet across the back of truck and SSG Brosset would have to seek cover and wait until a lull to try again. Eventually, he pulled out the mortar and engaged the top of TRP 7. This neutralized the enemy and allowed the ASG elements to move down the rest of the hilltop. As they passed through the mounted formation, they again came under attack by the same enemy engaging the ANA soldiers. The ASG element managed to stay together under the control of Canuck 1 and they were able to make it back to the ORP unscathed.

While this continued, my vehicle and the southern vehicle suppressed the enemy in the west. At this time though, TRP 21 remained unprotected by our mortars because the 120mm lay cold. I attempted to radio the southern truck, but I received no response. I immediately ran the 100m from my truck to the other truck to tell the Soldier to cover TRP 21 with their .50 cal. machine gun. The gunner had trouble hearing me and I pointed out exactly where I wanted him to cover. As I pointed up to TRP, I noticed an enemy MG team setup on top of the mountain. I then noticed that I was standing in an open field completely exposed. I then looked back at my truck, which provided my only cover, and decided that getting back there as fast as possible was my best option because the enemy machine gunner lay protected and distanced over five hundred meters away behind good cover. I watched as the enemy gunner pointed his weapon directly at me and then took off.

I hadn't realized how close I had been to getting shot until I moved back to my truck and my gunner told me that the enemy machine gun walked its rounds in on me and that the rounds came within one foot of me. I knew that the rounds had impacted close to me, but I didn't know that they had been so close. At this point, all of the enemy positions in the west fired accurately and began to overwhelm the gunners. I didn't have to order any soldiers out of their trucks, because they all dismounted by themselves and followed the engagement priorities list down to a tee. Even our interpreter began to fire in defense of himself. Dismounts engaged other [enemy] dismounts within 300 meters. The heavy guns mounted on the trucks stayed on MG teams 300 meters and beyond, as well as RPG teams 150 meters and nearer. These simple engagement priorities ensured that we could destroy the biggest threats first without any target overkill. Other priorities existed, but we encountered only these two types of enemies during this fight. Eventually, we suppressed the enemy and prevented the envelopment of the entire platoon.

Meanwhile, when the ANA soldiers fled to Chino 1, they directly ran into 2nd Squad's field of fire in the north. This presented a significant problem because the enemy still actively engaged them and 2nd Squad from a hilltop above the ANA soldiers. Also, someone now had to go rally the ANA. Major Cannata's fire team saw where they [ANA] went and could quickly reach them. He recommended to me that they should go get them. I told them to go do it and the fire team proceeded to move to the ANA positions. I wasn't happy about it, but to suppress the enemy while Major Cannata's team moved up to the ANA soldiers, I had 2nd Squad fire over the ANA element.

The village of Chino 1 sat in some low ground and the enemy location provided enough distance away from friendly forces. This allowed the gunners to engage only the enemy on the high ground, with friendly forces out of the beaten zone. The situation thrilled no one, but the rate and accuracy of the enemy's fire indicated that no suppression on Major Cannata's team would pose a greater risk than firing on the enemy and over friendly positions. Major Cannata bounded himself and his team from their position a couple of hundred meters toward the ANA position. Even with the suppression, the team came under heavy fire and Major Cannata used the M249 SAW gunner as a local support by fire to finish his movement to the ANA positions. Eventually, the team made it to the ANA soldiers and rallied them. Major Cannata then moved the ANA soldiers back to the ORP, once again under fire. All the more impressive, the fire team accomplished this without using an interpreter.

Once the ANA element and ASG element returned to the ORP, the mounted elements began to move back. All the enemy on TRP 7 and on the western line had been suppressed, but the enemy to the north still positioned itself to continue fighting. I moved the trucks up to a position near the ORP where the trucks could use cover and suppress the final remnants of the enemy. Up until this point, the air assets remained unused because every time we walked the air onto the targets, the enemy would either displace or hide, leaving the CAS and CCA with no targets. This last engagement showed no difference. Just as we walked the

Apaches onto the targets, the enemy displaced, and the Apaches could not positively identify targets. Cave systems and large boulders provided the enemy excellent cover and concealment. This made it extremely difficult for air assets to engage targets not just during this fight but for the remainder of the deployment.

During this final engagement a bullet wounded a child, hiding in a field, in his leg. We didn't know that this had happened at the time. It wasn't until his grandfather brought him to the COP several hours after we had returned. We turned this unfortunate incident into a positive though. Our actions of caring for the wounded child and saving his leg led to the grandfather providing us a considerable amount of information on the local Taliban.

Once we had suppressed the final enemy to the north, the mounted elements moved back to the ORP. At the ORP, we reconsolidated and reorganized, and began to move back to the COP. The movement started out very well. Then about halfway, everybody's energy level crashed. Once everybody's adrenaline had subsided, the dismounts became walking zombies, and the [Afghan] soldiers in the trucks struggled to stay awake. Normally, the Afghans could walk around the rugged terrain all day and all night, without showing any fatigue. By the time we reached the Bazaar though, 2000 meters away from the COP, they had to stop and call the ANP to come pick up the ASG and ANA elements, with their ANP pickup trucks. Around 2100 hours, we finally made it back with all of our personnel and equipment.

I held an AAR [55] immediately after the mission, against my NCOs' wishes, because I wanted the information to be fresh. We also structured it in a very simple way to keep the AAR from becoming just a war story forum and kept it to a device where we could pull actual lessons learned. I structured the AAR in the following manner: I briefed our original plan, then an NCO would brief what actually happened up to an important part of the mission. At these parts [of the AAR], such as when we reached the ORP or when we came under fire, the platoon would identify three things we could improve and three things we would sustain. The "improves" for the mission included that someone always needs to be with the ANA soldiers, because even though they say they understand, they may not fully. We also identified that we all needed to improve our

---

[55] AAR: After Action Review

use of CAS [56] and CCA. We didn't take full advantage of these assets during the mission and they could have been critical in destroying all of the enemy forces. This AAR point actually led to us getting a joint tactical air controller (JTAC) to come out to the COP and teach us how to better use these assets.

The biggest sustain we identified covered the use of controlled violence. Through the strong identification of sectors of fires and engagement priorities, we maintained an ability to destroy or repel enemy forces without producing large amounts of collateral damage. During mission, we hadn't damaged or destroyed any buildings or property. We had successfully MEDEVAC'd the young child with the bullet wound in his leg, and he returned to the area completely healthy. We also identified the strong communication between all the elements and that really came from rehearsals. The rehearsals put everybody on the same page and made communications much easier.

Overall, we succeeded in our mission. Everybody made it back uninjured, several enemy perished, and we seized a large amount of drugs and weapons. We also identified several lessons that would improve our platoon throughout our deployment. This would not be the last fight we had in the area, and in fact, in another large fight in the area, three Soldiers sustained injuries and earned Purple Hearts. Yet, this fight sent a message to the Taliban that if they wanted to fight us, we would not just run away but would violently engage them and make them pay for attacking us.

This battle also provided us larger access to the Dauvdzay area. That led to the Dauvdzay elder eventually attending shuras [57], and by the end of the deployment, the elder [of the area] informed us that the Taliban had left the Dauvdzay area. For me, this experience proved incredible. At only 24 years of age, I learned the surreal feeling of an actual firefight.

The hardest part about writing this story though comes in articulating how the planning of the operation commenced and then trying to describe the incredible work of the Soldiers under my leadership. I can't say enough about those Soldiers. In our society we only see warriors as grizzled Special Forces Soldiers than can kill a man with a stare.

---

[56] CAS: Close Air Support
[57] Shuras: village/tribal meetings

Those guys are great, but the men of 2nd Platoon, Alpha Company, 1-4 IN are the Soldiers to look up to. I tell this story through my perspective and with my inner monologue, but without those men none of this happened. These guys endured a 270 degree ambush where the enemy had the high ground and attacked us at our most vulnerable, and my Soldiers held their ground, repealed the enemy and brought everyone home safely. I held responsibility and command, but any credit for victory must go to those Soldiers and their display of a true warrior character.

(Special Note: This account originally appeared as part of his time in the Army Captain's Career Course. This excerpt has been edited for content and clarity.)

ALEX BENTLEY-FREEMAN [2009]

(Special Note: Alex died in a car accident a few days after submitting his story for the book project. He will be deeply missed by those who knew him and those with whom he served.)

It was October at some point, I will have to look at my award paperwork to be sure when. We rolled out of the wire at COP (combat outpost) Mizan before the sun had risen to conduct a KLE (key leader engagement) in a town that I can't remember the name of for the life of me. The KLE was uneventful as they usually were. We had already picked up our sniper OP (observation post) and were on our way back to the COP. My truck consisted of the LT , SPC M. as the driver, SPC T. as the gunner, the terp that we called Rocky and myself the medic. We were about a kilometer away from base when I heard T. yell that an explosion went off in front of a vehicle approximately 3 trucks back from us in the convoy. At that time, I had no idea whether anybody had been hurt or not.

At that point, T. yelled out *"CONTACT! 3 o'clock."* He began to fire his m240B but it jammed; he was having a hell of a time getting it back up and at that point we could all hear rounds ricocheting off of the turret as he yelled out about a rocket propelled grenade flying by his head.

The ANA (Afghan National Army) truck in front of us screeched to a halt and started firing its DShK (Russian anti-aircraft machine gun) while the soldiers piled out of the back of the truck to push towards the enemy who we couldn't see. In step with the present situation, LT had called up to Mizan base and called in a 120mm strike on TRP 3 I think it was. I will never forget the sound that round made. You could hear the explosion, but what came after that haunted us while the shredding sound of the shrapnel cut through the air so close to us.

I remember looking across the Humvee out the window and seeing a local national peeking his head out of his hut., right before the impact and then running back inside when he heard the initial explosion. He looked to be about 20. I do not know if he got hit or not, but seeing as he never came to the base to receive treatment from me, I am assuming he did not.

At this point the LT screamed into the radio that we needed to get moving – and fast. We and all of the ANA (minus the truck that the soldiers had poured out of) started to push through the ambush. I will never forget what happened when we rounded the corner of the mountain. The LT, frustrated with the situation to put it lightly, started punching the BFT and yelling, *"Goddamnit!"* repeatedly. On the third time he shouted out, everything faded into a haze for a second. It seemed as though all of the moon dust that had been building up in these vehicles over the past couple of years of use had decided to dance in the daylight around us.

I looked around and my training kicked in. I started putting my hands on everyone in the truck and asking them if they had been hurt. The external blast blew open the doors of the Humvee. The terp, LT and driver told me they were fine, so I told them to get out of the truck. At this point I heard T. up in the turret yell down at me *"DOC!!!! I'M SQUIRTIN!!"* I told him to put his hand on it and I would be up there in a minute. I climbed up into the hatch and noticed his Kevlar nowhere to be seen as he held his right hand to the right side of his face. I told him to take his hand off of it so I could see. When he did this, I saw a laceration about 6 inches long and the wound squirted blood out of it, hitting the glass in the gunners hatch. I told him to put his hand back on it and get out of the truck. I later found out that he had severed a facial nerve. I also didn't realize with everything occurring at the time that the rest of the platoon laid down some serious hate and malice into the ridgeline right next to us.

I proceeded to get out of the truck after grabbing my aide bag and went over to T. to start working on him. As I began to wrap his face with gauze our mechanic mentioned *"Doc, you know you're bleeding on him, right?!"* I yelled back asking what the fuck he was talking about and he pointed to his forehead. I reached up and felt the left side of my forehead, realizing a twinge of pain as I did so. I told T. to hold the gauze I had been using on his face and proceeded to wrap my own forehead. At that point, I realized I did not have my helmet either. I completed the wound dressing on T. and we loaded up into another vehicle while everyone else was either firing at the ridgeline, or hooking up our crippled Humvee to drag it home.

After we arrived back to the base and called up a medevac while re-dressing wounds, we realized that M. (our driver) suffered from a traumatic brain injury. When the bird [58] arrived we all loaded up. While we were flying towards FOB (forward operating base) Lagman the flight medic tried initiating a saline lock on M. and he slapped him. M. sat between my legs and I told him to chill and explained what was

---

[58] Bird: slang word for helicopter

happening so the flight medic could work. The rest of the flight proved uneventful.

T. and I got off at Lagman to go to the FST (forward surgical team) and M. continued on to KAF (Kandahar Airfield) for further evaluation. While T. and I walked to the FST we saw a smoke pit right outside the door and asked if we could smoke first. Everyone told us to shut the hell up and get inside. As we entered to be treated, my senior medic, SGT M. told me something hilarious when he first saw me, "*Damn it, Bentley. I told you not to get hurt.*" I don't remember if I actually responded or just thought "*Yeah, cause I meant to do this shit.*" I was getting sutures put into my forehead and I heard a commotion from where Toups was. The people working on T. were trying to tell him that he had bitten off half of his tongue in the blast.

Now let me preface the rest of this by explaining T. to you. He is a Cajun, born with half of a tongue, so he couldn't speak for shit to begin with. As the medical personnel were yelling that he bit off half of his tongue, he was yelling back unintelligibly that that was the way he was born. He got fed up with them not understanding and slapped all their hands away and pulled together the wound on his face, and proceeded to speak as slowly and clearly as he could "*No mother fuckers, that's how I was born, I was a crack baby.*" I almost lost my shit. While this was going on I was being told that I may have a bit of a scar, and I proceeded to say that I didn't give a fuck because bitches love scars. One female NCO medic got offended, and then a female Major said "*What?! We do!*"

And that there is the story of the day I earned my Harry Potter scar. When I went back out to the COP 4 days later I got to see the Humvee, the entire trunk had been destroyed and the blast shield had been pushed forward from a secondary blast of the ammunition in the trunk. I just count myself lucky that I didn't get my back broken, which would have been the least that would have happened had I been wearing a seatbelt on that mission.

SEAN STACY [2010]

TUESDAY 23 MAR 2010

During the evening I found myself talking to the Afghan Army Soldiers through the use of an interpreter out of sheer boredom. One way or another, throughout the conversation, I mentioned that the Americans had been to the moon, and to this day our flag still flies there. This brought about hysterical laughter, and I feel that they thought I was completely making this up to play a practical joke on them. The more serious and adamant I was, the funnier it seemed to them. It is as if the very concept, of a group of people via the use of technology and motivation from the space race with the Russians, would find themselves with the capabilities of going to the moon, was completely alien and unbelievable. At conversations end I am positive that they thought I was attempting to make a joke at their dispense and to this day none of those men actually believe that there is an American flag on the moon. It just goes to show the difference in culture between our two societies.

THURSDAY 25 MAR 2010

Still being kept busy with details. Today a Command Sergeant Major and a Colonel came unannounced to check on us from the 82nd Airborne. We are attached to them and belong to Task Force Fury. He was upset to say the least and claimed we were going "native" on him. Among his complaints were our lack of bloused boots, unshaved faces, and improper wear of the uniform. Although I realize the important of discipline in a professional army, it still humors me how these big shots show up and expect us to be in a garrison mind frame. He accused us of hording food since we have piles of boxed food. We do not even want it and have sent up multiple requests that the supply trucks stopping bring us rations but these have all gone ignored.

It is annoying to be woken up in the middle of the night to download supplies and rations that we do not even need, and then on top of that to be chewed out for having too much of it. At any time another unit can come and help themselves to most of this crap and they won't hear a complaint out of anyone of us. The amount of water we get is a problem too. Most of it goes bad from being in the sun before we have a chance to drink it. The oils in the plastic break done and leave the water with a fuel aftertaste. We try to keep most of it in the shade but we cannot fit all of it underneath the platforms that we are building. We were instructed upon our arrival to open and smell each bottle of water before we start to drink from it. If it has a slight scent of oil, we are not to drink it because that would mean that the plastic has started to decompose (due to sunlight) back into its oil derivative. An obvious indicator is when the labeling has faded from the bottle. We would use these bottles for washing ourselves.

I suppose it could always be worse and instead of having too much we could not have enough. When I was attached to the 101st during my first deployment and they never showed up at our FOB or told us how to behave. I do appreciate the fact that I had a chance to have been attached to two of the most famous units in the Army. I have TOC duty again tonight and who knows what else they have planned for us tomorrow. The worst part of this deployment so far is the complete lack of schedule. The higher ups within the platoon attempt to keep us informed of what is going on but they themselves are often left in the dark. Routine, regardless of the op tempo, can be a comforting factor out here.

TUESDAY 30 MAR 2010

The amount of fuel that is required to fill this FOB is staggering. I can't imagine how much fuel is used on a daily basis to maintain operations of the hundreds of FOBs throughout this country. I have also come to realize how lazy Romanians are. They literally sit around all day and play board games and cards. Almost every one of them is overweight and lack in personal hygiene. At chow they eat two or three portions. Although we have make-shift toilets, they prefer to relieve themselves in holes in the ground. My last deployment we were forced to go to the bathroom in plastic bags and then throw them in the burn pit, so I appreciate being able to use a toilet. On the other hand we didn't have to use toilets last time, so there was less of a mess to clean up after.

WEDNESDAY 31 MAR 2010

Went on a mission today in a town called Nawrak. My platoon along with another one that came from FOB Lagman joined to together and encircled the town. We put 31 people into the biometric system. I was assigned as a M1151 [59] driver for the CO at the last minute. I'm not usually a driver so I had mixed feelings. As an infantryman, I prefer to dismount and go

---

[59] M1151: A type of Humvee

into town rather than stay behind with the gunner and the truck. Our role with the vehicles is to provide security for the town while our guys are talking to the elders in an attempt to gain information about the Taliban.

While searching the town we found a dried up well they were concealing. There were tire tracks leading us to it and the edges were worn down indicating that people went in and out of it. A search turned up nothing. From talking to the villagers we learned that the local police chief, whose compound was only 500 meters away, had been supposedly mistreating them. One villager ran up to us with the police in pursuit and told us the police were trying to steal his money. Other villagers told us they came drunk at nights and mistreated women and robbed the men. A father told us they came and took his son three days before and he hadn't seen him since. It was implied he was taken with the intention to be sodomized by the police chief.

After hearing this, we turned our target on to the police compound. We surrounded the compound and trained our weapons on them. It was an awkward moment and I could feel the tension in the air. Afghans are very proud people and I was glad when they didn't resist. We entered and did a search, resulting in finding heroin. The plan was to tell the police chief to either leave town or be removed from his position. We didn't know how he would react, so that is why we came in heavy-handed.

Before the CO and his escort went in the compound, he instructed me and the vehicle gunner that if we heard any gunshots to drive the vehicle through the gate and start shooting any one not wearing a US Army uniform. After that we returned to base and discussed what had happened. At the time there was very little information being passed on so I was left in the dark wondering what the hell was really going on. I have an early guard shift tonight and will be able to go to sleep at a decent hour. Hopefully I will be able to contact my family from the TOC computer, which was returned after being taken away because an NCO was using it to look at indecent material while he was on duty.

THURSDAY 01 APR 2010

Got back from another day mission today. We went to a village called Gajuy about 4 km away to conduct a key leader's engagement and enroll more villagers in our biometrics. It was a larger village right off HWY1 with a bazaar nearby. One platoon surrounded the village while mine went in to conduct the mission. I was assigned to pull dismounted security in the village.

Part way through the mission I was told to accompany our LT with a few other guys to walk through the village and check for anything suspicious, which we did not find. After talking to the elders and taking biometrics from 51 villagers we mounted up and returned to the FOB. I haven't talked to my family for a few days now and hope they don't think I am ignoring them; I just haven't had the chance to get to a computer to contact them.

Escrow closed on the house we purchased and my wife has been fixing it up the last couple of weeks. I think she is putting too much into it in terms of repair, and every time I get a chance to check my email she is telling me about the latest thing she has changed. I do not agree with all the changes but there is little I can do from here except to mention my thoughts and hope she listens to me. I realize she is creating her nest to raise our children, so it does not bother me much. If anything I feel guilty for her having to deal with all the details on her own. She is competent so I am sure everything will work out.

WEDNESDAY 07 APR 2010

The ANA have recently acquired our weapons and seem to lack in training in the use of them. An advantage of them using American weapons is that the Taliban cannot benefit from the sale of ammunition by corrupt Afghan police and Army personnel. While out here, I read a report about how over 70 percent of ammunition taken from the Taliban had matching serial and lot numbers of the ammunition that we provide Afghan police and military to provide security for this country.

If this war goes on long even the M16 and M4 will replace the weapon of choice of insurgents throughout the world that currently rely on the AK47 produced by the Soviet Union and their allies. Our weapons are more accurate, but they do require more maintenance. Watching some of the Afghans work with American weapons had me wondering if them switching over is a good idea. Either choice has its pros and cons. I'm sure the decision makers have a lot more knowledge of the situation then I do.

THURSDAY 08 APR 2010

Returned from a dismounted mission to Kuh-E-Lala-Shahid (rough English translation, pronounced as sounded), a mountain about 10K away from our FOB. It took my squad most of the day to reach the summit, which was over 6200 feet, so we could set up an OP and monitor enemy activity in the valley below. We brought a 240B machine gun and a 60mm mortar tube with us. Every person, eight in total, brought three mortar rounds with them. There were about seven ANA soldiers with us, but they kept a distance and did their own thing.

The hike definitely showed a few people that they need to work on getting in better shape. Before we left we even decided that a couple people shouldn't go because the two individuals would slow us down and hamper our ability to move, actually being a liability instead of an asset. Around evening we started heading down and a few hours later linked up with our mounted element and returned back to base.

While we were there we discovered a female sheep that had separated from her herd so she could give birth to her lamb. The place she decided to do her business was not the best location since there was no food or water and the little one was not able to follow her down the mountain because of the steepness. The Afghan soldiers picked up the lamb and, with the sheep following them, brought them back the village on the way down. I have always thought that if you handle a baby animal as too young of an age that the mother would reject it, but I figure since these people have been handling animals since the times of Jesus that they probably knew a lot more about this type of thing then I did.

So far we haven't encountered the enemy where I am. At my previous FOB last year, we got into an hours-long firefight within hours of arriving. I remember thinking that was to be expected on a daily basis since it was my first time in combat and so soon after I arrived. The Taliban mortared and attacked us with small arms on multiple sides. I couldn't make much out because there were orchards around us. As the sun set and I turned on my night vision goggles, I was able to see their muzzle flashes and was surprised by both how many of them were attacking, and how close they were to us. We blanketed the entire tree line with MK19 rounds and eventually the attack died down.

The next morning we went out to the areas they attacked from but found no bodies. We did however find body parts and areas with a lot of dark blood, indicating arterial bleeding along with bloody man dresses. The local villages told us shortly after the attack the Taliban came through their villages asking for water and food for their trip back to Pakistan and that they had both dead and wounded with them. Although we engaged the enemy many times after that, it wasn't on a daily basis like I thought it would be. However, from that night on I always made sure my rifle was close at night, and for a while, some even slept with their rifles on their bunks.

I cannot understand why the Taliban had attacked our fortified positions when they could have decided to instead ambush one of our dismounted squads during the following days of us arriving. They would have caught us in the open with under ten personnel, most of them being privates [60] fresh from basic training. Whenever they are successful during their attacks, they use the same tactics and doctrine that we use. They establish a support by fire and maneuver with a flanking element. Had they attacked us shortly after they arrived, instead of wasting manpower and resources on the FOB attack, it would have not been a good situation for us.

Like I mentioned previously, due to the amount of inexperience by us, it is sketchy at best how we would have reacted. Besides two or three of our NCOs that had previous experience, for the rest of us, it would have been our first baptism by fire. The enemy could have chosen the time and place for the attack and not initiated the ambush until everything was in their favor. They would have also had the advantage of knowing the terrain, which in the first couple weeks we did not.

WEDNESDAY 14 APR 2010

Went on a dismounted mission yesterday with 1st squad and about seven ANA soldiers. We traveled about three kilometers south up to a riverbed and then walked about eight kilometers west, looking for potential crossings for military vehicles. We only found two but wrote down the grids for future reference.

The mission was more of an area recon than anything else. We are still learning the area we have been assigned to. While walking I looked down and noticed an old pineapple grenade. I wrote down the grid and sent it up to my chain of command. Another member in my squad also found

---

[60] Private: lowest Army rank; brand new Soldier

two mines out there. We arrived on a bridge and attempted to make a communications link-up with our base using the TACSAT radio, which did not work. When working properly, the TACSAT is capable of communicating across large distances. Due to us being a far distance from our base and not having communication, our LT decided to have us head back.

When we got back to base, I noticed within an hour that there was something funny about the Romanians. Apparently they got some alcohol from home, or where ever. They were up until about 5 a.m. going crazy. They remind me of stories you hear about American Indians, how whatever they get they drink it until it's gone and get completely annihilated. They kept most of us up all night, but I didn't mind, I thought it was funny hearing them laugh until they cried, although I would say they were making complete fools of themselves. At one point, SPC M. got fed up and decided to say something to them.

The only thing separating our living space from theirs was a wood wall that stopped a few feet short of the ceiling. He set up a chair so he could stand on it to speak to them. When he popped his head over the wall he saw three Romanians. One was dressed in nothing but his underwear, and the other two were splashing water on him and hitting him with a whip. At first shocked, he mentioned that it was close to 3AM and that in the next couple hours we would have to wake up to go on a mission. He told them they were being too loud and that we were having trouble going to sleep. They responded by laughing hysterically and throwing a picture of a nun at him. Sounds completely random, but it happened. M. gave up, crawled back to his bed shaking his head, and realized that neither he nor the rest of us were going to end up getting any sleep that night.

SUNDAY 18 APR 2010

Received rocket fire while at FOB Warrior escorting a convoy of ANA soldiers. A Polish military K9 almost attacked our interpreter, most likely because the dog was trained to not like Afghans in general. Our interpreter, xxxxx, was even more upset that rather than sticking up for him we all just started laughing and teasing him. We give the terps so much harassment and talk a lot of shit to them. I'm sure most of them wonder why they are even helping us. We constantly try to feed them pork, which is against their religion. It's almost like a game – they cannot read English, and whenever they ask us what a food product says, we tell them it is harmless beef. We have even gotten away with feeding them canned dog food by telling them it was a rare delicacy in America. Once they eat it we start laughing and tell them they ate pork and will not get the 72 virgins they were expecting. We are lucky they don't place a grenade under our bunks.

Most American FOBs have pet dogs even though we are not supposed to. They bring up morale and learn to be weary of anyone not in American uniforms. Unfortunately when replacing units take over a FOB at the end of a tour the Commanders often have the animals shot. Shortly after that they eventually get a dog of their own and the process repeats itself. We have a dog that the men named Jimmy and hopefully he will make it through a couple different units before his time comes. He hates the Afghan Army that stays with us and will chase them whenever they get too close to the American compound. They are terrified of him and run as soon as they realize he is heading in their direction. It probably doesn't help that a lot of the Americans encourage the dog to act this way. The Afghans don't help either by throwing rocks at the dog when they think there are no Americans watching.

TUESDAY 27 APR 2010

I got back to Al Masak yesterday after being gone for nine days because of an injury. On the 15th or 16th of this month we went on a mounted patrol to another FOB to exchange vehicles for the newest model. On the way back, I was in the lead vehicle and we hit an IED. The blast was a 300lb bomb underneath the asphalt. The Taliban heated up the road, peeled back the asphalt, laid the bomb and put the asphalt back down again. It was command detonated and was triggered from someone about 300 meters away to the south. He had run the wire through a field, down a ravine, across a river, and into a tree line. The blast threw our vehicle in the air and we landed upside down. I was thrown around inside the vehicle and was the only person in the back. I hit my face on something, most likely the padded seat across from me (since I didn't shatter my facial bones) and was knocked out. I had "carpet" burns across my face which also makes me think I hit the seat across from me. I also crushed my leg due to the fact that the ammunition for the MK19 was not tied down. There had to be 15-20 cans, and I would assume each one weighed at least 35 lbs. It was not my assigned vehicle.

While we were in Lagman our vehicle was dead-lined because of a mechanical issue. At the last minute, they told me I would be riding in a vehicle with another crew. When I came to, I realized that we had hit an IED and that I was bleeding from my nose and mouth. Luckily no one in the vehicle was seriously injured. I looked up and saw that our gunner was dangling upside down – only held in place by the safety harness that prevented him from being thrown from the vehicle. His head was probably less than six inches from the pavement. We exited the vehicle and set up security in case there was an ambush.

I was out of it for a few minutes because of the concussion. I remember people asking me questions but even though I was answering in my head I was unable for a few minutes to answer verbally. The other people in the vehicle with me were SPC B., SSG S., and SPC P. The PL [61] called up on the net that our vehicle was a catastrophic kill. For the vehicles in the back it must have looked like we were done. Eventually some of them came up and helped us establish security. In the meantime another convoy from a different unit happened to be going in the opposite direction and helped us set up a perimeter while we investigated the blast site to determine where the trigger man had been located. It also took a while for us to recover the parts of the vehicle that had been blown off during the blast.

Within a few hours a wrecker vehicle arrived to tow our truck back to a recovery bay. They took us back to the FOB we had just come from and took us to medical and behavior health. I developed the largest bruise I've ever had in my life behind my right thigh, basically covering the whole thing. They told us no duty for 72 hours but it took over a week for them to find us a ride back. We spent the time reading books and playing cards.

FOB Lagman has a computer room with Internet so we were able to catch up with events going on back at home. I was told to call my wife and tell her I was involved with a combat-related injury and that I was okay. No other details were to be mentioned. It reminded me of the time when I was in basic training and I was given a note that I was to read off to the person I called. I had to say only what was on the note, and not deviate a single word. No bye, I love you, or anything. "*Hello dear sir or ma'am. This is PFC Stacy, roster number 348. I am assigned to Alpha Company 1-50. I am alive and well. I will call you later with further details.*" As soon as the last word was said I was supposed to hang up, and there was a drill sergeant

---

[61] PL: platoon leader

standing within a foot of me to make sure it went according to plan. I decided to call my mom instead of my wife. She was married to a Marine 30 years ago and I figured she would understand better. Regarding the IED, I decided to call my wife this time. Of course a wife is going to be upset about that type of information. Eventually we got a ride back aboard a Blackhawk and arrived around evening, just in time to prep for the next mission that was to take place at 0400 the next morning.

TUESDAY 11 MAY 2010

One of our Grenadiers is SPC B. He is about 30 years old, white, and is from Kansas. He is married with a daughter and is also an Infantryman. He came from Ft. Campbell with the 101st and has deployed to Iraq. We are good friends, which is odd because we are political opposites. I am constantly teasing him about his views on homosexual marriage, gun rights, abortion, etc. He is also an atheist. He is a bleeding heart liberal, which is very strange when you consider what we do for a living out here. He is a good guy and one of the few I have meet in the Army that I can actually have an intelligent conversation with.

He has some college and has a lot more general knowledge then the other people out here. He plans on working for the DEA when he gets out in a couple years, another subject that I put him down about, being that it is part of "big" government. He plans on re-classing to CID once he gets back to Germany. He complains about the infantry mentality, which I do not blame him for. He is one of those types of people you can recommend a good book to and he will actually read it, which I have found is an anomaly in our line of work.

Most people in our field have no idea how old America is, our current Vice President, or the most basic questions relevant to our country or history. Infantrymen are physically tough, but as a general rule of thumb are dumber than a sack of rocks. People like B. are an exception to this rule. I actually learn things from the conversations we share.

TUESDAY 18 MAY 2010

I have been on QRF (quick reaction force) for about a week now. A couple of times we were called to DEFCON 1 (be ready within 15 minutes) but eventually were told we would not be going out. We are in support of Operation Eagle Claw. At random times in the night our platoon sergeant conducts drills, not mentioning it is a drill until after we are suited up and ready roll. He is trying to time us and see how good we are.

I am on this detail with a different squad from my own, along with one other person. Every time activation is called, we are awoken and in a mad rush try to put on our equipment and run to the vehicles. It can be frustrating when we realize it was just a drill after the fact. A lot of the guys get pissed off, but I can see why our leadership feels that it is important to conduct these drills. They tell us to keep our equipment in the vehicles, but I never do this.

After being in the military for a few years I have experienced how soldiers treat other people's gear. They toss it around without care of what happens, and our body armor plates crack and as a result provide less protection against enemy rounds. If someone is missing a piece of equipment they are likely to simply take it off of someone else's kit so that when the time comes to turn in the equipment they will not be held responsible for not having the things that they are signed for. Besides, putting on my equipment inside of my tent and then mounting up inside the vehicle takes no less time than running to the truck and pulling my equipment out, putting it on, and getting into my assigned seat

SATURDAY 05 JUN 2010

Went on a mission this morning to a town near checkpoint six alpha called Taziraba. We investigated an IED crater in the road and went to the town since it was close. We talked to a farmer who said he saw the Taliban set up the bomb and then run off when it detonated on an ISAF convoy. He claimed there were three of them involved.

We bought a falcon from the village for six dollars and brought him back to the FOB. I don't know what they plan on doing with it. Yesterday we conducted a mission to FOB Bullard. From there five other soldiers and I flew in a Chinook helicopter to FOB Lagman to pick up two MRAP vehicles and drive them back to our FOB during the night. I was in the gun turret on the way back. These vehicles are an older model and we have no use for them. They will probably sit in the motor pool and collect dust.

I received an email from an Army officer in Europe trying to recruit me to psychological operations. He reviewed my entry test scores and civilian education and said I would make a good candidate and was interested if I wanted to switch jobs. I haven't replied, and probably won't since it will most likely require me to extend my commitment in time for the military and I'm not sure at this point if that is something I want to do.

I spent the evening rearranging my gear. The way we carry our equipment is different from person to person. We are required to carry at least seven magazines, a first aid kit, a pouch for our night vision goggles, and a tourniquet. Anything after that is optional, unless you are a team leader, and in that case you need to have a radio to keep in contact with the other leadership. Team leaders also generally carry a map, compass, and protractor. As a grenadier I usually carry around eight 40MM grenades. Five of those are HEDP and the others are various smoke marking colors along with a parachute flare. I also have on my vest a multi-tool, GPS, flashlight, headlamp, spare batteries, notepad with pens, and a few pictures of my family. Attached to my rifle I have the M203 launcher, the leaf sight that allows me to have a good idea where the rounds will land, and a PAC15 infrared laser for use at night. The use of night vision goggles does not allow us to aim through the weapon sight so we use the IR laser to determine where our rounds will land at night

I also replaced my issued Trijicon ACOG for a personal EOTech. The ACOG has the advantage that it magnifies with a four-power scope. I prefer the EOTech, which is a red dot, as it allows me to acquire targets faster.

MONDAY 07 JUN 2010

It has almost been a month with no running water. We have been bathing with bottled water with a hole in the cap so it can spray. Understandably getting a water pump out here is not a priority to the Army. We suspect the Afghan Army has been stealing fuel for some time now. Power outages are also becoming more common. The logistics involved in keeping even the smallest of outposts running is mind-boggling. The supply trucks and helicopters, both civilian and military, are always under threat of constant attack and require an armed escort.

TUESDAY 08 JUN 2010

Back today following a long and eventful mission. Yesterday morning we left to link up with Afghan police near checkpoint 6. We were to go with them south along a dirt road to conduct a KLE of a small town. The ANP told us before we left that the area we intended to go to was known to have IEDs. About four kilometers towards the town, the road came to a point where there were walls on both sides. As the lead MATV was going through the dirt walled alley it hit an IED. The crew inside was unharmed. We pulled security and attempted to back up another vehicle to hook up to the damaged one and tow it out of the kill zone. As the other vehicle backed up it too hit an IED.

The Afghan police started shooting, which added to the chaos. The AK47 has a distinct sound and is the same weapon that the Taliban use. This caused some of us to think we were receiving fire from a short distance. The area we were in was heavily wooded and left me wondering what the hell was going on. No one in the convoy was seriously injured. We did have a Soldier take a piece of shrapnel to his front plate. He also took a hit to his arm that shaved a part of his tattoo off.

We had to pull security for hours until EOD arrived to check out the situation. While pulling security on the east side of the blast site, an Afghan policeman came and sat down next to me. He started talking to me like I was supposed to understand his language. After a while he pulled out a bag of hash, broke it up, rolled it into a joint and started smoking it. He handed it to me a couple times, but I tried to show him with hand signals that I would get in a lot of trouble if someone found out. I don't have anything against people getting stoned, but it wasn't the best time as we had just triggered two IEDs and were supposed to be on the lookout for a small arms attack.

Supposedly hashish is banned within the police department and army here, but in my experience they almost all smoke it. Shortly after EOD showed up, other elements from our platoon came to reinforce us. We then moved in to a nearby village to ask them if they had any information. Some of them were openly sympathetic to the Taliban and did not want to speak with us. I put about 17 military-aged males into our biometric system. It is very clear that there is Taliban activity in that town. It is located in an area where a lot of US Forces are being hit with IEDs. Hopefully the higher ups take this into consideration and plan more future missions in that area to disrupt enemy movement.

FRIDAY 11 JUN 2010

Went to FOB Bullard today to pick up the guys in our platoon who had to fly out to Lagman because of the IED blasts. While we were there the FOB got mortared. Mortars landed both behind and in front of us. No one was injured that I know of. They implied a communication blackout on our FOB today because earlier a PRT [62] team out of Bullard went on a mission to the bazaar. While they were there a suicide bomber detonated next to the team and two Americans were killed and one seriously injured.

I have not had a communication blackout since my last deployment, which saw a lot more action then I have seen so far on this one. About half way through my last deployment two squads, including my own went on a mission to a village called Tangey Kalay. While we were conducting a KLE, iCom [63] traffic stated that the Taliban knew we were in the area and were setting up an ambush for us on our return trip. As soon as we left the town we came under fire and found ourselves in a 30-minute firefight. We had the Afghan Police with us.

After we called in an airstrike on the mountain we were taking fire from, we started to head back to FOB Baylough. 2nd squad, which had inserted into an OP the night before and on foot were ordered to link up with us at the vehicles for our push back. We came under fire a second time and had to drive extremely slowly so the dismounted soldiers in our element could walk alongside the armored vehicles and use them for cover since we were exposed in a valley.

The commanding officer of Charlie Company (Capt. H.) was with us at the time and was the TC of my vehicle. During the second firefight he stepped out of the vehicle and before he could walk five steps he was hit multiple times in the lower body with an RPK machine gun. We got him back into the vehicle and continued back towards the FOB, ignoring the

---

[62] PRT: Provincial Reconstruction Team
[63] iCom: type of hand-held communication device

ambush. After another couple kilometers we found our self under attack for the third time. We continued to push there because at this point we were out of ammunition because of the last two encounters.

About an hour later we reached the FOB. The helicopter was already waiting at the landing strip because of how long it took us to return. Upon returning I counted the bullet holes in the vehicle I was traveling in and counted 28. Shortly after that our Battle Captain, Major Mescal, was killed as a result of hitting an IED driving from Lagman to Kandahar Air Field. In his vehicle were four other Soldiers, three of whom also died and one who became paralyzed from the neck down.

During the deployment of Bravo Company, which relieved us, their Commanding Officer was killed in action when the vehicle he was riding in hit an IED. Two EOD technicians who were with him were also killed. Charlie Company also lost PFC Ngo when he was shot in the head while manning a machine gun in the torrent of a HUMVEE. He survived the initial injury and later died while in surgery in Kandahar.

TUESDAY 15 JUN 2010

Gearing up for another mission. I set aside some time to listen to 'Sweet Child of Mine' by Aerosmith. I have made it a habit lately to listen to this song before every mission. I think of my daughter. It is one of those songs written by a father to his daughter, and anyone who listens to it will understand. She even fits the physical description in the song. I think of family often, and how much I look forward to seeing them again one day.

MONDAY 21 JUN 2010

Went to the local Afghan police station with our CO and five other soldiers. They had two suspects detained and accused of scouting out areas to emplace IEDs at the bazaar in Shajoy. In the jail cell they also put in an undercover person in civilian Afghan clothes as an arrested Taliban in the hopes of tricking the two other suspects into revealing any information. We entered the two suspects, who were from Kandahar, into our biometrics system. One of them claimed to repair old cell phones for a living. That would give him the necessary know-how to make remote detonated IEDs.

We sat down to a traditional Afghan lunch with the police chief. He told us that earlier in the week a local Taliban militia captured one of his sergeants. The police chief, with his men, went to the Taliban leader's house and told his aging father that he will kill the family if the policeman was not returned. Shortly after that the sergeant was released.

Shortly after our unit arrived to the area to relieve the 82nd (Airborne), an incident cost their platoon leader his life at FOB Bullard. An IED was located north of the local bazaar by the Afghan Army. A squad from the 82nd went out to confirm if it was a legitimate threat. Once they made a positive confirmation they radioed for EOD. While waiting for EOD to show, up the LT attempted to mark the location of the IED with a chem light. Somehow the IED, or another IED located very close by, went off and killed him. It affected the morale of the platoon from the 82nd. They were slotted to go home within days. It also had an effect on our men from 1-4 because they gave them an idea of what to expect for the rest of their deployment.

THURSDAY 24 JUN 2010

Today we did a dismounted mission to the local bazaar in Shajoy. The mission was to enter at least five shopkeepers into our biometrics systems and get general information about where they are from and what they sell. Our squad moved in and set up security at an intersection. We blocked off all traffic, which we are not allowed to do. Our current rules of engagement do not allow us to restrict civilian traffic. It is a joke and demoralizes our soldiers.

A suicide bomber killed two Americans in the same place within the last month ago. Less than twenty minutes after we returned an IED went off which killed an Afghan soldier 20 meters from the path we took entering the bazaar. A couple of hours after I got back I was woken up and told the ANA found another IED a couple kilometers south of our FOB.

I had to man a machine gun on a vehicle and go out to confirm it was an IED so we could fly EOD [64] to the location. We confirmed it was an IED, waited in place for 4 hours, and came back to pick up EOD from the landing zone. While EOD did their job I was tasked out to block all traffic. A truck driver ignored repeated attempts to have him stop using hand

---

[64] EOD: Explosive Ordinance Disposal; bomb squad

signals. I shot a pen flare, which bounced off his windshield, and he continued to drive anyways.

If he had been a suicide bomber he could have blown us up. If I shot at him and he didn't have a bomb I could possibly face jail time. In a place such as Afghanistan, people only understand fear and power, and to these people we do not possess either. We have our hands tied behind our back and the enemy has every advantage.

The EOD did a controlled detonation and the IED was so large it blew up the entire road. It was a remote detonation IED that could be activated by cell phone. If it had hit an American vehicle like it was supposed to, it would have killed everyone in the vehicle regardless of the armor. I felt the concussion of the blast from about 600 meters away. While I was gone, the rest of my squad went back into the bazaar and interviewed a few more shopkeepers. Hopefully we will go back to Al Masak soon, I am tired of living out of a bag, but at the same time appreciate having running water.

SATURDAY 10 JUL 2010

As we waited for EOD we were told the Army Rangers needed our help a couple miles north of our position. When we arrived we were told they made contact resulting in five dead Taliban. They had to leave and we were tasked with collecting up the evidence and bodies as well as destroying the IED the Taliban were emplacing when they were engaged. They [Taliban] had a RPG, machine gun, and a couple of AK47s. We were able to trace the wire since they did not have the chance to bury it yet enroute to a culvert. Other IED making material was located there as well.

It was good for the morale of our platoon to be able to deal with the Taliban on our own terms rather than theirs. All too often we are on the receiving end and because of the enemy tactics they more often than not get away. We brought the bodies in body bags to the local ANA checkpoint but they did not want to take them. After failing to convince them, we ended up leaving the bodies on a dirt road leading to the closest village. The treatment the bodies received from us was the complete opposite of what we can expect if the situation was reversed. The Taliban are known to mutilate bodies and bury them without ever notifying anyone. Although they do not deserve it, we intentionally placed the

90

bodies so the locals can locate, identify, and provide them with a proper burial.

As a result of the Army killing these insurgents, HWY 1 [65] will undoubtedly a little safer even if for a short time. The guys caught emplacing the IED probably had been doing similar activities for a while, and most likely didn't have any intentions of stopping any time soon. When we were investigating the area we saw that they were in the middle of completing a remote-detonated bomb. The IED was already emplaced in the road, probably a day or so prior. They had returned to run the wire and the other Afghans were there to provide security while the supposed triggerman laid the copper wire. One Taliban was killed with the wire running directly to him and leading up to the bombsite. He was emplacing two separate wires, probably as a precaution in case one did not detonate when he triggered it with an electric charge from a battery.

The remaining dead Taliban fighter clearly showed that they put up a fight. There was a pile of brass from an RPK that lead me to believe that he attempted to fire on the helicopters as they landed or fired at him. The insurgent who was laying the wire clearly tried to run from the firing helicopters. I could see the path he took and the rounds that were impacting on the dirt right behind him. From his footprints I could see that he was running at a dead sprint and didn't even slow down as he approached a ditch at least ten feet deep. As a result of him jumping into the ditch at a sprint he broke both ankles and had compound fractures to both of his ankles from him hitting the ground from so high and at a high speed. The bones from his leg were protruding from his ankles that lead me to initially assume he had been shot in the ankles until I looked a little closer. He had a couple small entry wounds from large caliber rounds (assumedly from the Apaches or Chinook door gunners), and the exits wounds were very large and exposed most of his organs.

The violent death he suffered resulted in his clothes being torn away and exposing his entire body. Two of his other buddies were almost covered in dirt as a result of the fire they received. Obviously they were at the edge of a wadi[66], which collapsed due to the intense firepower from aircraft up above. From examining their bodies we could see that they too were hit directly with rounds. Their entire party was basically caught in

---

[65] HWY 1: The main highway in Afghanistan
[66] Wadi: similar to a covered ditch on the side of a road

the open with hostile intentions. The helicopters out here in combat operations fly so low you wouldn't realize they were coming until they were basically already on top of you.

I found it interesting that although they had only been dead for a short period that they already looked as though they were made of wax and that rigor mortis had already set in. I found myself pitying him and what I considered his warped philosophy on life. Maybe in under different circumstances he could have been a productive member of society and contributed to the human race. At the same time I admired him for dying for something he believed in, for fighting against a numerically and technologically superior force.
Regardless of him being right or wrong, he was a man of principle, along with his buddies who died with him that day. He believed in something, and was willing to die for it. I did not feel sorry for him, and in fact was glad he had died. I'm sure he had been responsible for prior American deaths, and only the fact that he had died would prevent him from taking any other American lives.

In a country as primitive as Afghanistan, I wondered if his family would know how he died and what he was doing at that time. If he was from one of the local villages, there is a chance they would. However, if he was like most Taliban, who travel the country in search of opportunities to attack ISAF forces, there is a good chance that they will never know. The fact that they were emplacing the IED in the middle of the day, when HWY 1 is populated with traffic, showed that they had been doing similar activity for a while and long enough that they felt comfortable to do it during high traffic daylight hours.

Hopefully Americans and NATO forces who died at these peoples' hands were in a twisted way avenged today, although I realize that will bring little to no satisfaction to their surviving family members. It was one of those rare occasions that brought a sense of accomplishment to those of us involved, who were able to see the results of our airpower instead of the results of Taliban insurgents IEDs that wounded and killed our comrades.

The Taliban have a recorded history of taking revenge on anyone who gives us information. Interpreters who work for us often cover their faces and some have told me that they do not even tell their parents what they do for a living. At least half of the ones I have worked with from this deployment (and the last) claim they were students at the University in Kabul before the Taliban took over. The fact that they speak English shows they are more educated than the typical Afghan. Most have an ultimate goal of helping the Americans enough to get a visa to either live in America or Europe. Any Afghan with an ounce of education probably realized just how backwards their country is and their only chance of being successful in life is to move away and start anew.

SATURDAY 31 JUL 2010

[PREVIOUS INFORMATION REDACTED]

Hopefully the ANP will realize the confrontation was the result of a single stressed out kid who represented his own self and not our attitude in general towards them. This particular ANP commander is an honest Taliban-hating man who I have had lunch with while with the CO in Bullard. I remember him telling us of a recent incident when the Taliban kidnapped one of his officers at gunpoint on a makeshift middle of the night roadside checkpoint. He knew of the Taliban commander and went to his local village and arrested the insurgent's father. He put word out in the village that if any harm came to his officer then he would execute the Taliban commander's father.

Shortly after that the officer was released. He based his officer's worth on the amount of Taliban he had personally killed in his career. Its people like this ANP Commander that are going to allow both the Americans to leave on a successful note one day and Afghan government to operate on its own. When we were finally done with all the missions for the day we pulled up to our FOB.

The Romanians are responsible for manning the guard towers which makes all of us worry just how secure we really are. The Romanian at the front tower is the one who is supposed to come down and move their vehicle, which prevents the front gate from opening from the outside. We had to honk our horns and sit there for a few minutes. It was obvious that the guards were sleeping since they didn't see or hear us less than ten feet from their place of duty.

When the guard finally woke up he went to the vehicle and instead of going in reverse he went forward crashing into the gate. He attempted to fix the gears on the vehicle but instead went forward again and almost hit our vehicle. When he finally figured out how to back up his HUMVEE, which the Americans gave them, it was damaged and leaking fuel. He backed up and then ran into a wall. He was drunk and due to our complete lack of faith in them he didn't even get in trouble because it is almost to the point that behavior like that is expected of them.

SUNDAY 01 AUG 2010

The news is saying this is the deadliest month for Americans since the war started. This is the third month in a row that they are saying this. Each month more Americans died then the last with most of the deaths result from IEDs. IEDs are bad because you have no warning at all until the blast goes off and in most cases that is too late. I preferred my last deployment when we had to worry about ambushes instead. In those situations I felt that I at least had a fighting chance. The terrain out there didn't allow for much use of vehicles so almost all the patrols we did were on foot. When I look back now and remember how at times I would bitch to myself about having to walk everywhere we went I now realize how good I had it compared to driving up and down the highway.

The Generals in the news are saying that the reason for such high numbers of deaths is because of the increase in the amount of troops. As a result the Taliban are being forced to engage the Americans more often. The soldiers meet this with a mixed reaction and in my experience I would say that most of them blame the deaths on the ROE that gives the enemy an advantage.

Also while heading to the piss tubes today I noticed movement out of the corner of my eye and realize it was the back end of a snake going under a piece of wood. I pointed it out to some of the Afghan soldiers who happened to be standing by and they moved the wood and killed the snake with a pole. It was some type of viper and I plan on being more careful walking around at night with just my flip-flops on.

I decided to go to the Internet tent and look up the snake that I had seen. I decided from comparing it against the two possible snakes it could have been that it was a "carpet" viper. The article I read described it as one of the deadliest snakes in the world. Although there are snakes with more potent venom, this particular snake is located in regions of the world with little to no medical services available. I warned a couple of the guys to my sighting of the snake and the information I read about it.

WEDNESDAY 04 AUG 2010

We had another soldier today go coward on us. *SPC xxxxx* told the leadership that he couldn't handle going on missions anymore. The last couple of mission he went on the other soldiers were getting upset with his constant complaining of him being in fear of dying. Our PL sent him on a convoy to Bullard to fly out to Kandahar. He probably got the idea when he saw how easy it was for xxxxx to get out of here when he had similar complaints. No wonder this Army cannot win this war. Even if a soldier is scared to go on a mission he should have to go regardless. Everyone out here is probably scared at one point or another, but they make the decision to keep it to their selves and continue with the mission.

It seems some men join the Army because they think the idea and concept sound good but when they are hit with reality they cannot handle it. I would be embarrassed and ashamed if I found myself doing something like that. Whenever I looked back to my time in the military it would be a stain. It is a waste of taxpayers' money to spend on their training and equipment if the Soldier fails to perform once they get into combat.

If any of these weakling Soldiers received a bonus or any type of perk when they enlisted in the Army it should be given back. When they tell people that they served in Afghanistan they should mention that they found a loophole out and could not handle it, but of course I am sure they won't. It makes me wonder how history would have been different if men of similar character were allowed to simply quit when the going got tough. The platoon will still have to conduct the same amount of mission and pull the same amount of weight but we will have to do it with two less people now.

The villagers that we talk to are constantly saying that they have no idea about enemy movements or what they are up to. Obviously the Taliban are going to local towns to get food and fuel in order to continue operations against us. However, the common person out here is hesitant to tell us due to retaliation by the enemy. Even though we have the tactical advantage while we are in their town, they are smart enough to realize that as soon as we leave the Taliban are the biggest kid on the block. For all they know, it will be weeks, if not months, if not ever, before we come back again to ask them more questions. The Taliban in the meantime will be there on a daily basis and will be upset with anyone who took the time out of their day to tell us anything that can remotely help us. The landscape is too large and our forces too small to effectively police an area as remotely and spread out as the one that we are currently assigned to.

SATURDAY 07 AUG 2010

What is left of the platoon erected another tent this morning. The tents we use out here are large and can hold 15 men or more and are elevated on a wood platform a couple feet above the ground that we build. We were officially told via a letter from our Battalion Commander that our unit would stop deploying after Christmas. The Company relieving us will only bring a little more than two platoons. We are trying to improve the FOB so that they will be more comfortable when they get here. Half of them will probably go to FOB Bullard.

SATURDAY 21 AUG 2010

My squad went out in the morning to conduct a KLE at a village just south of the highway around checkpoint six alpha. The town seemed abandoned but when we searched it we found that three males and one female lived there. A gun battle between the ANA and Taliban took place right outside the village during the night before we showed up. Although the ANA ambushed them from two different sides the Taliban all got away and no one was killed. The female in the town was elderly a looked like a fairy tale witch. She was wearing a hood and had a large mole on her chin. The only teeth she had were two lower ones. She was actually trying to talk to us, which is unusual since she is a female, and not being able to understand her it sounded like she was trying to put a spell on us.

MONDAY 23 AUG 2010

It was nice to be able to take a shower and do our laundry with washing machines. The chow hall is also a treat since in Al Masak all we have to eat are MREs and their big brother, UGRAs. Taking a shit without holding a bag up to your ass and throwing it in a burn pit also helped us feel more civilized.

TUESDAY 07 SEP 2010

Charlie Company is finally here. We went and picked up their platoon in the morning. They were flown in on helicopters to FOB Bullard. About half our platoon loaded up in the same birds before they left. We rolled with skeleton crews so we would have room for passengers to take back to Al Masak. Because every truck was only able to load two or three passengers, and we needed to move 44 Soldiers, it took up four trips back and forth. If everything goes according to schedule I should fly out on the next bird on the 12th. I only knew two people from C Co. who were with them when I was reassigned to Delta. It's a completely different Company now. While we were taking them back and forth the Romanians from our FOB hit an IED at checkpoint six. A couple of them were injured but everyone survived. Yesterday an IED also went off just north of Bullard but we haven't heard any details or know who was hit.

TUESDAY 14 SEP 2010

We have been in KAF for a couple days now. C Co. took us to Bullard and we were picked up by a Chinook and landed in Lagman. After a couple of hours another bird took us the remaining way to KAF. Nothing is planned for about a week, and the first thing to do is going to be customs. They will lay out all our personal belonging and make sure we are not trying to take anything back that is not allowed. The guys have been taking advantage of the down time. In between meals at the chow hall, which are a hundred times better to the food we are used to, we are in and out of the gyms. Other guys use their time to relax and watch movies.

There are also shops out here that sell souvenirs and creature comforts and a lot of guys can be found spending some of the money they have saved up since we have been out here. The men and woman who are stationed here can barely call this a deployment. The Kandahar boardwalk reminds me of a mall, which probably about thirty or forty shops to waste your money on. The various chow halls have different themes, as in European chow, American, Indian, etc. You can purchase almost any creature comfort that you want, and it even has its own little black market to purchase hashish and alcohol. A lot of soldiers stationed here even have their own cars to get about, and receive tickets from the military police if they do not obey the traffic laws.

There are multiple locations where any Soldier or civilian can either use the Internet, watch a movie, or play a game of ping-pong or pool. The Canadians are the main effort when it comes to FOB defense and running missions in Kandahar city. It is basically a logistics base for American processing personnel and manpower. It is one of the main air bases that soldiers who are arriving or leaving in country go through. I am in no rush to leave this place, in fact I'm hoping to at least wait until the end of the month so that I receive the extra combat and family separation pay.

TUESDAY 21 SEP 2010

The Company arrived in Germany a couple days ago. We flew in from Kyrgyzstan (Manas Air Force Base) after staying for a day. We had to go through US Customs that were stationed in Kyrgyzstan. We did a complete dump of all equipment and a personal pat down. Didn't seem too invasive and I'm sure a lot of guys brought back things they weren't supposed to, as they did in every war before this. There are strict rules allowing what is legally allowed to be returned. A bag of sand, melted down ammunition brass transformed into a souvenir by the Afghans, exotic bugs native to the region within a glass sphere, and Soviet war items left behind are just a few examples of what is banned from being brought back. Any form of weaponry is also strictly forbidden.

The US military stationed Manas have a good assignment similar to those in Kandahar. There is little to no threat of an attack. They have nice chow, reliable Internet and recreation facilities, and are even allowed to drink alcohol. People going through temporarily do not have access to some of these luxuries. For the past year there have been news reports and rumors that this place will be closing down shortly because of complaints from Russia of us having a military base in their backyard. While we are here they are still constructing new buildings and working on improvements so only time will tell if the rumors become a reality. The majority of the workers were local nationals.

After about a 7-hour flight, buses were waiting at the airport in Nuremburg to take us back to our home coming ceremony in Hohenfels. There were Army personal on standby to sort out logistics. We were given room keys, meal cards, and anything else that was needed to reintegrate our stay back in the garrison life. This was done in order to allow us to be released to our families once a quick ceremony was completed to mark our arrival. Family members of people that we had lost during the deployment had sandwiches and American soft drinks waiting for us upon exiting of the plane.

The ceremony located in the high school gym right past the main gate of the base. Like my last deployment, it is a weird feeling driving through civilization. They escorted us with military police and fire truck vehicles, spraying hoses and blaring sirens. Children from the schools were lined on the road cheering and holding flags, a ritual all too common on this post as the units arrive back.

After staying in a country of unpredictability, it was nice to not have to worry about every piece of trash on the road having the potential to conceal a roadside bomb. These thoughts are something that will only take time for the guys of this deployment to retrain their brains and process of thoughts.

The families of married soldiers were all waiting for us and after a short speech, the Commander released us to our families. Being a geographic bachelor myself, I quickly left the area as I felt awkward standing around while a lot of other people were being reunited with their families. Upon returning to the barracks, we have found that Lee's wife (lost her husband with us in an IED attack along with two other soldiers) had put a six-pack of Corona beer inside of every soldier's refrigerator. Normally they do not let us drink for a couple weeks after we get back because our alcohol tolerance is so low.

The people in charge decided they would make an exception and change the rule. We didn't have to report to work until the next afternoon so the guys in the barracks had a good time. Due to a couple soldiers who abused this, it is doubtful that the chain of command will repeat this privilege. It was hard to see the family members of the guys we lost waiting there for the rest of us to return. It was as if they were a part of our family, and were clinging on to the last friends their husband had before they went to meet their maker.

STEPHEN HAMILTON [2010]

MONDAY 07 JUN 2010

What should have been a regular KLE mission turned out to be one of the scariest days of my life. We ran KLE missions all the time. KLE stands for Key Leader Engagement. Basically, we would roll up into a village and engage their leaders and see if they needed anything or if the Taliban has given them any trouble. I, as the medic, would screen the elderly and children. It was all pretty routine and normal, until 07 June 2010.

In Afghanistan US forces cannot conduct operations without their local national counterparts. So we usually had some ANA or ANP with us on missions. We informed the ANA that we were going to conduct a KLE in the village of Narwabad and needed a few crews from them to do so. They said they would help us out like usual. This mission was originally set for 5 June 2010, but on that day after we were ready to roll out, the ANA forces were gone. Apparently they had gotten other orders from their higher command and couldn't spare anyone for our mission. No big deal, we understood. We'll just do it tomorrow.

SUNDAY 06 JUN 2010

The time came and again no ANA not even a single Afghan soldier left to tell us where they went. Guess we'll try again tomorrow. That fateful day came and again, no ANA. Looking back at in retrospect this should have been a red flag from the get go. Why were the ANA soldiers so scared to go with us to Narwabad? We were about to learn why.

After the third time with no ANA support and the mission had already been pushed back twice, our command said get it done anyway. Someone remembered there was an ANP checkpoint not far from our objective and maybe they could give us a crew or two? So we rolled out. I was in the third vehicle along with Specialists M., S., and H. and Staff Sergeant L. We made it to the ANP checkpoint and they agreed to give us two crews. SSG L. told us the news as he got back in the truck and he said the ANP informed the leadership that there are IEDs heading into Narwabad. M. spoke up, *"Whatever, we hear that shit all the time and nothing ever happens."*

Now, I'm not a superstitious person but I believe there are two things in the military you should never do when in a combat zone. Do not carry a lucky charm. If you do carry a lucky charm do not forget it. Turns out, M. and H. had lucky charms. And they both forgot them that day.

The layout of Narwabad was kind of odd. The village was to the east on higher ground, separated by a wadi (dry riverbed); to the west of the wadi was an orchard that was walled-in by like a four foot mud wall. West of the wall was the road you had to take that led to a bridge that led into the village. There was another wall on the other side of the road, which kind of made the road act like a funnel.

We had the ANP crews up front followed by our four vehicles. The ANP drove Ford Rangers like you see on the streets back in the States all the time. We drove the super heavy and up armored MATVs. The ANP's trucks went through that funneled area first and nothing happened. It was time for us to follow.

The first truck drove into the funnel. You know the saying people use when something shocks them so quickly, "*It feels like my heart sank into my gut*"? I was about to learn what that felt like. Not long after the first truck entered that funnel we all heard a deafening boom. My heart dropped. M. was the only one in my truck to speak and he said a single word, "*shit*". Then after what felt like forever but was probably mere seconds, the radio crackled "*IED IED IED!*" I wanted out of the truck to go check on my guys. I am the medic let me do my job! SSG L. wouldn't let me out of the truck until we had 360 security set. The second truck moved to the west and then dropped dismounts and my truck moved to the east into the orchard and the rear truck stayed put while the ANP covered the north.

I was a mental mess. I had five guys just get blown up and I want to get out of the truck and get to work. As my truck moved into its security position, the turret nailed some low-hanging branches that knocked off some of the fruit and H. said, "*OOO BERRIES!*" Then H. let off a red star cluster from the turret which filled the cab with smoke. SSG L. and SPC S. got out of our vehicle but [I] being the medic and an asset they made me stay put. After what felt like hours I was finally allowed out to go do my job. SSG L. let me out and told us we were going to use our truck to try and self-recover the disabled truck in the funnel. I asked where the injured soldiers were and was told they were on the other side of the funnel, so I began making my way through the orchard while M. and H. started backing around the orchard walls toward the disabled vehicle and into the funnel.

I reached the far wall of the orchard right as M. and H. had entered the funnel. I decided to let them pass before I hopped over the wall and into the funnel myself. They passed. I hopped over. For some reason I looked back at my truck and my crew. I was about ten feet away from them and the truck.......BOOOM! As I flew in the air I saw my aid bag come off my right shoulder while I screamed, "WHAT THE FUCK!" Then I felt my left knee hit the ground and pop and I thought, "That fucking hurt." Then my head smacked the ground and I was out.

When I came to I grabbed my junk to make sure it was still there. It was. I couldn't really hear or see anything, everything around me was a brown/grey haze and the ringing in my ears was piercing. My first thought was, "Shit M. and H. are still in the truck!" so I got up and took one step toward them and that's when all hell broke loose. AK-47s, M-4s and M-16s going off everywhere. I thought, "Fucking seriously" as I grabbed my aid bag and threw it against the mud wall I had just hopped over a second ago. I took up a position facing the orchard and the village, but I still couldn't see shit and we had dismounts in the orchard so I didn't fire. Then I heard SSG B. calling for a cease fire and things got quiet. He then barked at all of us to get out of the road which after what had just happened seemed like common sense.

At this point I noticed the hood to truck was blown forward and I realized that if it had come all the way off I would have been taken out of this world for sure, but the equipment did its job. The blast had blown H.'s .50 cal onto the engine block and his SAW was nowhere to be found. M. told H. to climb out through the turret but he decided to go over the radios. So me and M. pulled H. out of the truck and H. starts freaking out because he feels a warm liquid on his body. "The mouth piece to your camelback just came off retard." We three hopped over the wall and into the orchard and made our way down.

I had M., H. and our wounded interpreter with me and the other wounded from the first blast were gathered elsewhere. I went to go check on the other guys when I hear, "Hey Doc? I've got blood." M.'s arm was fucked up and so was H.'s. At first glance the wounds seemed identical but on a more thorough exam later, H. had more of a puncture wound. I handed of some of my equipment to our mechanic and began to take care of my guys. That's when I realized it had only been fifteen minutes since the first IED went off. From boom one to boom two and a fire fight.....just fifteen fucking minutes of my life here in Afghanistan.

In total, I believe eleven of us were wounded that day but we all survived. I patched up the ones that needed treatment and kept the concussed ones awake. A skeleton crew of our guys and Romanians came out for QRF, we regrouped and went into Narwabad on foot and finished the mission. I'll never forget the Battle in Narwabad, even the silly things that we did to find humor to get us through that day or how pissed everyone was that they didn't bring enough smokes because the mission was only supposed to last so long. The images in my memory of that day are just as vivid today as I write this, and if you asked me if I would do it again I'd say yes. As long as I'm with 1-4.

GAMPIERO SCATTALON [2010]

Scattolon's Afghanistan story

While deployed in Afghanistan in the summer of 2010 my life changed because of the things I saw and experienced there. Particularly with one event that occurred at the gates of our Forward Operating Base (FOB) in Afghanistan. We lived surrounded by a handful of villages in the mountains of the Zabul province of Afghanistan (Southern part of Afghanistan). Within the walls of our FOB with the aid of pumps, generators and other expensive electronics, we, the Soldiers, had the comforts of running water, electricity, air conditioning, and even internet access. There was very little suffering that I had witness up to this point.

However, one afternoon a group of village elders from a nearby village came to our gates begging for urgent medical care. The men seem to be overcome with a sense of pain and sadness in their faces and voices. In my mind, I remember thinking that there was no need for me to understand the utterances in their native language (Pashto). Because I knew that something had gone terribly wrong. Indeed, soon enough the men brought to us three young, children in agony wrapped in white sheets.

These young boys were small, perhaps they were no more than ten years of age. I saw them first laid out on the dusty ground partially covered by white sheets and what was left of their shalwar kameez (pajama-like traditional clothing). Their faces and exposed skin were covered with burn marks and dried blood. The children were awake, however they seemed not fully present, or in a manner of speaking not fully alive. They seemed to be in shock with their eyes not focusing on anything; looking through us as if we were not even there. Their facial muscles were twitching; perhaps because of the overwhelming pain from having some of their flesh scorched. Their eyes were dried as if they had run out of tears. Nevertheless, the tears they had cried earlier had left their mark as they had washed some of the dust from their faces.

I have three children and for some reason I could see the faces of my children in the faces of the three little boys lying on the ground. Part of me wanted to run to them and hold them, but that was not my job. My job was to remain vigilant providing security for the medics who were treating the boys. I was doing just fine holding my composure until I saw the medics as they continued to examine the little bodies and found that their little hands were severely burned and had missing fingers caused

104

by an explosive device. I could not hold the tears back. Soon enough that moment was over for us soldiers, as the helicopters came and evacuated the three young children.

I never knew what ended up happening to the three young boys. Most of us will never know what happened to all those men, women, and children that were wounded by the calamities of war. Some of us, if not all who were there in the field of battle, will forever carry scars that no one will ever see.

SCOTT FREDERIKSEN [2010]

SUNDAY 04 JUL 2010

This day was great. I woke up and was informed I was on KP [67]. Hell yeah. All I had to do was cook and wash dishes. All my vehicles were out on mission so it was just me Doc Hamilton and SSG Butler. Well the damn Taliban or al Qaeda fighters had a different plan for us. They decided to give us a 4th of July fireworks show. It lasted all day at random times. They'd fire a mortar round here, one there, and a rocket at this time or that time.

Well that evening after dinner chow was done and my chores were done me and the Doc decided to watch a movie so I asked Doc *"Hey you ever seen Kiss Kiss Bang Bang?"* He said no so I said *"Dude you're gonna laugh your ass off."* So we started it and got a few minutes into it and then we hear the distinct sound of a mortar flying overhead. So we grab our shit and do like we usually did and climbed the Hesco barriers to our position. After we were given the all clear we went back to the movie. The damn movie was over. So we started it all over again. Then I'll be damned if it didn't happen again. So we grabbed our shit. Again. And went to our spot. Again.

We were then given the all clear so we went back to our movie. Then son of a bitch it happened again. So we sat there a second and I looked over at Doc and said *"Stay put maybe B. didn't hear that one."* We started laughing and then SSG B. ran in and yelled *"Didn't ya'll fucking hear that. Get your fucking gear on. Let's go!"* So we got our crap on again but this time I had the brilliant idea of pausing the movie first. I said *"Hey Doc, where do you want me to stop the movie at?"* He said *"I don't care."* So I said *"How about the part where we see her tits?"* So we start laughing damn hard and walk to the shelter instead of on top of the Hesco this time. We wait, and wait and wait some more. Finally we hear over the radio *"All clear. Somebody left a spray can of some kind in the burn pit."* We started laughing and I said *"Son of a bitch, you mean I coulda been looking at tits this whole time?!*

---

[67] KP: Kitchen Prep; kitchen duty

VANTAGE POINTS

War functions much like a puzzle box in which each person holds individual pieces that reveal the final picture of any event. Each piece of the puzzle shapes the vantage point through which we understand a sequence of events. There is often more to a story or an event when we open up to the realization that multiple interpretations of the same event can occur simultaneously. Every story or action in life possesses multiple vantage points.

The culmination of each of the following stories highlight an incident in which we lost three great Warriors in Afghanistan through their ultimate sacrifice. Each story offers a piece to complete the puzzle. You will experience each individual's response as the incident unfolded. From frontline to home front, each piece of the narrative forms a picture of the untimely loss of some of our Warriors.

LEVI WILCOX [2010]

When it comes to remembering July 06, 2010, that day will be seared into my memory for many coming years. A lot of overwhelming emotions flood my head just recalling that day.

I had been assigned as an RTO (radio transmission operator) in the TOC (Tactical Operations Center) at FOB (forward operating base) Lagman. As the call about KIAs came in, I don't remember much of anything except for just trying to get air support to their location as quickly as possible. As I watched the UAV (unarmed aerial vehicle) feed, the radio echoed *"break, break, break..."* to clear all other non-essential radio traffic and focus on the TIC (troops in contact) on the ground.

As information began to pour in, roster numbers came across the radio net. Once I found out that one of the battle rosters was Roger Lee, I began to weep. At that point, the CO [68], XO [69], 1SG [70], and OIC [71] stood behind me listening to the information and I realized that I needed to keep my emotions together at least long enough to get the KIA extracted and the other soldiers on the ground back to safety and out of harm's way.

The hardest event I have faced in my life was having to watch my friends die while all I could do is transfer information between the CASEVAC team and the TOC. Just a few hours prior, I had eaten a meal with Roger before those guys left on their convoy back to Bullard. We talked about going home and working on my car and laughed just like during any other meal. Before being sent to Lagman to work in the TOC, I had been in Roger's platoon and the thought hit me hard in the gut that I would have been the driver of the vehicle that suffered three KIAs – instead of Pridham.

As more information about the KIAs passed through the radio, the updated reports confirmed that the driver (Pridham) and the TC (Arizmendez) had likely been killed instantly while the gunner (Lee) had been nearly chopped in half but still clinged to life. I was on the LZ CASEVAC crew and when the chopper came in with Lee, my 1SG wouldn't let me go because he knew how close Lee and I had been and

---

[68] CO: Commanding Officer
[69] XO: Executive Officer
[70] 1SG: First Sergeant
[71] OIC: Officer in Charge

didn't want me to see him that way. Later, we found out that Lee had passed away en route to Lagman.

After everything calmed down a little more, our mechanics along with our 1SG and XO went to recover the wreckage. The convoy truck needed to be cleaned so that we could send it back to KAF and exchange the truck for a replacement. 1SG and the XO would not let anyone else look at the vehicle and took it upon themselves to shoulder the burden of that scarring event. They were amazing leaders that I am proud to have served under.

After the CO had written letters to the families of the KIAs, I carried the sealed letters with me to KAF via helicopter. I tucked the letters inside the pocket of my body armor to keep them safe and after I landed, I gave them to our armorer who would pass the letters on as soon as it was safe enough to fly again. Most of the air traffic at that time had been grounded due to heavy enemy contact in the area.

Recalling these memories, I've cried like a baby. I am in disbelief that it has been more than seven years since we lost those amazing men – Arizmendez, Lee, and Pridham.

STEVEN "DOC" PRICE [2010]

THE BYPASS

The 6th of July in 2010 is perhaps the most significant experience, both spiritually and emotionally, in my life. While I can remember many details of this incident vividly, my mind has also suppressed much of what I used to recollect. This incident happened in Zabul Province, Afghanistan while I was deployed with White Tank of D Company, 1st Battalion, 4th Infantry Regiment.

On this day, I was a part of a routine convoy mission to pick up supplies from Forward Operating Base (FOB) Lagman and return to our shanty away from home, Combat Outpost (COP) Bullard. The Convoy to the FOB felt like purgatory. It was very uneventful and everything looked the same, like we weren't going anywhere. I did notice a broken-down semi-truck the Afghans used for shipping on the way over though. That stuck out to me at least. Once we finally arrived at our destination, we parked the convoy, and while we were "hurrying up and waiting" we took the time to relax. FOB Lagman at this time had a tiny shop that opened recently, and a Green Beans coffee shop right with the MWR [72] internet café. Some of us went to go eat at the chow hall or to just stay with the trucks and get some precious sleep.

I can recall heading to the motor pool on the FOB trying to offer a hand where I could, but if I wasn't working on a patient I was mostly useless. Staff Sergeant (SSG) Arizmendez was also there getting eyes on some of the parts we needed for the trucks back at Bullard. SSG Arizmendez was my squad leader, but in all the time I had spent with him, I had never seen him sleep. The guy was always looking for something to do. Always diligent. If he had a beard, a battle-axe and an extra 100 pounds, he would have been an excellent casting choice for "The Lord of the Rings". After helping a bit there, I went to the trucks and just sat there bullshitting with the rest of the guys. I think I drank five or so triple-shot iced coffees that day. Best waste of money. Ever.

After a few hours had passed and after loading the trucks, we had to reshuffle our own seating arrangements. The convoy consisted of three MATVs and one MRAP. MATVs were a newer model of vehicle that took the IED-resilient hull of an MRAP and married that with the design influence of the Humvee. It had four seats and a gunner's position, and

---

[72] MWR: Morale, Wellness, and Recreation

110

resembled a Militarized pickup truck. The MRAP was the designated vehicle for casualties, since it could carry more. But it was also crammed with other supplies we needed, so I was moved from that truck into the Platoon Sergeant's, Sergeant First Class (SFC) A.'s, MATV. We had to make some more adjustments but once it was all settled we were ready to go; however, we had to wait for one final briefing before we went back outside the wire.

The briefing was still the same standard one we had all heard time and again. The truck order in the convoy, who was where, weather and road conditions, rules of engagement, and one final detail that had put us on the alert. One the same day for the past three consecutive weeks, there were successful IED strikes on convoys leaving FOB Lagman on the same route we had to take to return to COP Bullard. There was a noticeable change in everyone's demeanor after that little nugget of information. Everyone seemed to have tensed up; some people were visibly uncomfortable with knowing that. I personally felt nauseated. SFC A. let that sink in for a moment, and then did his best to reassure us and continued for a moment longer, communicating the need to be as thorough as we can be in our scanning of the roadways and terrain, as we always were. And with that we locked and loaded and were ready to go.

The route back to COP Bullard was slower than before. It was a convoy that, to me, seemed to become cautious and methodical in our advance as we crept closer and closer to the area described in our briefing. The same road we took to get there. The same bridge bypass we had to take. Again. The front vehicle relayed on the radio what they saw on the bypass. There was what looked like massive oil stain on the earth in the center of the makeshift artery. Everybody had already prepared themselves for the worst.

Our dismount team did what they did. They approached the area and began to look at anything and everything for evidence of an IED being present. It was a very vigorous search and some of them even dug into the ground in places they felt were likely to hold a command wire, or a receiver, or anything to set the damn thing off. The area was a bridge under construction going over a wadi, which is just a cut in the side of a hill/cliff face that protects from rain and flash flooding. A bypass was made to go around it. It is a natural choice for ambushing or emplacing IEDs. The wadi ran down the side of the cliff face under the bridge and bypass into a larger one. Out in the distance there was a little plateau maybe 500+ meters or more away from us. It looked like an orchard was on it. It was a good position to see the truck on the roads to remote detonate a bomb. It seemed like an eternity but after several minutes of vigorous searching, our dismounts rejoined the trucks. No evidence. No one saw a spotter in the orchard either.

Erring to caution, our trucks went across the bypass one by one. As fast as possible. The first two went by with ease. But when the third vehicle, the MRAP directly in front of me, started to cross, BOOM! Our driver began to reverse as fast as he could back uphill and onto the road. All that was visible in front of us was a sudden flash and a cloud of dust. Before the cloud engulfed the truck, I could see the front end lift off the ground. There were bits of metal, tires and other debris scattering about from the blast. The only recognizable part I could immediately see from the explosion was a door. Once the dust settled the dismount team went back out to find establish security around the blast. The trucks made an outer cordon to keep security as well. Once the dust settled I dismounted the vehicle, grabbed my aid bag, and was able to see the extent of the damage.

There was a massive crater from the IED in the center of the road - easily six to seven feet deep and at least twice that in diameter. Before I could even finish running down to the blast site, SSG A., the leader of first squad, was already hailing me down to the two casualties he had there. The dismount team had already run down there and secured the site and casualties by the time I got there. Specialist (SPC) W. was one of the casualties. He only had minor cuts and scrapes. Lucky bastard. And our interpreter had what looked like a shrapnel wound to his leg and later we discovered he also had a broken leg.

He and W. were in the back of the MRAP which we observed had been ripped off from its chassis and thrown into the ravine below. He dragged the interpreter out to where they were now. Neither were in any visible pain at the time. I took care of them and looked back towards the blast site. I needed to go up and check on the rest of the guys in the truck; SSG Arizmendez, SPC Lee, Private First Class (PFC) Pridham. SSG A. and another member of his squad, SPC S., helped W. and me carry the interpreter on a litter to the helicopter as it arrived. W. had to go as well, despite such minor injuries. There was a risk for a concussion, and other passengers had died. Better to examine him now and be safe rather than sorry later on.

Once we got out of the ravine where the helicopter had landed and up the hill to the crater, I saw SSG Arizmendez. He had died instantly but his body thrown some 20-30 feet away from the point of the blast. He was in a sitting position. I was not expecting to ever see that. PFC Pridham was also deceased, likely instantly or within minutes, he had a cut into his inguinal area and a leg broken in a couple of places. I carefully moved him away from the crater so I could tend to SPC Lee, who for some miraculous reason was still breathing. Shallow breaths. Still fighting to survive.

The rear axle of the MRAP was inside the crater, and Lee was dangling over it. I think he must have landed on it after being ejected from the gunner's position. We had to untangle him and drag him out of the crater. His body armor took most of the damage, but a few of his ribs were still broken. Almost all of the damage to Lee was internal. I could only secure his airway and splint his broken limbs and put him on a litter. Everything else needed to be done at the Medical Station on Lagman.

In my training before my deployment, I focused significantly on stopping extremity bleeding, since it was the most easily preventable type of death. So having patients with internal bleeding was a mind fuck to me for a split second. It's a race to get on an operating table. The only thing that can be done on site is an IV [73], but you pose the risk of the patient dying. An IV would have raised the blood pressure, causing a faster bleed out. Allowing the body to shunt, while the blood pressure is decreased, it keeps the blood to the core organs of the body. This is permissive hypotension.

While I was treating Lee, SSG A., and a couple of other people helped me work on him. Everybody wanted Lee to pull through. We wanted a fucking miracle. SFC A. was on the radio with the MEDEVAC, keeping us informed on how far out the bird was. Once he was on the helicopter and off to the Naval Field Surgical Team, we went back to take care of Pridham and Arizmendez. I was physically and mentally exhausted from this. We had to stay to gather what we could so the enemy couldn't use it against us. It took us hours.

We didn't get back until the morning of July 7th .That's when we learned that Lee didn't make it. After a few moments, crestfallen, I took my gear off and walked to the other side of the COP [74]. I went to the chow hall we had there, which was nothing more than a wooden shack with benches and a kitchen. SPC P. was a cook with the 82nd (Airborne) that stayed back for a little while to basically just cook for us. He caught wind about

---

[73] IV: Intravenous bag delivering medicine, for example
[74] COP: Combat Outpost

what happened and just sat there with me and we just talked about bullshit to help me get my mind off of things.

We had our own little memorial service at the COP for the three of them. We mourned as best as we could manage, but we still had work to do. You can't really stop in an environment like a warzone and cope with your emotions. You wind up bottling them up, pushing them aside and drive on to the next mission, the next objective.

STEPHEN HAMILTON [2010]

06 JULY 2010

It began as any other ordinary day in Afghanistan. White Tank was running a mission to Lagman and I had just come from an op order [75] for a mission that was set to go off at zero dark thirty. Nothing new there.

It was going to be a big operation, probably one of the biggest I would ever be a part of. The thing is, it got scrubbed. After the op order those of us that were going to roll out were told to get some chow and try to rest. I went and ate as instructed. As I was walking to throw my tray away I saw Specialist L. come out of the hard stand latrines and he looked to have been crying. I jokingly asked him: "*Who died*? "That's when he turned and said White [platoon] had three KIAs. About two seconds later someone come out of the TOC screaming: "*QRF!*"

My counterpart O., was the medic for the QRF that day since I was the medic for the mission in the morning. I ran to tell O. to kit up and I donned my kit too just in case. I was told to remain on the COP and man the TOC. I didn't know how bad things were and I felt useless not going with the rest of the guys. Everything was still a mad scramble to gain some clarity in all the chaos.

I made my way to the TOC and immediately looked at the communication log. That's where I read and found out who our fallen brothers were: SSG Arizmendez, SPC Lee and PFC Pridham. Also noted were the survivors: the interpreter and SPC W.. We had sent W. to the rear to get some dental issues fixed and White Tank was picking him up and bringing him back as part of their mission. My heart sank. And I was about to learn how difficult being a Soldier could truly be.

The hardest thing I ever had to do was put duty first and emotions second and openly lie to one of my best friends. Shortly after I made it to the TOC, I was pulled away for a Blue Tank platoon meeting. The point of the meeting was to inform everybody of what happened and what was about to happen. Everyone was there, except our mechanic SPC F. One of the fallen, SSG Arizmendez, was the lead mechanic and one of SPC F.'s best friends. They played guitar together and didn't treat each as superior or inferior. They were always joking around but working hard. We all knew this. We all knew how much SSG Arizmendez meant to F. That's

---

[75] Op order: Operations order for a mission

why he wasn't there when the news was dropped and why the rest of the platoon couldn't say anything to him. We were put on a gag order to specifically not tell him. F. was damn good at his job and we needed him to do it without being emotionally compromised.

I can't imagine how hard things were for F. To have to go recover the vehicle one of your best friends was just killed in, that's gut- wrenching enough. I remember passing F. as they were about to roll out and he asked me if I knew who the fallen were. I had to lie. I just told him it'll be alright and to keep his head on a swivel and that I'll see him when he gets back. What was a calm evening in Afghanistan turned into the worst day of many of people's lives in mere seconds.

It was near dawn when the radio in the TOC crackled and everyone was coming home, the recovery process was complete. But we all knew there was still more to be done. At least things were calm for now. Blue and White had come in and everyone was taking gear off and trying to grasp reality. You could see the same look in every man's eyes. Tired and exhausted physically, emotionally and mentally. All hoping this was some kind of fucked-up dream. But all of us knew the truth. It was war, we knew this was part of the deal and we all signed the same contract.

I was eventually relieved in the TOC. On my way back to the tent, as the sun began to rise I passed F. He now knew who the fallen were. I could tell he'd been crying and as he walked passed me I saw he had a nose bleed. Like when you're crying and snot runs, I guess he rubbed his nose too hard. The PRT aid station was close to us so I grabbed F. by the shoulder and led him into the aid station. I found a roll of kerlix and opened it and handed it to him. He held it up to his nose to slow the bleeding, I hugged him and I began to cry. We just held each other for a moment. The duty part was over for now. It was safe to have emotions.

SCOTT FREDERIKSEN [2010]

TUESDAY 06 JUL 2010

This has taken me a very long time to speak about except to a few people. But these are my recollections of my worst day in Afghanistan. Losing my mentor, a leader, and a brother in arms (or wrenches in our case) but most of all a friend.

That day started like any other day for me at Bullard. As usual, I would write down (the night before) what needed to be fixed and then get on the ball due to us always either going on mission or being on QRF. I had it in my head that my vehicles would always be running at 100% even if I was dog tired from a late-night mission or burning the midnight oil fixing and then getting a list of needed parts so I could quit Freddy-rigging things because I couldn't get the parts I needed.

Well that moment we got the call for QRF I was balls deep inside a truck working on a turret. All I'd heard was that I needed to grab my gear and then I'd heard the words *"Get some body bags."* When I heard those words all I could think of was SSG Arizmendez. Well on my way to the tent I ran into Doc H. and I said *"I hope SSG A is alright."* As I was leaving he said *"You'll be alright Fred. I'll see ya when you get back."* At this point I'd already heard a rumor from a certain NCO that one of the KIAs [76] was SSG A., but I didn't believe it. It just couldn't be.

As we were leaving, I was hopping up into my place behind the .50 [machine gun] and the TC SGT E. told me and PVT M. that we were his dismounts and he didn't want us on the .50 cal . I didn't think anything of it but I had this knot in my gut at the moment that was telling me something was wrong. Well, night fell and we were still on the road and over the radio I hear the words that somebody was placing bags of fertilizer in the bridge. So we dismounted and quickly came across two haji's placing the bags and a young boy maybe ten years old give or take a few years.

Well, the interpreter went and spoke with them and it turns out they were using the bags to drive over this big ass hole in a section of the bridge. Fuckers got lucky they didn't get lit up in all honesty. So SPC S. was putting their info into the system and I was told to watch them since S. was fiddling around with that gizmo and his weapon was slung on his

---

[76] KIA: Killed in Action

shoulder. So I was there with my weapon on them and I was getting ready to unload on them because I was so pissed off that my mentor and friend was possibly dead. Then from behind me was SGT A. and he told me to lower my weapon and get in the truck before I did something stupid. All I could think about was that it couldn't be my friend.

After we left there we got to our destination and I was getting ready to dismount and over the radio CPT R. told SGT E. to keep me in the truck. So I stayed in the truck and decided to go to sleep, but it didn't happen. When we got back to Bullard it was morning. The sun was shining and I was standing on top of my truck watching all of White Platoon's vehicles come in and the men leaving the trucks. I didn't see SSG A. leave his vehicle. It couldn't be true. I thought maybe I missed a vehicle and he's already drinking a monster. When all of Blue Platoon was back at our tents CPT R. gathered us all for a meeting to break the news. That knot came back all of a sudden. He said that we lost three brothers in an IED yesterday. He named them off: PFC Pridham, SPC Lee and SSG Arizmendez.

I threw my water bottle at the nearest sand bag and started crying. SSG B. came up to me and put his hand on my shoulder and told me "*It's alright, Fred. We're here. It'll be alright.*" SPC G. came up to me and did the same thing. I was told to keep it together, and to go see the chaplain. So I did and he told me to go to work to keep my mind off of it. Well I started to work and was then told to go catch some sleep and to take a day off. I tried to sleep, it didn't happen. All I could do was cry. I tried to not cry loud and to keep it from everyone but I'm sure everyone heard. Later I went outside and met up with Doc H. and we talked for a few minutes and smoked quite a few cigarettes. Wish I coulda had a few drinks but tobacco and a Rip-It energy drink would have to do.

About a year later after I'd been out of the Army for a while I'd kept in touch with Barbara [Arizmendez] and I was invited to go with her and the kids to Arlington. I jumped on it. I wanted to say goodbye and pay my respects. I was more embarrassed that our last conversation was about how he wanted me to go to the promotion board and all I wanted to do was to get out and go back to Texas. When we got to his grave Barbara gave me a few minutes to myself. Justin (her son) stayed with me. I got down on my knee and put my hand on his tombstone and started crying again. Then for as young as Justin was he said "*Fred, why are you crying?*" I told him how I missed his father and wish he was still around. He then got down with me and said "*I miss him too, but he's in a better place now and he's still watching over us."* I was amazed at how such a young person had a better perspective on matters than I did.

SEAN STACY [2010]

WEDNESDAY 07 JUL 2010 (JOURNAL ENTRY)

Yesterday morning we were spun up as QRF. During the early morning hours an ASG convoy hit two IEDS and came under RPG fire at the local bazaar. Another IED was found a little way up the HWY by the ANA. We went out there to confirm it but EOD refused to fly out because the ANA attempted to destroy the IED by lighting it on fire, which didn't work. They supposedly have a policy that they won't work on an IED that has already been tampered with. A mission planned for hours of darkness was cancelled because of tragic circumstances. A patrol from FOB Bullard was struck by an IED resulted in three American KIAs.

They were driving in a MRAP and were fourth in the order of march. The driver was PFC Pridham. He had been in the Army less than a year and was a tanker. The gunner was SPC Lee. He deployed with me with Charlie Company last year and came with me to Delta Company. The TC was SSG Arizmendez, a mechanic attached to Delta from HHC. All three were killed in the initial blast. SPC W., who is in my squad, along with an interpreter who was riding in the back were wounded.

The insurgent used a command detonation IED. The wire, buried six inches deep, was traced back a couple hundred meters south to a mud hut and as usual he got away. The convoy came across a damaged bridge and took a dirt road bypass to get across. The IED was placed in a part of the road that formed a funnel and forced traffic to go through the make-shift kill zone. My squad was tasked out to drive to their location and offer assistance. While in route we came to a bridge during the night with a truck parked in the middle. Booth and myself dismounted the vehicle to investigate and surprised two Afghans behind the vehicle as they didn't hear or see us coming since we drive without lights at night (the driver uses a thermal display to allow us to maintain daylight speeds).

They had gotten stuck in a hole on the bridge and were stuffing the hole with fertilizer so they could back up. Fertilizer is the biggest ingredient in bombs out here so it caused instant suspicion, but upon further questioning it was determined that these guys were legit. They just happened to be transporting fertilizer and it was all they have available to attempt to patch the hole in the bridge. After helping them move their truck we allowed them to leave so we could cross the damaged bridge ourselves in order to link up with the disabled convoy and to bring them back with us to FOB Bullard. All three causalities had children and two of them were married. A communication black out was put into effect for the soldiers in our AO until the victims' families could be notified.

BARBARA ARIZMENDEZ [2010]

2009.

We were happy to be back in Hohenfels. It was a great community and many of our friends were still there. Fast forward to March 1, 2010, Marc left for Afghanistan with Delta Company. I heard from him here and there when he had time to call. Knowing him he always was busy fixing things, but it was always important for me to let him know that we are right here waiting for him.

Fast forward again to July 7, 2010, in the morning. My sister had spent the night and she let me sleep in as she was getting breakfast for the kids. I remember that I heard Justin saying *"Mom, Mom, you have to get up."* I looked at him and he said again, *"Mom, you have to get up, there are two guys at the door and they want to talk to you."* I thought it might be the painters because they had just gotten done with the house the day before and maybe they had forgotten something.

I got up and dressed real quick and walked to the door. As I walked to the door I got a glance of dress uniforms. Everyone in the military knows what that means. My heart dropped. I felt as if I was walking in slow motion with the last few steps to the door.

I opened the door and saw two men in dress uniforms standing there. *"Mrs. Arizmendez, may we come in?"* I let them come in basically knowing what they would say. My knees got really weak. I sat down. I started hearing only pieces of words: *"... regret to inform you... your husband was KIA... in Afghanistan on July 6th."*

I understood everything he was saying, but couldn't make myself listen. I was just thinking to myself: *'I was just talking to him on the 5th. He was fine, he was ok just really busy.'* My sister came into the room and tried to understand what was going on. I told her Marc is not coming home anymore. From that time on for the next few days everything was a daze. I kind of did everything on auto pilot in order to finish the necessary tasks ahead of me.

These next few weeks were hard. First I flew to Dover for the Dignified Transfer. It was hard not to be able to see Marc. It felt wrong to me just to leave him there. We put papers in for the request to have him laid to rest in Arlington National Cemetery, which got approved. I got told that he is viewable and I would be able to see him and we will be able to have a viewing before his funeral.

After I returned to Germany, the paperwork started. And then the memorial service in Hohenfels for Marc, Roger and Mikey took place. I am still amazed of how many people were there and grateful for all the messages written to me and the children into the memorial service books.

On August 10th, we left for Arlington. The viewing was supposed to be on the 10th and the funeral on the 11th. The morning of the 10th I had to find out that we had received some incorrect information and Marc was not viewable. We still did a gathering with family and friends what had come out to support us.

August 11th came around and it was a really sunny and hot day for Marc's funeral. It was a hard day, but I am thankful to everyone who came and flew or drove many hours just to be there for us.

In the end I wanted to thank my CAO and his family, some really close friends who were there for us for days and nights, and everyone in the Hohenfels community. All the Soldiers and their families in 1-4 Infantry, thank you from the bottom of my heart for all the support you all have given to us! I could not have stayed as strong without all of you!

Marc will always stay alive in our memories and heart. He is gone but will NEVER be forgotten!!

Thank you, Hohenfels. Thank you 1-4. Thank you D-CO. You all will always have a special place in my heart.

INTERPRETER STORIES

Without interpreters, we would be lost in war and our ability to communicate. Our interpreters played an instrumental support role in allowing us to connect with local villages and the Afghan people as we sought to root out Taliban and other enemy forces that wreaked havoc upon the populace and led them into a destabilized way of life. Our interpreters came from a variety of different backgrounds and many of them held their intentions to be for a better and safer Afghanistan for their families and friends. Many interpreters become lifelong friends of some Soldiers. Ours became our family.

While some of our interpreters have escaped their circumstances in life and found new beginnings in other countries, not all of them have been so fortunate. As conflict rages on with a more limited US military presence as compared to the height of the war, some of our interpreters still remain in unsafe conditions within Afghanistan. Our interpreters sacrificed their personal safety on the hope of a better future for themselves and their country. Side by side on daily missions, they augmented our patrols and provided us with a connection to the Afghan people.

As Shakespeare is often attributed with writing:

All the world's a stage,
And all the men and women merely players;
They have their exits and their entrances;
And one man in his time plays many parts

Our interpreters played many roles. The fought with words as men of action.

INTERPRETER STORY # 1

It my pleasure to share my experience and stories with the 1-4 book project. I wanted to mention that I really enjoyed working with 1-4 infantry regiment soldiers from August 2007 to October 2010 in Mizan, Day Chopan districts of Zabul province Afghanistan.

We all were working as a team and all four Companies: Alpha, Bravo, Delta, and Charlie had good leadership and brave soldiers. As an interpreter, I was always trying to be an honest, distinguished and combat-proven interpreter for all 1-4 teams. My real name is xxxxx. My teams called me Happy Feet and there was a reason and a story behind why they were calling me Happy Feet.

During my first week of deployment while I was a new interpreter, I went out with my team on a long mission in a dangerous, remote village which was full of Taliban. We got engaged by the enemy in an ambush at the time. My I-com radio battery died and we had no connection with ANA (Afghan National Army) so the team captain told me to tell the ANA soldiers to not pass the river because the enemy was hiding behind huge rocks on the other side of river and our gunner wanted to shoot that spot.

As I got of our Humvee and started running toward the ANA truck to pass the message, the enemy started shooting at me when I became visible to them in an open field. Bullets were impacting around my legs and I was randomly jumping and moving like dancing so I tried not to get hit. And, I did not have combat military boots. Instead I had long, black, fancy and shiny shoes on me. After I made it to the truck, I felt a hot and burning sensation while our gunner was shooting and the empty brass of the M240 (machine gun) was falling onto my feet when I was sitting on the back seat of Humvee truck. When we arrived back to the FOB they gave me the nickname of Happy Feet.

On behalf of my friends, I say thanks and appreciate our teams that they didn't leave us behind. The SIV program support for Afghan interpreters who put their life in great danger and served alongside US Army is a great opportunity and I am glad that now I live in US with my family and kids.

INTERPRETER # 2

During my 2 years working with the United States Army as an interpreter I have many memories .First, my job was to listen the Taliban I-com during the mission and translate what my commander spoke when he was talking with the people of Afghanistan. Our team helped the people every day in any time. We were getting a lot of incoming mortar from the enemy of humans. They were doing a lots of cowardly actions against humans. Me and my team were trying to help the people. Many time we were ambushed by the Taliban in Zabul district, fortunately without any casualties.

One day is unforgettable for me. We had a mission in a village of a district. We got into contact with the Taliban without any casualty but the Taliban were talking with each other in the I-com that they killed our people. But that was not true. When I told my commander that the fucking Taliban said: *"We killed all of them."* we positioned ourselves on a hilltop. On the hilltop there was a big rock that I moved. It was right in front of us. When we had gone back to the FOB my commander start laughing at me. He said: *"How could you move that big rock when we were not even able to move our heads up?"*

We had a lot of missions together working as a family and we shared our problems with each other. Sometimes the Taliban would talk about me and say: *"If we catch that fat interpreter we will cut him to pieces."* My commander told me: *"Don't worry about the fucking Taliban. They can't do anything to us."* We had different missions (mounted and dismounted) and one night my commander comes to my room and he told me: *"xxxxx, you must go with us on tonight's mission."* I told him: *"Okay. No problem, sir."* despite that it was not my turn to go.

He started our mission briefing. After starting our mission, we reached a point where there was a river. We had to move from that river. It was a very dark night. Suddenly one of our sergeant's legs slid on a rock. His leg was displaced. He was moving a lot of ammunition in a big bag. My commander asked me: *"xxxxx, can you do me a favor?"* I told him: *"Of course, sir."* He said: *"Get the bag from the sergeant and you will be the ammo man."* I told him: *"Alright, sir."* It was around 11 pm when we arrived in our position. We just got to rest for a few minutes when my commander said: *"xxxxx, do you see that high mountain?"* I said: *"Yes, sir."* He told me to climb that mountain. The bag was very heavy. I then told to my lieutenant that if I would move this bag up mountains day or night because everyone wants to survive.

INTERPRETER # 3

The Story of Unarmed Warriors.

Time: 2007- 2010.
Locations: FOB, Mizan, Lane, Baylough and Lagman, Zabul Province, Afghanistan.

This is how I got the job as an interpreter:

I passed an English Proficiency Exam at Camp Phoenix, Kabul, Afghanistan in 2007 and received a great score and was assigned in Zabul Province and worked with 1st Battalion, 4th Infantry Regiment stationed in Camp Lagman with great honor and enthusiasm as their Translator/Interpreter. I served this Unit from 2007 until 2010. In 2010, I was transferred from Zabul Province to Camp Eggers, Kabul, Afghanistan and worked there as a Translator/Interpreter for NATO Training Mission -Afghanistan (NTM-A)/Combined Security Transition Command-Afghanistan (CSTC-A) until 2013.

When I served the US Armed Forces in Zabul Province, I accompanied my team in many mounted and dismounted combat missions and we have been in many face-to-face contacts. Besides that I accompanied my team to the village elders' councils, seminars, conferences and other social gatherings. My American and Afghan friends lost their lives in the battlefield and I am still living with their memories. They paid the ultimate price to respect and support the Operation Enduring Freedom campaign. Their sacrifices will be respected from generation to generation and their memories will not be forgotten.

Most of the local interpreters/translators were untrained warriors. Working with the well-trained warriors who were equipped with the most developed technology in the world was challenging, but we never gave up. Some of the interpreters weren't familiar with military terminologies. Interpreters kept working with the teams and started learning military terminologies day by day. It wasn't easy for us in the beginning, but later on we learned lots of stuff from our teammates.

We as interpreters joined the US military to assist in the war which was launched to eliminate terrorism from the face of the earth especially from our country Afghanistan. Most of us left high schools, colleges, and universities only to serve our country and to secure a better future for the next generation; on the other hand, the US Army needed us in the battlefield so we took the opportunity and got ready to deliver our language skills to accomplish the mission. We knew that this war will benefit us and those who were/are the victims of terrorism. It was obvious to me and others that one day death will come after all living creatures that live in the universe so why not die for a reason. We considered the job as our moral responsibility.

The following is one of my memories in Deh Chopan District, Zabul Province, Afghanistan.

FOB Baylough, November 2007, we had a dismount mission and were out of the FOB at 10:00 PM local time. All of my teammates had night vision and easily could see the way, but I didn't have one so one of the sergeants (I don't remember his name) told me to be careful because I didn't have night vision. He said "*This mission is very important and we have to do it without any mistakes.*" I replied: "*Don't worry. I am born and raised in this country and I know how to deal with it.*" He told me the same thing three times. He was about to say the same thing again, but he couldn't complete his statement because he himself fell down in a ditch and twisted his ankle. The mission was cancelled and we did the mission in the following night.

Special thanks to those men and women who took/take part in to secure freedom and security of others.

Best Regards,

xxxxx

INTERVIEWS

In order to help understand the realities of war and its effects on the thoughts of Soldiers who have been directly engaged in combat operations, the following section presents anonymous answers from some of the Warriors themselves and offers a personal look into their minds. The goal is to provide objective and unedited responses that promote an honest approach to the questions asked. The Warriors come from all walks of life and educational, spiritual, and personal backgrounds.

How would you describe the differences between military and civilian life?

In civilian life, you have the illusion that you have a choice.... Nah, the difference is in the types of stupid that you have to deal with.

There is a huge lack in comradery in the civilian world. No one looks out for each other. People are nice to your face in the civilian but will stab you in the back for their benefit. In the military, you could hate another motherfucker, but you would still catch a bullet for his ass.

Having to decide what to wear every morning is a surprising burden. I would obsess over what I would and could wear when I went home. I was trying to woo a girl that cared very deeply about fashion and I would buy clothes offline and send them to her house in anticipation of having control over my destiny. Now I dread having to figure out what to wear to work every morning. I care about my appearance but I am irked by the possibility that I am being judged for wearing the same pair of slacks for 5 days in a row with only a few different shirt and tie combinations. The rest of my life is like this, I feel like I am constantly stumbling out of bed into decisions that I anticipated but now dread having to make. I long for the meritocracy of military life.

Military life is too easy! Well that is if you like to be treated as a two-year-old and trust me rank and time in service means nothing! But really the ole saying of being in the right uniform at the right time and in the right place is the staple of military service. Civilian life is a little more complex and the responsibilities associated with it are often too difficult for some to handle fresh out of the service.

Finish the sentence: God is_____.

Alive and well.

A personal form of control over an absurd universe.

Something I want to believe in.

My savior and protector! God is great!

Good

Non-existent.

A useful concept for some, they say that God loves the infantry but thus far I have seen no evidence of that. Certainly, we will not have the chance to ask him in the next life, but neither will the people that we have killed.

Since the time that you have deployed, do you feel that the world (or any specific part of it is worth fighting for?

No not at all. I guess if I really thought about it I would say in order to stop the spread of something truly evil (i.e. the Nazis). But all this we see today is just political not for the right reasons.

Knowledge and understanding. Everything else is simply a way of keeping your own group alive, so that they can continue to breed and dominate.

I believe that all people deserve a chance. That if the people wish for a better life and want to help themselves of course it's worth fighting for. I just wish there weren't so many lies that spread and create conflict where there might not be otherwise. There are too many greedy people and politicians in the world that just want what they don't need. If that makes any sense.

The truth about me and many of the men that I served with was simple; we didn't fight because we were naive enough to think that a decade of war was actually good for the American people and our loved ones. We fought because we were Soldiers. Some of us liked fighting and were good at it; some of us felt that being a warrior was a valid career choice; some of us just fought for the people next to us. I think that all the patriotism and love of the country stuff is all well and good, but it's not running through anyone's mind when they're fighting.

How did you dispose of trash while you were deployed?

While deployed, trash disposal consisted of being carried out to a large fire pit in the back left side of FOB Bullard. Not only was trash disposed of in this location but also human excrement, such as feces. We kept the fire burning day and night and sent people to watch it occasionally, to ensure spreading was not an issue.

Every bit of trash we had went straight to the burning pits. Then we dug a second burn pit at Al Masak. We didn't have anything to put on the trash to spread the fire, so I handed a jug of something over that said "Flammable" on it. Well, next thing you know, that fluid combined with an incendiary grenade made for one hell of a fire starter.

How much water did you drink in a typical day?

In Afghanistan? Three or four of those small bottles plus whatever was in my camelback. In Iraq I didn't drink the water because it made my stomach churn, so it was Gatorade and Rip-Its.

Way too much. I can't say for sure, but I still don't like water because of all the hydration over there.

Fuck if I know. A lot. It was 140 degrees, what do you think I was going to do?

A lot, I was on a sniper team and we climbed those crazy high mountains. I remember carrying IV packs just in case we had to force hydrate via infusion which we did at one point back in 2008 I think.

Honestly, I don't even remember how much water I drank, but I can tell you it was enough water to the point where my piss was clear at all times.

My daily goal was a 12 pack of those 20oz (?) bottles. If we didn't have those then I'd try to get a 6 pack of the 1 liter bottles. I loved the plentiful supply of bottled water! To this day, I still sniff the bottled drink before drinking it. Old habits never die! My wife doesn't understand!

Water? I didn't even know water existed while deployed, I thought we only had the mini cans of holy juice called Rip Its. Ok, on a serious note, I consumed about 5 liters of water a day, considering that my camel back was 2L, and I would empty it about 2 and a half times daily.

Do you keep track of military conflicts throughout the world? If so, did your perspective of conflicts change after you returned from Afghanistan?

My perspective changed on my first deployment to Iraq so when I got to Afghanistan I understood that the US military was being asked to do the impossible. We just did not have the training and understanding to affect any change.

Yes, I do. And yes, it did change. Being from the South, the stereotype is fuck Muslims, but that pissed me off. The only Islamic or Muslim people I had issue with were the ones trying to kill me. The majority of the local people were hospitable. To come home to the South and hear such hate from people who had not interacted with those of Islamic faith and hearing how they talked just pissed me off.

Yes, I try to keep up with as much news/politics as possible. You could say I am more jaded now. I always try to look at the reason behind the reason on why this conflict is started. Which corporation is benefiting in the name of "freedom" or "democracy." Tin foil hat I know.

Yes. You realize very quickly that our news is no different than the propaganda our psyops [77] units put out in other countries. I have realized that can't trust what you get from Fox, CNN, Washington Post, or Times. You have to dig for the truth if you want it.

Sometimes on and off, and I honestly don't have an opinion about this.

I do with great interest follow all military conflicts but I am aware of the sacrifice now. You see a report of a conflict and you associate it with your own blood, sweat and tears. Those conflicts became personal.

To be honest, I lost a lot of respect for the world after both of my deployments not only to Afghanistan but to Iraq also. You never realize how political and how much these conflicts are really just like a business. I mean lives become like liabilities for HR or something. Some things that happened were morally wrong and will never be known but to the individuals that witnessed them. Things of this nature really made me change my perspective and lose respect, and only want to focus on the bigger picture, and that is saving our people as a whole.

Republican, Democrat, or who-gives-a-damn?

Common sense. I wrote in Daffy Duck on the last Presidential election and voted for local, state, and county stuff. I felt like Trump was

---

[77] Psyops: Psychological Operations

incompetent and Hillary untrustworthy. And I did not like the independent candidates either. But I still exercise my right to vote on state and local legislature.

My give a damn on this is basically busted, I represent the best person that fulfils and meets my needs. Now I will say that on average, Democrats, and third parties such as Liberals usually meet my criteria best.

More Republican/who-gives-a-damn. I guess just the way i was raised makes me see democrats as a bunch of pussies. But I think if people could just work together more problems could be solved faster and easier. Someone always has a bigger ego to fill.

Deciding what party matters is costing us our country. Why does it really matter what party it is? These two parties have the job description, and that is representing the people of your state. These congressmen, governors, mayors, and many others should be our voice to the states. Many of these people are only doing it for the benefits. During the election time, these people will do every possible way to be elected or re-elected. These people will lie just to get your vote. The people have been waiting for a change to our country.

Libertarian.

I think it is wrong to pick either corrupt political party. I have more views of a libertarian, but would vote for the best person regardless of political party. I initially liked Obama's message of working with both parties and uniting the nation.

Monarchist, the ideal of the Philosopher King.

Republican.

Republican with Libertarian tendencies.

Left-leaning Independent.

Doesn't matter to me, just give me an honest government and I'll be ready.

I've always identified myself as a Republican, but after this last election, I'm more on the page that says they are all corrupt and trying to line their pockets.

Democrat, hard-core lefty liberal.

Have you rescued or saved the life of someone else while deployed? If so, who was it – a soldier, a child, a local, etc.?

I personally did not.

Yes. I saved an SF Terp and maybe even a 1-year-old due to taking the kid back to Lane for a week for feedings and educating his father on the care of a child.

Part of me wants to say yes and part of me wants to say no. In a way, there are too many to count. And in a way, I don't want to talk about it. It should be known that I was a medic. And maybe in some way the people around me saved me.

A soldier and received a BSM-V [78] for it.

Yes. I was a medic I saved soldier and LN [79] alike.

This is not a comfortable question, I'll pass.

I treated a bunch of locals throughout my career, mostly IED or gunshot-related injuries. I kept most of them alive for the duration of my care but never heard about what happened to them after they were medevac'd, mostly didn't care. I have treated a few American casualties. I was the first responder to a nasty double amputation, he later thanked me for saving his life, but that's a long story.

Finish the sentence: Flying out of Afghanistan was _____.

Relieving.

---

[78] BSM-V: Bronze Star Medal with Valor
[79] LN: Local National

Surreal. The first two times, being a single soldier, it was almost depressing coming back. You ask yourself: what am I coming back to, what do I do now? As a married soldier coming back from my last deployments, it was a much more joyous occasion.

Good/bad. Crazy to say I miss it over there. Three deployments and I miss the action, the feeling of making a difference every day.
Great. It's the first flight I've ever been on that I was able to sleep through.

A feeling of mixed emotions. Mostly happy ones but knowing we were coming home with less guys than we left with was something I was not happy about.

The greatest day of my life.

A little sad because I grew to like the country.

The same – when I landed and the wind blew and I had dirt in my eye. I said, "Fuck this place." The feeling was the same coming into and leaving Afghanistan.

In general: How do you feel about the President (as the Commander-in-Chief) not having any background in international conflicts or combat? Does that influence war in a negative, positive, or even neutral way?

I think it is neutral, because while the President may not have experience in those fields, those advising him do.

I think it should be a requirement to become President. Hopefully it'll positively influence the war. What I hope for is that he'll take the leash off the dog and let them do what needs to be done instead of having to play nice, so to speak.

For a long time now our POTUS has been nothing more than a figure head or spokesperson. A glorified Walmart greeter. Some have been respected on a global scale more than others. When the POTUS isn't respected it makes our country look weak and thus it opens the door for others to attack. The media more than anything impacts war. It influences rules of engagement etc. Civilians say that they want to know what is going on, but when they find out how ugly war is, they turn away and demand change. Sadly, this change weakens our ability to achieve success sometimes.

I don't think it really matters. He has so many analysts and advisors. Even if he did serve he would be so out of touch. It matters more that he listens to his Generals and advisors.

I think that the President not having any military experience is not a bad thing. However, he (or she) should absolutely have experience with international conflicts, this experience can be practical or academic, but having an understanding of international affairs is very important.

What comes to mind when you think of Rip-Its?

Fuck that.

A lot of nostalgia, little cans of energy, way too sweet, sought after.

Nasty. Many other better energy drinks out there. But made for fun. Ever try the rip-it challenge?

High heart rate, probably chemicals we don't want to know about.

Rip-or-ade! A can of orange Rip-It and a bottle of red Gatorade! SSG Arizmendez taught me that one.

The many sleepless nights in a guard shack wondering if that was going to be the shift you could let loose on the M240B!! But really they were my life line, when we ran out I would supplement my cravings with Gatorade protein shakes and when those ran out I would go for the java energy drink they gave us! But the damn Romanians would constantly be stealing drinks by the case from our connex, I'm surprised we never established a guard!

God's gift to life and survival haha.

Liquid hate. And excitement. I pretty much get a hard on when I find them at the convenience stores here at home.

I laugh every time when I see them in a store or gas-station, memories of CDS drops and trying to get to the Rip-Its while they still cold.

What did you do in your downtime to keep yourself occupied while deployed?

Watch movies, shot the shit with friends. We did stupid shit – empty water bottles about 20 meters out and threw rocks at them to see who could knock them down. Pretty much whatever you could.

I actually started writing a book, I completed around 78 pages of a fictional novel, though I never completed the book. I also studied physics and geography, which has prepared me for my current life now.

Books, movies, and porn.

Sleep, read, Rock Band with the boys, and general fucking around. Movies, skype calls, and working out were among the top contenders. I also volunteered my time with the mechanics, I love working on trucks so I would help them as much as I could. That's where I built my bond with SSG Arizmendez.

Masturbated, wrote letters, masturbated, video games, masturbated, watched lots of shitty DVDs of American shows, masturbated, gym, masturbated.

What is military humor to you? Can you give an example?

Military humor huh? So we now get safety briefings every fucking weekend so it's humorous to me to whisper to someone else about how I'd rather slit my wrist or go hang myself than to have to be told not to beat my wife this weekend. So yeah that's a form of military humor. If I said that to a civilian, I feel I'd be in handcuffs on a hospital bed with padded walls surrounding me.

Fucked up. And I can give an example: I never understood military humor until I read a certain book from high school – and in the book a soldier stepped on a landmine and was blown to pieces and two soldiers were tasked to get his body parts. The soldier's name was Lemon and one of the two soldiers started singing the song Lemon Drop when picking up the body parts.

Dark, morbid obscene.

140

Military humor is crude and warped. Starting a story off with "And there I was standing balls deep in your sister" etc...

Haha. To me, military humor is either dark, crude, or offensive. It can also be the person being able to laugh at things or situations civilians would either be traumatized by or have them look at you with this weird look that says, "*This person needs help.*" Well, let's see if I can give ya a good one; here is an example of something funny to me and a few other guys that were there when it happened. One day, while at Bullard we were called out for QRF. (This is the short version). When we went to the location, the choppers were there and the men were getting back in. Needless to say, business was good that day. We ended up getting tasked to pick up the bodies and weapons.

Well, while there I was bending over to flip the dead fucker over and Doc xxxxx beat me to it. He flipped him over and the front of his face was gone. While flipping him, what's left of his brain and other body parts and blood fly onto me – head to toe! Well, a little later we go back to Bullard and I'm walking back to the tent and [two fellow soldiers; redacted] see me covered in blood and they thought I got hit. They yelled, "*Fred, where you hit at?*" I yelled back, "*No I ain't hit. I'm covered in fucking Achmed juice!*" It was a sad day. I put on a perfectly good pair of coveralls and a good pair of boots in the burn pit that had been with me since I enlisted in 2006. Not exactly what you're looking for, but when I talk with my Army buddies we normally end up laughing about this incident.

What influenced your decision to join the Army?

9/11 shit pissed me off. Had a chance to play college ball but decided the Army was better.

I actually joined the Army partially because I was gonna enlist anyways when I turned 18 because I didn't know what I wanted to do in life. The other reason I ended up joining at 17 was because at the time I had pissed my parents off enough that they were more than willing to sign the papers to let me join a year earlier.
To be honest, I joined at 17 years old with my parents signing the waiver, and it was all because I wanted out of my life at the time, and thought it would make me some billy bad ass.

A lot of things. I was sick as a child. I had a rare kidney disorder and was constantly in and out of the hospital and subject to all sorts of testing and got used to it and came to admire the people who had saved my life. And one of the things I always said to the question: *"What do you want to be when you grow up?"* was the person who gives IVs. I also am fond of history. I could use the military benefits to go on and study history. But I wound up staying the medical field after the Army.

I grew up in Cold War Germany, I saw US soldiers when I played in the woods or when I saw formations of soldiers doing PT while I was walking to school in my German hometown. I always knew that one day I will go to the States, become American and fight for the United States.

Hahahaha I wanted to jump out of planes and shoot shit. That's what I told my recruiter.

Bad breakup, college loans, always wanted to be a Soldier.

I believe it is where God wanted me at that point and time in my life.

What was the funniest story or event that happened to you while deployed?

One of the funniest things that happened was when I was teaching another mechanic how to change fire bottles in a new MAT-V truck. Well, I was laying down on top of the tight rear tire telling J. how to do it. Well, the problem we were having is that it was getting hot enough outside the heat was setting the bottles off. Well, he hooked it up and right when he hooked it up SGT xxxxx came over and started telling us something, so we started laughing and the next thing you know, J. forgot to do one step and the bottle went off and I couldn't get out of my position! I came out from there looking like an Oompa Loompa! I was purple literally from head to toe! (xxxxx has a picture of it somewhere, you'll have to ask him for it).

I don't have a sense of smell. At the time we didn't have working showers so we were using 5-gallon water cans. Well someone put JP8 in a water can that I showered with. As my eyes were burning, I asked a dude walking past if it smelled like gas and he said yes. So here I am, butt-naked rinsing off with 2 cases of water one bottle at a time out in the open. Wound up with chemicals blisters on my feet, made for fun patrols for the next week. Was pissed then, funny now. I'm just glad he didn't have a lit cigarette.

There was always some funny or stupid shit going on. When I was first attached to C Co, I was just a PFC and was hogtied with duct tape and set on the Company CQ desk before a platoon sergeant came by and told someone to get me off of the desk. I put in a good fight, but was no match for my whole squad. Shit, just saw you asked for a deployment story. ha! Birthdays in the Army are always fun if it's not yours. While deployed they go to the next level. We tied a guy up with zip ties, stripped him near naked, and dumped water on him. While he rolled in the mud we cut open glow sticks and sprayed the liquid on him. That is also an example of the humor in the Army.

Getting caught in contact. Hearing *"Contact in the rear!"* and then someone making the joke, *"Your mom got contact in the rear!"* (in the middle of a firefight).

What was the most dangerous moment during your service in the Army?

Getting shot at, at any point. The first time was as I was on guard duty. You never forget that first crack of the bullet going by your head and the poofs of concrete coming off the guard tower. That's when you realize what's going on and that maybe you should move. Another point was on mission/patrol when we had to get out of the trucks to assault a firing position. As we were moving forward, you just see the dirt kicking up at your feet and hear the gun shot from a distance.

During one of my tours I had to low crawl to and dig up a suspicious object that my rifleman had found with his metal detector. I pulled it up with my K-Bar and I remember the chills when I pulled a 155 artillery round up. It would have killed me and the rest of my squad.

Had a grenade land between me and a soldier I was in charge of, almost too many to count.
The day I was blown up in a complex ambush while dismounted on patrol.

The most dangerous was probably in Afghanistan. One day our FOB came under heavy rocket and mortar attack, and as everyone was running to the bunkers, I was gearing up running across base. As a mortar man, I did not have the luxury of hiding in the bunker like some of the

143

others. I had to make my way across base, while also taking the incoming attack, to the mortar pit to prep for counter battery.

Probably coming under direct fire while on patrol in an open area between 2 ridgelines.

Walking the riverbed on the second to last night at Mizan, we were coming back to the FOB so I was pumped up. As were walking I go to move from the river's edge and a explosion goes off behind me. I fell to the ground and when I came back to I was dazed and confused, the guys were calling my name so I got up and ran to the opposite side. I remember them asking if I was ok and I yelled the answer because the ringing in my ears was so loud! I thought I was a dead man. Later that night the mortars were shooting the 120mm and every time it went off I damn near hit the ground!

Was there anything that shocked you about Afghanistan?

The people and how they lived. So happy with little to nothing. It was a simple way of life and they accepted it, but then driving a few hours up the road and seeing a completely different lifestyle and culture. Also the pure beauty to the landscape, it truly is a nice looking country if you can look past the war-torn cities.

The people that weren't trying to kill us, were the true embodiment of what Southern hospitality is about. Also, on my first patrol I felt like I had stepped back to the time of Jesus. It reminded me of a much more down and dirty Charleston Heston Ten Commandments movie.
How archaic it seemed. You literally felt like you went back in time. You grow up in a first-world country with amenities, and it was hard to believe that people still live in conditions where they build their houses out of water, mud, and hay. And modern technologies are not present. It was like the Biblical era – even medieval England was probably more advanced.
Just how dirty the people are. The level of filth was mind-blowing.

I wasn't shocked a whole lot except for when me and xxxxx went to the terps' tent to drink tea when we walked in there were the terps and the shit truck driver all holding hands! Well, we walked in and walked right back out! I guess you could say I was shocked because I thought everyone was just joking about "Man Love Thursday", turns out they isn't joking about that.

Not really.

I grew up in El Paso, Texas, and I think what shocked me the most is how similar the landscape Afghanistan looked to home. That and the smell of Kandahar, which will live with most of us forever.

Was there a moment while deployed when you just wanted to go home?

Yeah, there were times when I wanted to go home. Partly to get a cold beer, but the only time I really wanted to leave was to go pay my respects and make it to SSG A.'s funeral.

While I was deployed my father was diagnosed with cancer and had surgery, he survived and I got to see him again, but when I found out, yes I wanted to be with him. We are very close. He is my hero.

No. As a single Soldier what would I have gone home to?

Not really. I wished some other people went home but otherwise I liked being deployed.
Of course! Primarily after every shitty mission where we would walk for hours on end only to not get into a firefight and would have to carry everything back to the COP.

Mostly around the holidays, weird how you can be sounded by 30 other guys but still feel lonely.

Got cheated on a few times... that wasn't pleasant. But by the end I didn't want to go home.

Did you suffer any serious injuries while deployed? If so, what were they?

Other than some mental issues and mTBI, thankfully no.

No physical injuries, however I did see behavioral health for quite some time after my first and second deployments. They said I have been labelled as having PTSD but it's not serious in my book.

The retina in my left eye was detached, TBI, left knee fucked up. But I am still moving.

I hurt my back fairly severely, I would end up becoming disabled from the injury. During my first tour I was underneath a Humvee during a mission trying to repair part of the drive train with a mechanic. We got ambushed and the recoil from the .50 Cal machine gun knocked the Humvee off the jack and onto my shoulder. It didn't pin me but after the tour I would learn that I had ruptured 4 discs in my back.

TBI.

Several post-blast traumas, concussions etc., strafe round to the chin, shrapnel, messed up discs in the back got medical retired 2014 but only because they re-classed me and wouldn't let me stay infantry, so I left. If I can't do what I love I can't do it.

Would you ever return to Afghanistan? If so, why?

Sure I'd return. I'd only return if it could be the same group of guys because we all became brothers and would do anything for each other. Plus, we all had a good time playing jokes on each other. It's hard to describe the loyalty we all have for each other.

I would, but only with the same group of motherfuckers that were with me on deployment. They could call me up and say that we will assault the gates of hell and we will die and I would say when and where.

If I could say with whom and where I was going as well as cut out the bullshit, then hell yeah! The guys I spent my time with became my brothers and I would love to make some more memories. Kinda miss some action too.
I would return for the food and the climate.

I miss it all the time.

I myself would go as a tourist, not as a Soldier, this falls into a category of I do not support some of the things that happened morally.

Well, no choice if the Army sends me. Otherwise nope! Too much risk.

Yes. To see if it is the same. To see if we had any impact at all.

What are your thoughts about the people of Afghanistan?

Very stubborn and not open for change.

Simple farmers and herders who just want to be left alone.

Most want to be left alone, just wish they would stand up and say enough and fight for their own country.

Now that I'm a civilian I can say that I'm sure they are good people with rich and varied lives. As a Soldier I didn't think about them.

Just different.

Very good, hospitable people. Just don't shoot at me and we won't have issues.

These people are just normal everyday people, I mean if you grew up in a nation that did not have so much you would be the same. And that is not even a true statement either. If you look back pre-wars, to like the 70s and etc., this country was striving and a great place. I think the people have just been put through so many conflicts that it has just tortured them to the point of breaking down mentally and physically.

I think they are caught between a rock and a hard place.

How has deployment shaped or changed your life after you returned?

I see things differently, maybe harsher. And don't have a problem seeing/watching violent things especially if the person it is happening to, deserves it.

It has affected my life a great deal. I will carry the things I have seen and done with me forever.

I nowadays don't sit in restaurants or other places with my back to the door. At times when driving I find myself driving in the middle of the road. There's times when branding cattle and I smell the burnt flesh I think about the burn pits and the god awful smell from some of the things that'd get burned.

Very dramatically. I found the fact that I need to feel a sense of need and purpose and I am better at taking care of others and immediately jumped into a relationship afterwards, and it wasn't right. But I am finally dealing with the military after Afghanistan. I immediately jumped into the first thing that gave me a sense of purpose and reason. And now I am trying to find myself after the war and the Army and it has still been five years and more. Lots of depression, anxiety, and paranoia. I am not sure who I am.

It has changed everything; I can't drive without thinking the road will blow up from under me! I watch for debris.

If I was being honest I would say deployment has made me so damn apathetic. It is hard to feel anything now.

Deployment made me realize the person I was, who I never wanted to be, and also showed me a path to take in life. That is why now I am not a Soldier, have an education, and am working at bettering the world.

Made me train my soldiers more realistically, and I focused on the things that matter the most.

How would you define the word "Soldier"?

I think about earning this title. And I think about what I had to do to get it. I remember the NIC (night infiltration course) and after all of that, there was a bonfire – a culmination of all of our training and all of us that made it through and then the ROPE ceremony [basic training ceremony]. We received the Army values dog tags and got to drink Gatorade for the first time in a long time. Ha-ha. And we all recited the Soldiers' Creed. Maybe I would define it as: someone more selfless than the average person.

Fresh out of basic: Brainwashed. Few years in: Open-minded, all about liberty. Making command: Power-hungry. That is just some, there is also the Soldier who is a strong willed individual that feels he is standing for what he believes in and wants to make a difference in the world.

Time warrior; shithead; civil servant; asshole; hardworking; takes initiative; worthless.

Most selfless person, the best the US has to offer who is willing to die for his brother, anytime and everywhere.

Lonely.

Anyone that is willing to fight, defend, and die for his fellow brothers in arms.

Someone who is willing to lay their life down for their country.
A man or woman who's willing to die in order to protect their country and free others from oppression.

Never really thought about it but I think it is a person willing to fight for their fellow human being.

Someone who toes the line, stands up and fights for change.

Protector.

A normal person that gives his mind and body to a belief bigger than himself.

What would you like civilians to know about war?

If they want to know they can go enlist. Otherwise know that war is ugly, we do bad and ugly things to protect them and this country. Please spare us your judgment.

It's more complex than anyone can imagine. It's fun, challenging, adventurous, absurd, funny and scary all at the same time.

It is not the movies. There are good times and bad times. I would like them to know that the war does not stop for us after we come home. Some of us can separate that life from this better than others, but even that has its downsides. Asking someone to go out and do something against their human nature, then asking them to turn around and be a perfectly normal member of society is not going to happen. We spend billions on war; let us spend the same taking care of the people who came home.

War will combine your worst and best emotions, feelings and fears in on single second for months at a time and will drain your soul.

It's not pretty and its filled with propaganda both good and bad.

Finish the sentence: War is _____.

A necessary evil. My logic behind it is that war breeds innovation and creation. We wouldn't have GPS in our phones if it was not for Vietnam. People would not be driving Jeep vehicles if it was not for WW II. Most technological advancements in medicine stem from war. As horrible as war is, it does benefit future generations through lessons learned. It is a necessary evil that I would like to go away, but we are human and it will happen again and continue to breed advancement.

Dark.

Freedom.

Hell.

Against human nature.

Where you will learn how much heart a man has.

Ugly but necessary.

An adrenaline rush at times but also at times filled by boredom.
The greatest sport devised by mankind.

A great time until it's not.
A whole bunch of emotions, depending on how it has affected you.

Brutal

Mancini, Adam. Conducting mortar fire. Personal Archive.

Mancini, Adam. Soldiers on patrol. Personal Archive.

Starnes, David. Resupply by airdrop. Personal Archive.

Mancini, Adam. A Soldier on watch. Personal Archive.

Johansen, Boyd. A Christmas portrait. Personal Archive.

Massagee, Ben. Supportive Afghan children. Personal Archive.

Stacy, Sean. **A medical evacuation. Personal Archive.**

Abernathy, Dakota. **Honoring the fallen. Personal Archive.**

Starnes, David. Bear (FOB dog) watches Soldiers. Personal Archive.

Mancini, Adam. On mission patrol. Personal Archive.

Mancini, Adam. Two worlds collide. Personal Archive.

Mancini, Adam. Over-watch and reflection. Personal Archive.

Johansen, Boyd. Mountains in the distance. Personal Archive.

Starnes, David. Preparing to return home. Personal Archive.

Massagee, Ben. Joint mission with Romanians. Personal
Archive.

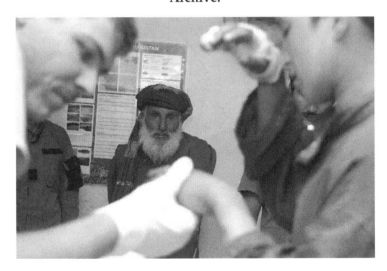

Starnes, David. Healing the wounded. Personal Archive.

Mancini, Adam. Soldiers on Patrol. Personal Archive.

Mancini, Adam. Soldiers on C-130. Personal Archive.

Mancini, Adam. Providing Over-watch. Personal Archive.

Mancini, Adam. Overlooking the terrain. Personal Archive.

Starnes, David. Human waste and a burn pit. Personal Archive.

Santiago, Roman. A modern band of brothers. Personal Archive.

Lee, John. Nighttime mortar mission. Personal Archive.

Slander, John. The middle of nowhere. Personal Archive.

UNCOMMON VALOR

During its Afghanistan deployments, Soldiers of 1-4 IN earned 20 BSMVs, 47 ARCOMVs [80], 1 SM [81] and 1 SS [82] through various actions. The following are the names of the Soldiers who earned these valor awards. Their rank, the type of award, and the deployment in which the Soldier earned the award are stated for reference in correspondence to the subsequent award citations. Some of the original award citations have been edited for clarity or to protect sensitive information.

Name	Rank	Award	Deployment
Lopez, Salvador	SSG	BSMV	B Co 2009
Mueller, Robert	SSG	BSMV	D Co 2008
Ritenour, Matthew	SSG	Silver Star	A Co 2007
Sher, Azhar	SSG	BSMV	B Co 2009
Giovanelli, Nicholas	SPC	ARCOMV	B Co 2009
Budinger, Matthew	SPC	ARCOMV	D Co 2008
Davis, Jeremy	SPC	ARCOMV	D Co 2008
Andrade, Javier	SPC	BSMV	B Co 2007
Cappo, Daniel	SPC	ARCOMV	B Co 2009
Widel, Curtis	SGT	ARCOMV	B Co 2009
Beck, Brian	SPC	ARCOMV	B Co 2009
Bugher, Adam	SPC	ARCOMV	B Co 2009
Daniels, William	SGT	BSMV	B Co 2007
Lopez, Salvador	SGT	BSMV	B Co 2007
Rubio, Jamie	SGT	BSMV	D Co 2008
Rubio, Jamie	SGT	ARCOMV	D Co 2008
Westfield, Edward	SGT	ARCOMV	B Co 2007
Kilson, Devon	SGT	ARCOMV	B Co 2009
Cisneros, Christian	SGT	ARCOMV	B Co 2009

[80] ARCOMV: Army Commendation Medal with Valor
[81] SM: Soldiers Medal
[82] SS: Silver Star

Sosa, Arturo	SGT	ARCOMV	B Co 2009
Gatewood, Wesley	PFC	ARCOMV	B Co 2009
Delashmidt, Ryan	PFC	ARCOMV	B Co 2009
Liberatore, Paul	PFC	ARCOMV	B Co 2009
Reyes, Miguel	PFC	ARCOMV	B Co 2009
Coleman, Jacob	PFC	ARCOMV	B Co 2009
Widel, Curtis	PFC	ARCOMV	B Co 2007
Macias, Antonio	PFC	ARCOMV	B Co 2009
Davidson, Jeremy	CPL	BSMV	B Co 2009
Berry, Spencer	PFC	ARCOMV	B Co 2009
Swintek, Philip	1LT	BSMV	D Co 2008
Basilides, Jason	1LT	BSMV	B Co 2009
Tomberlin, Jared	1LT	BSMV	B Co 2009
Stofan, Kevin	1LT	ARCOMV	B Co 2007
Greene, Marcel	SPC	BSMV	B Co 2007
Wright, Stephen	PV2	BSMV	B Co 2007
Houle, Seth	SPC	ARCOMV	C Co 2008
Cisneros, Christian	PFC	ARCOMV	B Co 2007
Ely, Fredrick	SPC	ARCOMV	B Co 2007
Goler, Alexander	SPC	ARCOMV	B Co 2007
Petry, Corde	PFC	ARCOMV	B Co 2007
Crosson, Clifton	PFC	ARCOMV	B Co 2007
Napier, William	PFC	ARCOMV	B Co 2007
Perez, Adrian	PFC	ARCOMV	B Co 2007
Summers, Edwin	SGT	ARCOMV	B Co 2007
Brown, Chancelor	SPC	ARCOMV	B Co 2007
Clark, Jackie	PFC	ARCOMV	B Co 2007
Larson, Christopher	SPC	ARCOMV	B Co 2007
Walker, Laroy	SPC	ARCOMV	B Co 2007
Zaehringer, Johnathan	PFC	BSMV	B Co 2007
Gilbert, Brian	PFC	ARCOMV	B Co 2007
Widel, Curtis	SGT	BSMV	B Co 2009
Cleland, Wade	1LT	BSMV	A Co 2007

Calloway, Isaiah	CPL	BSMV	C Co 2006
Weiskittel, Chris	SFC	ARCOMV	D Co 2005
Neighbors, Clifford	SSG	ARCOMV	UNK
Thom, Dustin	SGT	ARCOMV	B Co 2007
Thompson, Brent	SGT	ARCOMV	B Co 2007
Frungillo, Steven	SPC	ARCOMV	B Co 2007
Brown, Brennan	SPC	ARCOMV	C Co 2008
Ruehs, Alan	SGT	ARCOMV	C Co 2008
Westengerg, Shawn	1LT	ARCOMV	B Co 2007
Billig, Thomas	1LT	ARCOMV	B Co 2007
Thomasee, Nolan	SGT	ARCOMV	D Co 2005
Wright, Jordan	SPC	SM	B Co 2009
Bell, Scott	SGT	BSMV	A Co 2007
Clark, Matthew	PFC	BSMV	A Co 2007
Hargus, Shawn	PFC	ARCOMV	A Co 2007

1LT Jason V. Basilides
Team Blackfoot, 1-4 Infantry
April 2009

On 24 April 2009, 1LT Basilides was on a leader's reconnaissance patrol in the northern district of Day Chopan, Zabul Province, Afghanistan. Initially, the patrol consisted of the Company Commander, First Sergeant, 1LT Basilides, one of his fire teams, and the PL with two squads from 1st Platoon, Bravo Company, 1st Battalion, 4th Infantry Regiment. The patrol departed FOB Baylough at 1000 in the morning to conduct a route reconnaissance to Davudzay (42S xxxxx) in preparation for future Company-level operations. Davudzay is a known Taliban safe haven that coalition forces seldom go to. The patrol was clearing the route to the village of Chino 1 (42S xxxxx), approximately 6 km west of the FOB, when the patrol came under intense enemy fire.

The patrol stopped in a security halt at the base of a hilltop (42S xxxxx) just east of Chino 1 (42S xxxxx). 1LT Basilides, being the platoon leader responsible for the Day Chopan District, led the leaders on the patrol up the hill to get a better vantage point. While on top of the hill, the patrol received ICOM chatter that the Taliban was in position and ready to attack. 1LT Basilides knew from past SAF engagements in the area that contact would most likely come from the vicinity of TRP 7 or TRP 39. He immediately called back and had his mortar team lay the 120mm on TRP 7. The patrol had not reached the final objective, so I told 1LT Basilides that we needed to continue clearing west towards the town of Chino 1. 1LT Basilides linked up with his fire team, and they continued clearing the route dismounted in front of the vehicles across an open area with little cover or concealment. I called back to the TOC and had the QRF start moving towards our location to stage for the attack. The QRF consisted of one squad from 1st Platoon, one squad from 2nd Platoon, one ODA Team, and two squads of ANA.

The Taliban continued talking on the ICOMs saying that the attack would commence shortly. As the patrol reached the town of Chino 1, the ICOM chatter went silent. Contact was imminent, so I knew we had to gain the high ground as soon as possible. I told 1LT Basilides to occupy the high ground at 42S xxxxx with his team in order to establish an over watch of the town of Davudzay (42S xxxxx) and to be prepared for the attack. There was no good route to the high ground, only open terrain. 1LT Tomberlin positioned his vehicles to cover 1LT Basilides' movement from the west and southwest. 1LT Basilides had to maneuver 300m across an open field with no cover or concealment to reach the base of the 2454 meter hill that he had to climb. About 100 meters into 1LT Basilides' movement, the Taliban abruptly engaged 1LT Basilides and his team with a heavy barrage of AK-47 and PKM fire. He instinctively got down, returned fire, and rallied his Soldiers to continue bounding to the cover of the rocks at the base of the hill. Rounds were impacting within inches of 1LT Basilides and his team. 1LT Tomberlin continued to maneuver his platoon towards the initial contact in order to relieve the effective fire that the Taliban was placing on 1LT Basilides and his team. By this time however, there were enemy on the high ground to the south, vicinity TB xxxxx, TB xxxxx, and the base of the mountain (TB xxxxx) that 1LT Basilides was now attempting to occupy.

The persistent heavy volleys of small arms fire continued to rain down on 1LT Basilides and his Soldiers. As the patrol started to gain fire superiority, the enemy withdrew to new positions and began firing RPGs along with the AK-47s and PKMs. 1LT Basilides' disregard for his own safety and his "follow me" infantry mindset propelled him to set the example for his Soldiers and lead from the front. He bounded over and over towards the rocks as rounds impacted all around him. 1LT Basilides' Soldiers latched on to his steadfast leadership and continued bounding behind him. When 1LT Basilides was about 50m from the cover of the rocks, the QRF arrived and began engaging the Taliban who were on the southern end of the hill 1LT Basilides was about to climb. 1LT Basilides' courage and calmness under fire carried his men to the cover of the rocks.

The fight would rage on for several more hours as the patrol continued pushing west into the Davudzay bowl. Once the rest of 1st Platoon and the ODA from the QRF made their way to 1LT Tomberlin, they continued their assault to the orchards. At this point, the firefight had been ongoing for approximately 40 minutes. As the rest of the company started to move, 1LT Tomberlin and his elements again came under another barrage of RPG and machine gun fire. The fire was so intense and close that vehicles and Soldiers were taking shrapnel and a few shots impacted the body armor itself. The JTAC with the ODA element started dropping ordinance on the enemy positions while the rest of the company continued to engage and assault through into the town of Davudzay. Around this time, 1LT Basilides and his team made it to the top of the hill.

From this position, he was able to see the entire Davudzay bowl. He immediately began relaying to the JTAC enemy positions in the orchards and the ridgelines west and north of Davudzay. This enabled CAS and

CCA to destroy enemy reinforcements coming from the surrounding Taliban safe havens. His actions from the over-watch were crucial to the survivability of the patrol because ammunition was quickly becoming a concern, and it would be another hour before the ammo resupply arrived. 1LT Basilides was able to keep reinforcements at bay and give the rest of the patrol the ability to continue clearing the orchards.

Simply put, this mission would have failed without 1LT Basilides. His disregard for personal safety and ferocious audacity in the face of overwhelming enemy contact was the spark that inspired every Soldier on the mission to continue to fight. His clear visualization of the enemy situation, his sensible understanding of the patrol's situation and capabilities, and his tenacious focus on his mission allowed him to make sound, logical decisions and regain the initiative against the enemy. 1LT Basilides' steadfast example of courage under fire allowed him to fight off a fanatical enemy force, maneuver under fire to gain the key terrain to over watch the rest of the patrol, and ultimately, save the lives of his fellow Soldiers. His actions that day resulted in the destruction of 17 enemy killed and many more wounded. His valorous actions in combat reflect great credit upon himself, Task Force Zabul, Combined/Joint Task Force 101, and the United States Army.

1LT Philip Swintek
Team Dragon, 1-4 Infantry
June 2008

On the 14th and 15th of June 2008, 2nd Platoon was on a combat patrol to the southern end of the Chalikor Valley with an Operational Detachment Alpha (ODA), Embedded Training Team (ETT), Afghan National Army (ANA), and Afghan National Police (ANP) element. The patrol came under harassing anti-coalition forces (ACF) fire on the morning of the 15th at approximately 06:00 as they cleared the North end of Tangay Village (42S xxxxx) in the southern end of the Chalikor Valley. As the ANA completed clearing Tangay Village, A collective decision was made to continue to engage spotters and ACF small arms weapons teams positively identified and continuing to engage the patrol from the northwest. ODA repositioned into an over-watch position, ETT and ANA advanced beyond Tangay northwest toward Siratala (42S xxxxx) and 1LT Swintek maintained the center as he deployed two UAH's to cover rear security and the exfil route for the patrol. At approximately 09:30, the ANA and ETT were abruptly engaged with heavy volumes of ACF fire from RPG, SPG-9, PKM, AK-47 and Dragonov sniper fire. The ODA also became decisively engaged at their over-watch position sustaining vehicle mobility kills to one GMV. All communications between the three key elements became interrupted at this time and command and control of the fight became compromised.

1LT Philip Swintek observed that the ETT UAH's crew served weapon had jammed and was sustaining heavy suppressive fire. Unable to reach the ETT leader, CPT xxxxx, on the net, 1LT Swintek maneuvered his UAH into the ACF line of fire to shield the ETT UAH and allow them to attempt to repair their weapon. He then dismounted his vehicle, moved to the rear of the ETT UAH and made link-up with CPT Cline. SGT Rubio of 2nd PLT, Delta Company 1-4 was the gunner for the ETT UAH and, assessing that the repair to the crew-served weapon was impossible, dismounted and accompanied 1LT Swintek. After making contact with CPT xxxxx, assessing the situation and identifying possible Courses of Action (COA), 1LT Swintek determined that he would have to contact the ODA Team Leader, CPT xxxxx, face to face. Without regard for personal safety, 1LT Swintek dashed nearly 200m from CPT xxxxx's vehicle to CPT xxxxx's GMV through persistent volleys of heavy ACF small arms fire. Once 1LT Swintek made link-up with CPT xxxxx, he relayed the situation with the ETT UAH crew, and assisted in re-establishing FM communications between 2nd platoon elements and ODA. 1LT Swintek and CPT xxxxx considered COAs and determined a scheme of maneuver to develop the situation and resume the initiative versus the ACF. With a plan set, 1LT Swintek recovered SGT Rubio (who was helping an ODA NCO fire 60mm mortars), and again bounded through heavy fire back to his UAH over nearly 200m of rough terrain. Once he returned to his vehicle, he remounted and prepared for subsequent maneuvers.

Throughout his efforts to re-establish command and control of the Coalition Forces friendly effort, 1LT Swintek was concurrently aware of a situation developing to the unit's rear. An ANSF OP previously set over three kilometers to the rear to defend the patrol's exfil route had come into heavy contact. Through clear and succinct orders, 1LT Swintek dispatched a two UAH truck section to assist the OPs and maintain rear security. The 2nd PLT Platoon Sergeant, SFC Darryl Treadwell had established a platoon casualty collection point and mortar firing point to the rear. 1LT Swintek coordinated fires of the 60mm mortar and effectively began to suppress the ACF fighting positions with coordinated friendly Indirect Fire (IDF) and Small Arms Fire (SAF). He ordered his "wingman, "SSG Robert Mueller" to move his UAH into position to assist a disabled ODA GMV. The momentum of the fight shifted back in favor of the patrol just after 10:00. CAS arrived on station, 1LT Swintek assisted in directing the Close Air Support (CAS) on target, and ACF Battle Damage Assessment (BDA) was clearly observed. By 11:30, 1LT Swintek's UAH, along with his wingman and CPT xxxxx's UAH had moved with the ANA to a position northwest of the orchards and established an Attack by Fire Position (ABF) in order to consolidate and re-organize. ACF direct fire remained intense for over two more hours. By 13:00, ACF fire had slowed to sporadic engagements and the order to execute exfil came at approximately 13:45. ACF casualties due to direct fire were nearly 15 KIAs and an unknown number of WIAs. The ACF casualties due to CAS coordinated as a result of 1LT Swintek's actions were 10-15 KIAs and an unknown number of WIAs. There were no US or ANSF casualties after nearly seven hours of continuous contact.

Simply put, this mission would have failed without 1LT Swintek. His disregard for personal safety and ferocious audacity in the face of overwhelming ACF contact was the spark that inspired every Soldier on the mission to continue to fight. 1LT Swintek's clear visualization of the ACF situation, his sensible understanding of the patrol's situation and capabilities and his tenacious focus on his mission allowed him to make sound, logical decisions and regain the initiative against the ACF. His ability to command and control multiple elements throughout the battle demonstrated the tenacious flexibility of this talented, young Soldier. 1LT Swintek was directly responsible for saving the lives of his fellow platoon members and his actions resulted in destruction of numerous ACF. His steadfast example of courage under fire is in keeping with the finest traditions of military service, the Infantry Branch of which he is a member, and the Armor Unit with which he serves. His valorous actions in combat reflect great credit upon himself, Task Force Zabul, Regional Command (South), CJTF 101, CENTCOM, and the United States Army.

1LT Jared Tomberlin
Team Blackfoot, 1-4 Infantry
April 2009

On 24 April 2009, 1LT Tomberlin was conducting a joint dismounted combat patrol in the northern district of Day Chopan, Zabul Province, Afghanistan. The patrol consisted of the Company Commander, First Sergeant, 1LT Tomberlin and his two Squads from 1st Platoon, and the PL and a Squad from 2nd Platoon, Bravo Company, 1st Battalion, 4th Infantry Regiment. The patrol departed FOB Baylough at 1000 in the morning. The patrol was clearing the route to the village of Chino 1 (vicinity of 42S xxxxx), approximately 6 km west of the FOB, when the patrol came under intense enemy fire.

1LT Tomberlin had stopped his element in a security halt just south of Chino 1 (xxxxx). The Taliban were talking on the ICOMs saying that they were in position and that the attack would commence shortly. What had been a "Leaders' Recon" for future operations had now turned into a meeting engagement. The patrol had set up security on an intra-visibility line while CPT Garner formulated his plan. The QRF from FOB Baylough was launched, as well as, the ODA team. Contact was imminent, so CPT Garner told 1LT Basilides to occupy the high ground at xxxxx in order to establish an over watch of the town of Davudzay (xxxxx) and to be prepared for an attack. As 1LT Basilides started maneuvering across the open area, myself along with SFC Carney and SPC Redwine repositioned ourselves to over watch 1LT Basilides' move to the mountain top. Just as we were reaching a position to set up the M240, we were engaged by small arms fire, as well as 1LT Basilides and the squad he was moving with.

We immediately returned fire and established a base of fire. 1LT Tomberlin repositioned his platoon to support the dismounts in the open and the base of fire element. 1LT Tomberlin continued to maneuver his platoon towards the initial contact in order to relieve the effective fire that was being placed on 1LT Basilides. As fire superiority was gained, the enemy withdrew to new positions. 1LT Basilides was then able to move the three hundred or so meters to the base of the mountain and seek cover in the rocks. At this point, the QRF along with the ODA team were 500 meters behind the patrol. 1LT Tomberlin, not waiting for further guidance, took the initiative and moved forward to regain contact with the withdrawing enemy fighters. This time however, there were enemy on the high ground to the south, vicinity xxxxx, xxxxx, and the base of the

174

mountain (xxxxx) that 1LT Basilides was now attempting to occupy. The enemy fire was so intense that we established a support by fire with 60mm mortars, the eight UAH vehicles with assorted weapon systems, and the dismounts. 1LT Tomberlin then linked up with CPT Garner and was given his instructions on where he was to reposition to.

Under withering fire, 1LT Tomberlin ran to each of his vehicles and his dismounted men to ensure everyone knew the plan of attack. 1LT Tomberlin then picked up and started assaulting through the barrage of enemy fire across the open to establish his own support by fire position to facilitate the other elements ability to move. I then linked up with the ODA and had them tie in with 1st Platoon since the heaviest fighting was being waged to the south and west of them. Once ODA made their way to 1LT Tomberlin, they (ODA and 1st Platoon) continued their assault to the orchards. At this point, the firefight had been ongoing for approximately 40 minutes. The JTAC with the ODA element started dropping ordinance on the enemy positions while the rest of the company continued to engage and assault through.

As the rest of the company started to move, 1LT Tomberlin and his elements again came under another barrage of RPG and Machine gun fire. The fire was so intense and close that vehicles and Soldiers were taking shrapnel and a few shots impacted the body armor itself. 1LT Tomberlin, with complete disregard for his own safety ran to his Soldiers once again and motivated them to continue to fight through the barrage of bullets raining down on them. 1LT Tomberlin's actions were a decisive turning point in the battle, and through his actions, the company was able to occupy key terrain and force the enemy to withdraw. 1LT Tomberlin continued to call for fire and direct his men on where to engage the enemy until the initiative had been regained. Although the fight would rage for another couple hours, 1LT Tomberlin's actions were key to the successful outcome of the company as a whole. 1LT Tomberlin established a support by fire on the dominant terrain and had the ANA occupy the enemy positions on top of xxxxx in order to support the rest of the company sweeping through the town and orchards to clear the enemy out.

Even though the initial contact was a running gun battle 1LT Tomberlin kept his poise and demeanor to rally his inexperienced Soldiers in the midst of ferocious enemy fire, inspiring them through actions instead of words.

1LT Tomberlin's gallantry in action allowed him to fight off a fanatical enemy force and ultimately saved the lives of his fellow Soldiers. His actions on that day resulted in the destruction of 17 enemy killed and many more wounded. 1LT Tomberlin's actions and complete disregard for his own safety are in keeping with what makes the American Soldier the best in the world.

PFC Paul Liberatore
Team Blackfoot, 1-4 Infantry
May 2009

On 28 May 2009 PFC Paul C. Liberatore was on a Company mission in the Day Chopan District of Zabul Province, Afghanistan. PFC Liberatore was manning an observation point (OP) by the town of Vakil Kur, almost two kilometers in front of the assaulting force. Upon daylight, as the Company element and two Operational Detachment Alpha teams advanced towards Vakil Kur, an IED was set off in the vicinity of Ludin which is four kilometers south of the aforementioned town. Subsequently the assaulting force was halted in the vicinity of Tangay. The IED resulted in a disabled vehicle deterring the freedom of movement for the assaulting force, thus leaving PFC Liberatore and his squad significantly behind enemy lines with no friendly ground forces in route.

At first daylight, PFC Liberatore started identifying enemy positions moving towards the Company and ODA's main assaulting force. PFC Liberatore quickly alerted his Team Leader with an accurate description of the enemy combatants and their weapons systems, which included automatic machine guns, recoilless rifles and rocket propelled grenades (RPGs). PFC Liberatore repositioned himself and his M240B Gunner in order to have a better sector of fire towards the enemy. PFC Liberatore's accurate report on enemy positions deterred the enemy from setting up a hasty ambush on friendly forces. PFC Liberatore's M240B gunner killed an advancing combatant because of his accurate identification of the enemy's position. Due to PFC Liberatore's knowledge and skill of the M240B, he was able to conduct a barrel change while moving positions. PFC Liberatore's reporting and identification to his M240B gunner's fire was so effective and overwhelming that the enemy was unable to effectively engage the rest of the Patrol for the duration of the engagement.

Before the PFC Liberatore and his squad could move from their position, the enemy was able to conduct a counter-attack with multiple enemy reinforcements, whose techniques and equipment were extremely sophisticated; to include the use of smoke to conceal movement and the use of body armor and ballistic helmets. At one point, the enemy started engaging PFC Liberatore's position from three different sides; from his East on high ground, from his west just 300 meters away and from his North with recoilless rifle and RPK machine guns. PFC Liberatore once again identified an advancing enemy as they attempted to move towards the OP from the low ground in the riverbed. His actions resulted with the enemy being suppressed and killed.

Through PFC Liberatore's courageous action, he helped his Squad, Company elements and Operational Detachment Alpha Teams avoid any further serious damage or injuries to personnel and equipment while engaging the enemy in Vakil Kur and the Tangay Valley.

PFC Antonio Macias Jr.
Team Blackfoot, 1-4 Infantry
May 2009

On 28 May 2009, PFC Antonio Macias was on a Company mission in the Day Chopan District of Zabul Province, Afghanistan. PFC Macias was manning an observation point (OP) by the town of Vakil Kur, almost two kilometers in front of the assaulting force. Upon daylight as the Company element and two Operational Detachment Alpha teams advanced towards Vakil Kur, an IED was set off in the vicinity of Ludin, which is four kilometers south of the aforementioned town. Subsequently, the assaulting force was halted in the vicinity of Tangay. The IED resulted in a disabled vehicle deterring the freedom of movement for the assaulting force, thus leaving PFC Macias and his squad significantly behind enemy lines with no friendly ground forces in route.

At first daylight, PFC Macias started identifying enemy positions moving towards the Company and ODA's main assaulting force. PFC Macias quickly alerted his Team Leader with an accurate description of the enemy combatants and their weapons systems, which included automatic machine guns, recoilless rifles and rocket propelled grenades (RPGs). PFC Macias' accurate report on enemy positions was detrimental in deterring an enemy hasty ambush on the friendly force a few kilometers away.

During the engagement, PFC Macias identified five combatants who were attempting to flank their 3rd platoon counterparts. His reporting of the enemy location to his Team Leader, allowed the JTAC to drop munitions on that location. This resulted in enemy being destroyed by a 500 lb. JDAM.

Before PFC Macias and his squad could move from their position, the enemy was able to conduct a counter-attack with multiple enemy reinforcements, whose techniques and equipment were extremely sophisticated; to include the use of smoke to conceal movement and the use of body armor and ballistic helmets. At one point, the enemy started engaging PFC Macias from three different sides: from his east on high ground, from his west just 350 meters away and from his north with recoilless rifle and RPK machine guns. PFC Macias laid down heavy suppressive fire towards the enemy. The suppressive fire allowed his

Team Leader, SGT Westfield, and another Soldier, SPC Giovannelli, to reposition to a different covered location.

Through PFC Macias courageous action, he helped his Squad, Company elements and Operational Detachment Alpha Teams avoid any further serious damage or injuries to personnel and equipment while engaging the enemy in Vakil Kur and the Tangay Valley.

PFC Miguel Angel Reyes
Team Blackfoot, 1-4 Infantry
April 2009

During the morning of 24 April 2009, Blackfoot Company conducted a leader reconnaissance of the village of Davudzay, a known ACF safe haven. At approximately 14:00, the patrol came under heavy volumes of enemy fire from ranges of 300 to 400 meters to the north and west. Approximately 25-30 ACF fighters continuously poured effective RPG, PKM, and AK-47 fires into the patrol from the surrounding hillsides. Without hesitation, PFC Reyes began returning accurate fire on multiple enemy personnel as he bound directly into the incoming fires through open terrain. PFC Reyes immediate suppression of ACF forces allowed the also dismounted command element to move into a position where the Platoon Leader could regain communication with rest of the platoon. Without PFC Reyes' aggressive bounding, and suppressive fires, the platoon command element would have been pinned down and out of the fight. On multiple occasions, PFC Reyes' relentless engagement of enemy forces ensured command and control was never compromised.

Throughout the entire fight, which lasted approximately six hours, PFC Reyes was under enemy fire. During the three most intense ACF volleys, PFC Reyes was continually a valued target for ACF fighters. On multiple occasions, fires impacted within inches of PFC Reyes, and on one occasion PFC Reyes took fragmented SAF ricochets into his protective eye wear. Regardless of the personal danger he was in, PFC Reyes continually took the initiative to maneuver under accurate SAF, through open terrain to locations where he could provide suppressive fire allowing the command element to also bound forward.

In summary, PFC Reyes was vital to the combat success of coalition forces on the 24th of April 2009 in the village of Davudzay. He personally maneuvered directly into enemy fire on multiple occasions with no regard to his own safety. His selfless service and ability to put mission success and the welfare of his comrades before his own is heroic and admirable. PFC Reyes tactical aggression, composed demeanor under fire, and valorous actions are in keeping with the finest traditions of military service reflect great credit upon himself, Task Force Zabul, Combined/Joint Task Force 101, and the United States Army.

SGT Christian Cisneros
Team Blackfoot, 1-4 Infantry
May 2009

On 28 May 2009, SGT Christian M. Cisneros was on a Company mission in the Day Chopan District of Zabul Province, Afghanistan. SGT Cisneros was manning an observation point (OP) by the town of Vakil Kur, almost two kilometers in front of the assaulting force. Upon daylight as the Company element and two Operational Detachment Alpha teams advanced towards Vakil Kur, an IED was set off in the vicinity of Ludin which is four kilometers south of the aforementioned town. Subsequently, the assaulting force was halted in the vicinity of Tangay. The IED resulted in a disabled vehicle deterring the freedom of movement for the assaulting force, thus leaving SGT Cisneros and his squad significantly behind enemy lines with no friendly ground forces in route.

At first daylight, SGT Cisneros noticed enemy movement in the towns of Vakil Kur and Nowrah, consisting of eight and six enemy personnel respectively. Inside the town of Vakil Kur, the enemy combatants forced civilians out of their homes. SGT Cisneros quickly alerted his Squad Leader with an accurate description of the enemy combatants and their weapons systems, which included automatic machine guns, recoilless rifles and rocket propelled grenades (RPGs).

As the engagement began SGT Cisneros fires were so accurate, effective, and overwhelming, that the enemy was unable to effectively engage the rest of the patrol for the duration of the engagement. This caused the enemy to focus all of their attention to locating and destroying his position. At one point, the enemy started engaging SGT Cisneros position from three different sides, from his east on the high ground, from his west just 300 meters away and from his north with recoilless rifle and RPK machine guns. Throughout the battle SGT Cisneros continually guided an AH-64 Apache Attack helicopter on enemy positions destroying RPK machine gun positions.

Through SGT Cisneros's courageous action, he helped his squad, Company elements and Operational Detachment Alpha Teams avoid any further serious damage or injuries to personnel and equipment while engaging the enemy in Vakil Kur and the Tangay Valley.

SGT William Daniels
Team Blackfoot, 1-4 Infantry
July 2007

On the morning of 23 July 2007, SGT Daniels was conducting a routine mounted combat patrol in the Arghendab district of Zabul Province, Afghanistan. He was the Alpha Team Leader for 2nd Squad, 3rd Platoon, Bravo Company, 1-4 Infantry during the patrol to the local village of Barghantu to conduct a shura with the village elders. On the return trip back to Fire Base Lane, the five vehicle convoy came under heavy small arms, RPG, 82mm recoilless rifle, and PKM machine gun fire. SGT Daniels' UAH was located in the rear of the convoy when the platoon was ambushed by a group of 50- plus insurgents no more than 100 meters away off to the right side of the vehicles. The convoy stopped as per the platoon standard operating procedures in order to return fire and achieve fire superiority. Shortly thereafter, the call was given over the radio to break contact due to the overwhelming enemy firepower. Three of the UAHs in front of SGT Daniel's vehicle began to move around the lead vehicle. At the same time, SGT Daniels realized that the lead vehicle was smoking from an RPG blast. SGT Daniels made the selfless decision to move his vehicle up next to 1st squad's damaged UAH to render assistance.

SGT Daniels' first concern was to assist the Soldiers in the lead vehicle. The Soldiers in the damaged UAH were under such intense enemy fire that they could barely return fire. Once SGT Daniels' UAH pulled up next to the burning vehicle, he dismounted in the midst of withering enemy fire at the risk of his own life in order to render assistance to his fellow Soldiers next to the burning UAH. SGT Daniels then ordered his gunner to continue suppressing the enemy, while the medic went to render aid to the casualties in the first UAH. SGT Daniels then ordered the rest of his team to assist him in returning fire at the enemy ambush positions. SGT Daniels ran over to the 1st Squad Leader to assess the situation with the casualties. SGT Daniels was informed that one of his fellow Soldiers had died from the RPG blast. The other Soldier was in stable condition and SGT Daniels made the decision to put the casualties in his vehicle. While the casualties were being loaded in his vehicle, SGT Daniels and his automatic rifleman used the 60mm mortar in hand held mode to engage the enemy on the hill approximately 200 meters away.

While his automatic rifleman engaged the enemy with the 60mm mortar system, SGT Daniels located three enemy fighters trying to maneuver on their flank. Although he was completely exposed to the intense enemy fire, SGT Daniels fired an AT-4 at the three enemies, destroying at least two of them and injuring the third. SGT Daniels was able to effectively direct his team's fire in order to assist the Soldiers from 1st squad.

Meanwhile, the group of Soldiers started taking fire from a second group of enemy fighters from the left side of their vehicles in the orchards. SGT Daniels realized that they were being attacked from both sides and that their chances of survival were slim if they continued to fight in place. SGT Daniels recommended to the 1st squad leader that they gather as many sensitive items as possible from the burning UAH in order to break contact. SGT Daniels and his teammates continued to engage the enemy with 40mm M203 grenades, AT-4's, and 60mm mortar rounds in order to allow the Soldiers from 1st squad to gather the sensitive items. Through his direction, the Soldiers were able to repel another overwhelming enemy attack.

Once SGT Daniels was certain that the casualties and sensitive items were secure in his UAH, he ordered his driver to move slowly towards the platoon leader's vehicle position. SGT Daniels and the dismounted Soldiers continued to engage the enemy while moving under cover next to his UAH. SGT Daniels and the Soldiers from his team finally made link up with the platoon leader's vehicle and the decision was made to break contact to the designated area for air MEDEVAC. SGT Daniels was among the dismounted Soldiers who moved along the left side of the UAHs. As the vehicles made the turn towards the MEDEVAC site, the element immediately took an enormous amount of accurate enemy fire as soon as the vehicles came into view of the insurgent's field of fire. SGT Daniels continued to return fire, even though bullets were ricocheting off the UAHs next to him. SGT Daniels continued to support the platoon leader by controlling the fire direction of the gunners while moving to the MEDEVAC site. Although SGT Daniels suffered wounds from multiple ricochets, he continued to fight and lead his men with little concern to his own safety.

SGT Daniels' actions on that fateful day demonstrated absolute courage under intense enemy fire. Through his leadership and tactical expertise, SGT Daniels was able to turn a dire situation into one of hope. He remained calm under fire, flawlessly controlled a turbulent situation, and motivated his Soldiers to continue fighting even though the odds were against them. His valiant actions directly resulted in the destruction of more than 25 insurgent fighters and the evacuation of his fellow Soldiers. SGT Daniels' actions exhibit the epitome of valor in the most extreme of combat situations.

SGT Devon Kilson
Team Blackfoot, 1-4 Infantry
May 2009

On the morning of 25 May 2009, SGT Kilson was part of a joint combat patrol in the northern district of Day Chopan, Zabul Province, Afghanistan. The patrol consisted of elements from three different platoons of Blackfoot Company, two Operational Detachment Alphas (ODAs), and Afghan National Security Forces (ANSF). The patrol was forced to stop when the lead vehicle struck an Improvised Explosive Device at xxxxx. As the IED provided an early warning system for the Anti Coalition Fighters (ACF), the patrol hastily maneuvered into the Objective Rally Point (ORP). From this location, SGT Kilson's Squad dismounted for further movement into the village of Davudzay (42S xxxxx), a known ACF safe haven. At approximately 05:30, the patrol came under heavy enemy fire from 10 to 15 enemy fighters located 200 to 300 meters away, who unremittingly poured AK-47 and PKM fire into the patrol from an elevated rock outcropping and the orchards below.

As the lead elements of the patrol continued to push forward, they were pinned and under intense and concentrated enemy fire. Though momentarily pinned down behind a group of boulders by accurate enemy fire, in the midst of rounds impacting within inches of his location, SGT Kilson rallied his squad to bound forward into the incoming fire to establish a support by fire position, thus providing relief to the dismounted element that was now pinned down in the orchard by enemy fire that forcefully hacked the branches from the trees around the lead element. In an attempt to reestablish communication with the Platoon Leader (PL), who was trapped between the two elements, SGT Kilson, with complete disregard for his own safety, assaulted forward nearly 100 meters through open terrain into incoming enemy fire. SGT Kilson then linked up with the PL and was given his instructions while the intense firefight raged on around him, he moved back over the 100 meters of open terrain to relay the PL's guidance to his squad, and began bounding them into a position where they could better suppress the enemy, providing fires that saved the lives of those pinned down in the orchard.

As the fight continued, forward elements from 1st Platoon cleared a nearby compound to provide a defendable refuge for the remainder of the dismounted elements. SGT Kilson maneuvered his squad and an attached machine gun crew to this position, and quickly established security.

186

As 1st Platoon continued to push forward on an 1800 meter movement through enemy orchards and austere mountain terrain, and linkup with the Operational Detachment Alpha in vicinity of hilltop xxxxx (42S xxxxx) was made, again SGT Kilson established an over watch of Davudzay as members of ODA and ANSF began to clear through the village of Davudzay.

Soon after, a second IED exploded near the vehicle support by fire line at xxxxx. Within a short period of time after the second IED ignited, an IED material cache was found in the village of Davudzay. As fires were called in to destroy the compound, SGT Kilson, from his vantage point in the high ground in the over watch position, was able to relay the adjustments that needed to be made to bring the 120mm mortar fire on target.

After the IED cache was destroyed, the dismounted element moved back to the vehicle support by fire positions. However, once the patrol began to withdraw from the village, and the hilltop security positions that had been established had pulled off the mountaintops, 25-30 enemy fighters occupied these same mountaintop positions, and proceeded to deliver a powerful salvo of AK-47, PKM, and RPG fire that hammered down on the entire patrol from the hilltops in every direction. The enemy was so well concealed, and the fire was so intense, that 15 up-armored vehicles, numerous dismounted personnel with small arms, and Close Air Support (CAS), could not deter the enemy onslaught.

Due to only having front wheel drive capabilities, SGT Kilson's vehicle was being towed during the initial barrage of the ambush. However, the vehicle was unhooked, and SGT Kilson rallied both his squads vehicles to accompany the PL's vehicle in two separate assaults forward into concentrated enemy sniper, RPG, and PKM fire, before being called back due to being "danger close" in regards to coordination being made with the CAS on station, but not before effective fire was placed on the enemy which eventually allowed the patrol to break out of the kill zone.

In summary, SGT Kilson was essential to the combat success of coalition forces on the 25th of May 2009 in the village of Davudzay. He assaulted into withering enemy fire, calmly directed his Squad through intense salvos of SAF, and encouraged those around him to fight on through deadly enemy fire on multiple occasions with no regard for his own safety. His composed heroism and tactical poise were essential to the overall success of the mission. SGT Kilson's persistent courage under fire and heroic "lead from the front" mentality, are in keeping with the finest traditions of military service and reflect great credit upon himself,

Blackfoot Company, Task Force Zabul, Regional Command South, CJTT-101, and the United States Army.

SGT Salvador Lopez
Team Blackfoot, 1-4 Infantry
July 2007

On the morning of 23 July 2007, SGT Lopez was conducting a routine mounted combat patrol in the Arghendab district of Zabul Province, Afghanistan. He was the squad leader for 1st Squad, 3rd Platoon, Bravo Company, 1-4 Infantry during a patrol to the local village of Barghantu to conduct a shura with the village elders. On the return trip back to Fire Base Lane, the five-vehicle convoy came under heavy small arms, RPG, 82mm recoilless rifle and PKM machine gun fire. SGT Lopez was located in the passenger seat of the lead UAH when the convoy was ambushed by a group of 50-plus insurgents no more than 100 meters away. He stopped the convoy as per the platoon standard operating procedures in order to return fire and achieve fire superiority. Unknown to SGT Lopez, there were three enemy RPG gunners located 75 meters to the right side of his vehicle. They engaged SGT Lopez's UAH at close range, firing three RPGs at the front of the vehicle.

The first two RPGs detonated on the front windshield of his vehicle, however, the third RPG struck the UAH directly between the cross member of the windshield, impacting and detonating on the driver. The blast instantly killed his driver and wounded three other Soldiers inside of SGT Lopez's vehicle. Without hesitation and total disregard for his own safety, SGT Lopez immediately exited the burning UAH under a barrage of enemy fire in order to come around to the driver's side and pull out the two casualties located on that side of the vehicle. Although his bravo team leader and gunner were slightly injured from the blast, SGT Lopez directed them to engage the enemy while he assessed the injuries of his two other Soldiers. SGT Lopez knew immediately after assessing his driver's wounds that he was already dead.

During the initial stages of the ambush, his platoon leader's and alpha team leader's UAHs moved around SGT Lopez's position in order to flank the enemy ambush and engage the enemy fighters. At the same time, SGT Lopez was directing his gunner and bravo team leader's fire while treating his automatic rifleman's shrapnel wounds. SGT Lopez was also trying to put out the fire on his UAH while he stabilized his Soldier's wounds. The enemy continued to engage and move closer to SGT Lopez's vehicle when the alpha team leader of 2nd squad pulled his UAH up next to them to render assistance. Although he was facing overwhelming odds, SGT Lopez immediately took control of the situation by managing the aid of the casualties and directing the fire of his fellow Soldiers. He expertly controlled the rates of fire of the two gunners while engaging the enemy himself. At this time, the Soldiers involved in the recovery of the burning UAH became engaged by a second group of insurgents to the south of their position from the orchards. SGT Lopez directed some of his Soldiers to engage the new group of enemy insurgents with as much firepower as possible while he and two others continued to engage the first group of insurgents. SGT Lopez ordered two of his fellow Soldiers to engage the enemy with the 60mm mortar system in hand-held mode. While the 60mm mortar was being set up, SGT Lopez saw three enemies maneuvering down the hill to engage his position. He ran towards the nearest burm under withering enemy fire and engaged the insurgents with his rifle, destroying at least one of the enemies and injuring the other two.

Once SGT Lopez felt that the enemy fire was at a lull, he made the decision to leave the burning UAH in order to link up with his platoon leader's and alpha team leader's vehicles. SGT Lopez ordered two of his Soldiers to gather as many sensitive items as possible before they departed the burning UAH. Meanwhile, some of the other Soldiers loaded the casualties into the 2nd squad UAH while SGT Lopez continued to engage the enemy at close range. SGT Lopez ordered the functional 2nd squad UAH to move slowly so that the dismounted Soldiers could walk alongside the UAH for cover from enemy fire. Enemy fire picked up again from the original ambush site while the 2nd group of insurgents continued to maneuver on their position. SGT Lopez remained calm and directed fire in the appropriate directions in order to suppress and destroy numerous insurgents from both groups.

SGT Lopez's group of Soldiers finally made link up with the platoon leader's position after being overwhelmed by enemy forces on multiple occasions. Shortly thereafter, the decision was made to break contact towards the designated HLZ site for MEDEVAC. SGT Lopez was among the dismounted Soldiers who moved along the left side of the UAHs. As the vehicles made the turn towards the MEDEVAC site, the element immediately took an enormous amount of effective and accurate enemy fire as soon as the vehicles came into view of the insurgent's field of fire. SGT Lopez continued to return fire, even though bullets were ricocheting off the UAHs next to him. SGT Lopez continued to assist the platoon leader in controlling the group of Soldiers and vehicles as they made their way to the MEDEVAC site on higher ground out of the river bed. He remained dismounted outside of his vehicle for the duration of the fight, never once leaving any of his fellow Soldiers behind.

SGT Lopez's actions on that fateful day demonstrated absolute courage under intense enemy fire. Through his leadership and tactical expertise, SGT Lopez was able to turn a dire situation into one of hope. He remained calm under fire, flawlessly controlled a turbulent situation, and motivated his Soldiers to continue fighting even though the odds were against them. His valiant actions directly resulted in the destruction of more than 25 insurgent fighters and the evacuation of his fellow Soldiers. SGT Lopez's actions exhibit the epitome of valor in the most extreme of combat situations.

SPC Arturo Sosa
Team Blackfoot, 1-4 Infantry
May 2009

On the morning of the 25th of May 2009, SPC Sosa was part of joint combat patrol in the northern district of Day Chopan, Zabul Province, Afghanistan. The patrol consisted of elements from three different platoons of Blackfoot Company, two Operational Detachment Alphas (ODAs), and Afghan National Security Forces (ANSF). At approximately 05:00 an Improvised Explosive Device at xxxxx disabled the lead vehicle of the convoy. SPC Sosa's vehicle had stopped in a security halt west of the village of Chino 1 (xxxxx) in order to allow the dismounted element to begin their movement, when an intense barrage of enemy fire began to pour into the patrol. Without hesitation, SPC Sosa took the initiative to maneuver his vehicle into a location to best provide covering fire for the dismounted element that was pinned down. SPC Sosa's fires suppressed the enemy enough to allow the dismounted element to move out of the withering fire. As the fighting continued, SPC Sosa maintained his support by fire location 300 meters east of the village of Davudzay (xxxxx) supporting not only the Blackfoot Company dismounts in contact, but the ODA and ANSF forces as well.

Within a few hours a second IED had exploded at xxxxx, and a IED cache was destroyed in the village of Davudzay. As the patrol began to withdraw from the village, and the hilltop security positions that had been established pulled off the mountain tops, 25 to 30 enemy fighters occupied the same mountain top positions and proceeded to deliver a powerful salvo of AK-47, PKM, and RPG fire that hammered down on the entire patrol from the hilltops in every direction. The enemy was so well-concealed, and the fire was so intense, that 15 up-armored vehicles, numerous dismounted personnel with small arms, and Close Air Support (CAS), could not deter the enemy onslaught.

As fires intensified, with complete disregard for his own safety, SPC Sosa along with SPC Widel set in the platoon's 60mm mortar, and began to emplace high explosive mortars into suspected enemy positions. The indirect fires that SPC Sosa was placing on the enemy were so effective that they began to concentrate even more fires onto the mortar firing position. Several rounds began to impact the base plate of the mortar system within inches of SPC Sosa. For the next twenty minutes, withering fire from all directions continued to pour into the exhausted perimeter of the patrol. Though SPC Sosa had already fired fourteen high explosive 60mm mortar rounds into enemy positions, as well was firing with his M-4, he continued to seek out ways to engage the enemy. While the vehicles were receiving devastating fire that persistently impacted the outer armor of the vehicles, shattered windows, and flattened tires, SPC Sosa retrieved the M240B weapon system off his vehicles turret. With the machine gun, SPC Sosa engaged the enemy, directing his .50 caliber turrent gunner to mimic where he was placing fires. SPC Sosa then retrieved an AT-4 out of his vehicle, exposing himself to enemy fire in the process. With complete disregard for his own safety, SPC Sosa engaged a well-covered and concealed sniper position on hilltop xxxxx (xxxxx). Though revealing his location to the precise sniper fire he was able to destroy the threat with the shoulder-fired rocket.

While others took cover from the demoralizing fire, SPC Sosa exhausted every effort to engage and destroy the enemy, and did so in such an unnaturally calm manner that it was inspirational to those who fought around him. In summary, SPC Sosa's steadfast courage, and tactical poise was vital to the combat success of coalition forces on the 25th of May 2009 in the village of Davudzay. He maneuvered into enemy fire to support his fellow Soldiers, and inspired those around him to fight on through a seemingly endless barrage of destructive enemy fire with no regard for his own safety. His aggressive boldness, tactical competence, and situational awareness were essential to the overall success of the mission. SPC Sosa's valorous audacity under fire and heroic courage, are in keeping with the finest traditions of military service and reflect great credit upon himself, Blackfoot Company, Task Force Zabul, Regional Command South, CJTT-101, and the United States Army.

SSG Robert Mueller
Team Dragon, 1-4 Infantry
June 2008

On the 14th and 15th of June, 2nd Platoon was on a combat patrol to the southern end of the Chalikor Valley with Embedded Training Team (ETT), Operational Detachment Alpha (ODA), Afghan National Army (ANA), and Afghan National Police (ANP). The patrol came under harassing fire from Anti-Coalition Forces (ACF) on the morning of the 15th at approximately 06:00. SSG Mueller's two vehicles were immediately repositioned to the southeastern flank in order to provide security and engage the ACF. His squad's quick actions forced ACF to break contact and retreat north. At 0900, the patrol was engaged by ACF again, but this time by a much larger force. Approximately 40 to 50 ACF attacked the patrol from the north, east, and south in a complex attack with AK-47, PKM, SPG-9, RPG, and Dragonov fire.

Immediately, SSG Mueller was ordered to maneuver one of his vehicles directly into the fight, under heavy ACF fire, and suppress the ACF on the ridgeline to the East. Without hesitation, SSG Mueller repositioned his own vehicle northeast along a ridgeline and began suppressing the ACF with his MK-19. Within close proximity of his position, one of the ODA vehicles took an RPG round within 10 feet of the vehicle. It caused extensive damage to the vehicle and rendered the vehicle's crew-served weapon non-mission capable. SSG Mueller moved one of his vehicles to the ODA vehicle and picked up their sector of fire while providing a mechanic and a rifleman to help the crew fix their vehicle. He continued to return fire with all of his squad's weapons and effectively suppressed the ACF on the eastern flank.

To the rear, the platoon had established a mortar firing point. The vehicle at the mortar firing point came under heavy fire from a recoilless rifle and AK-47s. SSG Mueller immediately repositioned one of his vehicles back to their location. The vehicle returned fire with their .50 Caliber machine gun and M203 and suppressed the ACF forcing them to break contact from that location. Immediately after, ACF attempted to overrun the ANSF Observation Posts (OPs) approximately five kilometers to the rear. SSG Mueller sent his vehicle that had suppressed the ACF at the mortar firing point to the ANSF OP. As they came over the ridgeline upon the OP they engaged the ACF as they broke contact to the south. The vehicle remained with the ANSF in order to provide security to the south.

Intelligence reports that there were over 100 ACF to the south attempting to ambush the route home. The presence of one of SSG Mueller's vehicles was enough to deter the ACF from conducting a second ambush, thus saving multiple lives.

During the heaviest parts of the fighting, the platoon received extremely heavy ACF fire from the north. A number of weapons and vehicles had become non-mission capable during the battle and the ACF had fire superiority. SSG Mueller was ordered to maneuver his truck north directly under ACF fire on the ridgeline in order to better engage the ACF. SSG Mueller returned fire with his MK-19 and had his riflemen return fire with their personal weapons. As SSG Mueller's truck was taking heavy ACF fire, his MK-19 went down. He ordered his gunner to return fire with his secondary weapon, an M240B. SSG Mueller then climbed on the hood of his HMMWV and used his expertise as a former armorer to fix the MK-19 under direct fire. As he was fixing the weapon, ACF rounds were flying within inches of his face. SSG Mueller was able to fix the weapon and bring the combat power back into the fight. The MK-19 ended up going down two more times and both times; SSG Mueller climbed on his vehicle while under fire and fixed the weapon. Each time, SSG Mueller greatly risked his own personnel safety in order to fix his MK-19 and continue to engage the ACF.

In summary, Staff Sergeant Mueller was essential to the mission success of Coalition Forces in the Chalikor Valley on the 15th of June. He displayed courage, selfless service, and dedication to duty on numerous occasions throughout a seven hour long fire fight. He greatly risked his own safety to ensure that his squad was able to engage the ACF. SSG Mueller was directly responsible for saving the lives of his fellow platoon members and his actions resulted in destruction of numerous ACF. He is a steadfast example of courage under fire and his actions in combat are in keeping with the finest traditions of military service and reflect great credit upon himself, Task Force Zabul, Regional Command South, CJTF 101, and the United States Army.

SPC Daniel Cappo
Team Blackfoot, 1-4 Infantry
May 2009

During the morning of 05 May 2009, 1st Platoon, Blackfoot Company, was conducting a combat patrol through the Northern Arghendab District, enroute to the village of Morghabi. The austere terrain proved to be difficult for the up-armored HMMWVs to handle. Halfway through the mission SPC Cappo had already worked to replace a broken half shaft and assisted in towing two vehicles out of a ditch. In the process of recovery two vehicles that were wedged into a gully sustained damage, making them immobile.

After recovering the vehicles, they were in need of immediate repair. The patrol was unfortunately wedged inside a valley, and the terrain was extremely unsuitable for maintenance. As security was being pushed to the high ground in the immediate vicinity and assessments were being made on the vehicles, the patrol came under an intense barrage of small arms and RPG fire. Understanding the immense necessity of repairing the vehicles, SPC Cappo began to work on the downed trucks. With complete disregard to his own safety, SPC Cappo crawled through enemy fire, and underneath the vehicles on the side that the contact was coming from, to work on the broken components of the vehicles. RPGs began to impact within meters of the vehicles and AK-47 rounds were slamming into the turrets, as well as close proximity of the dismounted soldiers that were providing covering fire for the patrol. SPC Cappo relentlessly worked through the onslaught of enemy fire until the patrol was able to gain fire superiority, forcing the enemy fighters to break contact. During the brief lull in fighting, as SPC Cappo continued to work underneath one of the vehicles, the jack stand that he was using to hold the vehicle up broke and had it not been for the tire that SPC Cappo placed between him and the vehicle, he would have been crushed. After being drug from underneath the vehicle, SPC Cappo had to remove his body armor to get back underneath the vehicle to work on the still broken half shaft, rear differential, and number four and five cross members.

As SPC Cappo went back to work underneath the vehicles, the enemy fighters moved to the northern flank of the patrol and once again began pouring effective small arms fire into the platoon's defensive perimeter. Even as enemy fires were concentrated on the already damaged vehicles, SPC Cappo, who was still exposed to the enemy barrage without body armor, continued to work until the vehicles were once again mobile.

Throughout the entire fight SPC Cappo was under accurate small arms fire, but never gave a second though to leaving the vehicles until they were once again maneuverable.

In summary, SPC Cappo was vital to the combat success of coalition forces on the 5th of May 2009 in the Arghendab Valley. Without his courageous act of selfless service, the entire patrol would have remained fixed by enemy fire. SPC Cappo's ability to remain calm and perform his duties under intense enemy fire was unmistakably essential to 1st Platoon's ability to take the fight to the enemy. SPC Cappo's mechanical competence and heroic actions are in keeping with the finest traditions of military service and reflect great credit upon himself, Blackfoot Company, Task Force Zabul, Regional Command South, CJTT-101, and the United States Army.

SSG Salvador Lopez
Team Blackfoot, 1-4 Infantry
April 2009

During the morning of 24 April 2009 Blackfoot Company conducted a leader's reconnaissance of the village Davudzay, a known safe haven for Anti-Coalition Forces. As 1st Platoon began to establish a support by fire position just south of Chino 1, SSG Lopez emplaced two mortar firing points in order to over-watch a dismounted element from 2nd Platoon, which was moving through a field to a mountain top. Before the mortar positions were completely set in, the patrol came under intense PKM and AK-47 fire.

Without hesitation, SSG Lopez rallied his squad, and assaulted forward, as rounds impacted all around him. After establishing a local support by fire, SSG Lopez moved from position to position directing the fires of his squad. Simultaneously, SSG Lopez sent a vehicle to retrieve one of the mortar firing positions, and maneuvered them into a position where they could provide much needed suppressive fire to cover a dismounted element that was pinned down under an intense barrage of small-arms fire. The decisive maneuver of the mortar system and the vehicle's weapons platform was crucial to the Company's ability to gain fire superiority. The suppressive fires that SSG Lopez rallied caused the ACF to break contact, and ultimately saved the lives of 2nd platoon's pinned down element, as they were then able to move to the cover of the rocky hillside.

Seeking the initiative, SSG Lopez continued to bound his squad forward to regain contact with the enemy. The QRF that had been called for began to arrive on the scene, which brought two more trucks to the fight that SSG Lopez would maneuver. As SSG Lopez moved through sporadic gunfire on foot to link up with the platoon leader, RPGs were added to the enemy volley, and PKM bursts fell within feet of SSG Lopez on several occasions, as he zigzagged through the battlefield. Upon receiving guidance from the platoon leader, he then picked up and started assaulting through yet another barrage of enemy fire across the open to establish his own support by fire position, in order to facilitate the other elements' ability to also move. The enemy fire was so intense that a support by fire with 60mm mortars and the eight UAH vehicles with assorted weapon systems was established with the dismounts.

As the fighting intensified again, SSG Lopez, in conjunction with the ODA team that was part of the QRF, began to maneuver forward into the heaviest fighting of the battle on the south side of the valley. The fire was so concentrated and close, that vehicles and Soldiers were taking shrapnel and a few shots to the body armor itself. SSG Lopez, with complete disregard for his own well-being, dashed to each of his Soldiers in order to encourage them to fight through the barrage of bullets raining down on them. Throughout the entire fight, which would last nearly six hours, SSG Lopez was under direct enemy fire, and calmly maneuvered not only his element, but directed Afghan National Army elements, as well as personnel from a different squad.

In summary, SSG Lopez was absolutely vital to the combat success of coalition forces on the 24th of April 2009 in the village of Davudzay. He personally suppressed enemy forces, directed fires, and maneuvered directly into enemy fire on multiple occasions with no regard to his own safety. His tactical poise, aggressive decision making, and insightful guidance was critical to the overall success of the mission. SSG Lopez unwavering courage under intense enemy fire, precise tactical decision making, and courageous leadership in the face of danger are in keeping with the finest traditions of military service and reflect great credit upon himself, Blackfoot Company, Task Force Zabul, Regional Command South, CJTT 101, and the United States Army.

SGT Edward E. Westfield
Team Blackfoot, 1-4 Infantry
May 2009

On 28 May 2009, SGT Edward E. Westfield led his fire team on a Company mission in the Day Chopan District of Zabul Province, Afghanistan. SGT Westfield was manning an observation point (OP) by the town of Vakil Kur, almost two kilometers in front of the assaulting force. Upon daylight, as the Company element and two Operational Detachment Alpha teams advanced towards Vakil Kur, an IED was set off in the vicinity of the town of Ludin, four kilometers south of the aforementioned town. Subsequently, the assaulting force was halted in the vicinity of Tangay. The IED resulted in a disabled vehicle deterring the freedom of movement for the assaulting force, thus leaving SGT Westfield, his team and squad significantly behind enemy lines with no friendly ground forces in route.

At first daylight, SGT Westfield started identifying enemy positions and sixteen enemy combatants moving towards the main assaulting force while they were conducting vehicle recovery because of the aforementioned IED. SGT Westfield quickly alerted his platoon leader and company commander with an accurate description of the enemy combatants and their weapons systems, which included automatic machine guns, recoilless rifles and rocket propelled grenades. Upon observing the movement of the combatants, SGT Westfield quickly repositioned himself and M240B team into an effective position without giving away his position on the mountain top OP 8500 feet above sea level. SGT Westfield's accurate report on enemy positions was critical to deterring an enemy hasty ambush on the friendly force a few kilometers away. His fire was effective and placed deadly force upon the unsuspecting enemy combatants, whose focus was on attacking the main assault.

The enemy's focus shifted from the main assaulting force to finding and destroying the OP and SGT Westfield, who was employing deadly accuracy with his M-24 sniper rifle. At one point, the enemy started engaging SGT Westfield's position from three different sides: from his east on the high ground, from his west just 300 meters away and from his north with recoilless rifle and RPK machine guns. SGT Westfield quickly repositioned himself once again and started engaging the enemy with his M-24 sniper rifle killing both enemy personnel on the high ground.

Through SGT Westfield's courageous action, he helped his squad, Company elements and Operational Detachment Alpha Teams avoid any further serious damage or injuries to personnel and equipment while engaging the enemy in Vakil Kur and the Tangay Valley.

SPC Curtis Matthew Widel
Team Blackfoot, 1-4 Infantry
April 2009

During the morning of 24 April 2009, Blackfoot Company conducted a leader's reconnaissance of the village of Davudzay, a known ACF safe haven. At approximately 1400 [hours] the patrol came under heavy volumes of enemy fire from ranges of 300 to 400 meters to the north and west where 25-30 ACF fighters who continuously poured effective RPG, PKM, and AK-47 fires into the patrol from the surrounding hillsides. SPC Widel had already established a mortar firing point with the 60mm mortar as the position came under accurate SAF. With complete disregard for his own safety, SPC Widel remained in the open, placing effective direct mortar fire onto multiple enemy personnel and directing his team where to engage. SPC Widel provided extremely necessary suppressive fires with not only mortar fire, but also engaged enemy personnel with an AT-4 and his M-4. The covering fire that SPC Widel personally provided, and continually directed, saved the lives of the dismounted 2nd Platoon element that was pinned down in the open under intense enemy fire.

Throughout the entire fight, which lasted approximately six hours, SPC Widel was continually under fire. In attempt to reach a better mortar firing position, SPC Widel maneuvered the 60mm by foot under enemy SAF until a vehicle was able to retrieve him and his team, and transport them. Once in place, SPC Widel again set up the 60mm mortar system and began to place indirect mortar fire in support of the lead assault element, devastatingly suppressing the enemy in the orchards and surrounding hillsides.

As the fight continued, SPC Widel was split off from the platoon, and joined with the Company command element to maneuver into the north of the village of Davudzay in an attempt to recon potential routes to link the rest of the company together. SPC Widel and his team provided essential security, over-watch, and suppressive fires for the Company command element.

In summary, SPC Widel was vital to the combat success of coalition forces on the 24th of April 2009 in the village of Davudzay. He personally suppressed enemy forces, directed fires, and maneuvered directly into enemy fire on multiple occasions with no regard for his own safety. His aggressive heroism and tactical competence were essential to the overall success of the mission. SPC Widel's steadfast courage under fire and heroic "lead from the front" mentality are in keeping with the finest traditions of military service and reflect great credit upon himself, Blackfoot Company, Task Force Zabul, Regional Command South, CJTT-101, and the United States Army.

SPC Nicholas Giovannelli
Team Blackfoot, 1-4 Infantry
May 2009

On 28 May 2009, SPC Nicholas C. Giovannelli was on a Company mission in the Day Chopan District of Zabul Province, Afghanistan. SPC Giovannelli was manning an observation point (OP) by the town of Vakil Kur, almost two kilometers in front of the assaulting force. Upon daylight as the Company element and two Operational Detachment Alpha teams advanced towards Vakil Kur, an IED was set off in the vicinity of Ludin which is four kilometers south of the aforementioned town. Subsequently the assaulting force was halted in the vicinity of Tangay. The IED resulted in a disabled vehicle deterring the freedom of movement for the assaulting force, thus leaving SPC Giovannelli and his squad significantly behind enemy lines with no friendly ground forces in route.

At first daylight, SPC Giovannelli began engaging several enemy combatants with his M249 (SAW) near the town of Vakil Kur and its outskirts. SPC Giovannelli killed an enemy combatant in the central orchards of Vakil Kur as he attempted to engage the OP, which was located on a mountain top 8500 feet in elevation.

During the lull in fire, after the 120mm mortars were fired on the enemy positions near the town of Vakil Kur, SPC Giovannelli identified three enemy personnel a kilometer outside of Vakil Kur moving towards the river bed. While engaging them, SPC Giovannelli quickly alerted his team leader of the enemy's location and direction of travel. Subsequently, a fire mission was called in on the enemy allowing two AH-64 Apache Attack helicopters to destroy all of the enemy fighters.

Before SPC Giovannelli and his squad could move from their position, the enemy was able to conduct a counterattack with multiple enemy reinforcements, whose techniques and equipment were extremely sophisticated, to include the use of smoke to conceal movement and the use of body armor and ballistic helmets. Upon the enemy's attack, SPC Giovannelli laid down heavy suppressive fire towards the enemy who was firing at him from three different sides: from his east on the high ground, from his west just 300 meters away and from his north with recoilless rifle and RPK machine guns. Due to his accurate firing, the enemy specifically targeted SPC Giovannelli. He had to switch positions as the rocks he was behind and in front of him were being pummeled with enemy fire.

Through SPC Giovannelli courageous action, he helped his squad, Company elements and Operational Detachment Alpha Teams avoid any further serious damage or injuries to personnel and equipment while engaging the enemy in Vakil Kur and the Tangay Valley.

SSG Azhar M. Sher
Team Blackfoot, 1-4 Infantry
May 2009

On 28 May 2009, Staff Sergeant Sher led his squad on a dismounted combat patrol in the northern district of Day Chopan, Zabul Province, Afghanistan. The patrol consisted of two Operational Detachment Alpha (ODA) Teams, numerous Afghan National Army (ANA) Soldiers and elements from all three platoons of Bravo Company, 1st Battalion, 4th Infantry Regiment. As the lead element, SSG Sher and his Squad departed FOB Baylough at 2100 [hours] on the night of 27 May 2009. SSG Sher's task was to establish an observation post (OP) on the hilltop adjacent to Vakil Kur. Vakil Kur is a known Taliban safe haven that coalition forces seldom go to. SSG Sher was able to lead his squad, through the cover of darkness, five kilometers undetected up the rugged hilltop and establish the OP before daybreak. As soon as he was in position, SSG Sher immediately began to relay information on the current activity in the town to his Platoon Leader and Company Commander.

Upon daylight, the Company element, ODA teams and ANA advanced towards Vakil Kur. During their movement, an IED was set off in the vicinity of Ludin, which is four kilometers south of the Vakil Kur town. Subsequently, the main effort was halted in the vicinity of Tangay. The IED resulted in a disabled vehicle and greatly slowed the main effort's advancement. This left SSG Sher and his squad alone in an enemy safe haven with the main effort still kilometers away from reinforcing them.

After the IED was struck, SSG Sher observed enemy movement in the towns of Vakil Kur and Nowrah consisting of eight and six enemy personnel respectively. Inside the town of Vakil Kur, the enemy combatants forced civilians out of their homes and made them flee the village. SSG Sher quickly alerted his Platoon Leader with an accurate description of the enemy composition and their weapons systems, which included automatic machine guns, recoilless rifles and rocket propelled grenades (RPGs). The enemy combatants established a defensive position in the orchards south of Vakil Kur and sent an element further south towards the main effort. When the enemy passed SSG Sher's position and got close to the main effort, his squad started to engage them. SSG Sher's squad's fires were so accurate, effective and overwhelming, that the enemy was unable to effectively engage the rest of the patrol for the duration of the engagement. This caused the enemy to focus all of their attention to locating and destroying his position. At one point the enemy started engaging his squad from three different sides, from his east on the high ground, from his west just 300 meters away and from his north with recoilless rifle and PKM machine guns. SSG Sher got on his radio and guided an AH-64 Apache attack helicopter and A-10 Thunderbolts on the enemy positions and destroyed them. Even with the devastating attacks, the enemy was able to organize a counter-attack. They tried yet again to overrun the squad's position by attacking from the hilltops to the east and from the orchards near the village. SSG Sher once again guided the AH-64 Apaches and A-10 Thunderbolt's on the enemy, which successfully repelled them.

Simply put, this mission would have failed without SSG Sher. His disregard for personal safety and ferocious audacity in the face of overwhelming enemy contact was the spark that inspired his squad to continue to fight. His clear visualization of the enemy situation, his sensible understanding of the patrol's situation and capabilities, and his tenacious focus on his mission allowed him to make sound, logical decisions and regain the initiative against the enemy. SSG Sher's steadfast example of courage under fire allowed him to fight off a fanatical enemy force, maneuver under fire to gain and hold the key terrain to over watch the rest of the patrol, and ultimately, save the lives of his fellow soldiers. His actions that day resulted in the destruction of 35 enemy killed and many more wounded.

PFC Curtis Matthew Widel
Team Blackfoot, 1-4 Infantry
May 2007

On 23 May 2007, PFC Widel accompanied a mounted quick reaction force (QRF) as a MK19 gunner for one of the M1151 UAHs. Elements of Bravo Company, 1st Battalion, 4th Infantry Regiment were under attack from an overwhelming enemy force. PFC Widel and the QRF were dispatched from FOB Baylough in order to provide assistance. Once QRF arrived, PFC Widel destroyed several enemy positions, which secured the area to allow the element to push forward. During the course of the movement, enemy forces counter-attacked the Bravo Company elements in the valley with RPG fire. PFC Widel once again returned accurate fire destroying the enemy RPG strong hold. When the UAHs advanced to their blocking position, they once again came under heavy enemy fire. Despite concentrated enemy fire in his direction, PFC Widel would not take cover in his turret. He continued to fire with absolute disregard for his own life in order to suppress the enemy.

During the intense fire of RPGs, an 82mm recoilless rifle, and small arms fire PFC Widel's weapon began to malfunction causing him to resort to his secondary weapon. He continued to troubleshoot his primary weapon while returning effective fire with his M249. Once his primary weapon was again mission ready he began to effectively place rounds in front of the dismounted element allowing them to move into position and secure the high ground and push the entire enemy element out of the engagement area.

Through PFC Widel's gallant actions, Bravo Company elements were able to fight off the enemy attack. PFC Widel's selfless act was critical in saving the lives of his fellow Soldiers pinned down by enemy fire around the UAHs. He provided the necessary firepower to turn the tide of the battle in the favor of Bravo Company. PFC Widel's actions exemplify valor under the most extreme of combat conditions.

SGT Dustin Thom
Team Blackfoot, 1-4 Infantry
May 2007

On 25 May 2007, SGT Thom was conducting a joint dismounted combat patrol in the northern district of Day Chopan, Zabul Province, Afghanistan. First Squad from 2nd Platoon and Third Squad from 3rd Platoon, Bravo Company, 1st Battalion, 4th Infantry Regiment departed FOB Baylough early in the morning. The patrol was heading towards the village of Vakil Kur, approximately 6 km north of the FOB, when the patrol came under intense enemy fire. The squad from 2nd Platoon immediately suffered three friendly casualties and was pinned down by small arms and RPG fire from an ambush on the ridge to their northeast approximately 300 meters away. Within minutes, Third Squad, 3rd Platoon began to flank the enemy position by maneuvering up the southern portion of the ridge. Third Squad and SGT Thom's team ran up the steep slope undetected for approximately five minutes before the squad came under a heavy barrage of enemy fire. The squad quickly moved to cover behind some of the larger rocks to return fire and begin their bounding movements. Although he was completely exhausted from running up the side of a mountain, SGT Thom began to bound on his own as his Squad leader and team members were pinned down by enemy fire. After bounding 50 meters ahead of 3rd Squad and lobbing three M203 [grenade] rounds at the enemy's position, he began to maneuver his team on a frontal assault of the enemy position while B Team 3rd Squad flanked to the right to lay suppressive fire which destroyed one of the enemy positions. The enemy immediately broke contact and during the intense firefight, SSG Abdallah began to bound ahead of his squad leading them to the enemies' location. Seeing this, SGT Thom rushed up to his Squad Leader thrusting him to the ground and informing him, "*Let me do it Sergeant, you coordinate the battle field!*"

Through SGT Thom's gallant actions, his squad was able to destroy the enemy ambush. SGT Thom's selfless act caused the enemy to break contact, and allowed his squad to occupy the ridge. This key piece of terrain allowed 3rd Squad to effectively engage and destroy the enemy personnel that were putting effective fires on 1st Squad, 2nd Platoon. The destruction of enemy personnel saved the lives of his fellow Soldiers who were pinned down in the ambush and sustaining heavy casualties. SGT Thom's actions exemplify valor under the most extreme of combat conditions.

SPC Jackie E. Clark
Team Blackfoot, 1-4 Infantry
July 2007

On the morning of 23 July 2007, SPC Clark was conducting a routine mounted combat patrol in the Arghendab district of Zabul Province, Afghanistan. He was the automatic rifleman for 2nd Squad, 3rd Platoon, Bravo Company 1-4 Infantry during the patrol to the local village of Barghantu to conduct a shura with the village elders. On the return trip back to Firebase Lane, the five-vehicle convoy came under heavy small arms, RPG, 82mm recoilless rifle and PKM machine gun fire. SPC Clark was in the UAH located in the rear of the convoy when the platoon was ambushed by a group of 50-plus insurgents no more than 100 meters away off to the right side of the vehicles. The convoy stopped as per the platoon standard operating procedures in order to return fire and achieve fire superiority. Shortly thereafter, the call was given over the radio to break contact due to the overwhelming enemy firepower. Three of the up-armored UAHs in front of SPC Clark's vehicle began to move around the lead vehicle. At the same time, SPC Clark realized that the lead vehicle was smoking from an RPG blast.

As soon as SPC Clark's UAH pulled up next to 1st Squad's damaged UAH, he immediately dismounted without being told by his team leader to return fire. With total disregard for his own safety, SPC Clark exited the vehicle on the contact side under a barrage of accurate and effective enemy fire. He ran straight into enemy fire to take cover behind a burm and return fire with his M249 machine gun. SPC Clark engaged a group of insurgent fighters who were maneuvering towards their position, destroying at least two of them with accurate suppressive fire. Moments later, SPC Clark realized that 1st Squad had taken several casualties, including one that was fatally wounded. In order to cover and assist his medic, SPC Clark ran around the backside of his vehicle to grab the 60mm mortar tube while his team leader grabbed the rounds.

Completely exposed and with no fear whatsoever, SPC Clark engaged multiple enemy positions with the 60mm mortar system in handheld configuration. He was able to successfully lob three mortar rounds right on top of the enemy while taking accurate enemy fire. On the fourth round, SPC Clark took multiple rounds and ricochets within one meter of his position, causing him to lose balance right before firing the mortar tube. SPC Clark fired the tube anyway and the base plate dislodged, causing the tube to kick back on his left foot. SPC Clark didn't realize at the time that the tube had fractured his foot.

SPC Clark continued to fight back multiple enemy attacks even though his foot was injured. SPC Clark was informed by his team leader that they were going to leave the burning UAH in order to link up with the platoon leader's vehicle. While the other Soldiers gathered the sensitive items and casualties out of 1st squad's vehicle, SPC Clark moved around the vehicle to engage a second group of insurgents attempting to flank their position from the orchards to the south. Once again, SPC Clark was engaging the enemy with his M249 machine gun amidst a hail of enemy gunfire, causing the enemy to hunker down behind the trees. The enemy temporarily broke contact and his vehicle began moving slowly towards the platoon leader's position. SPC Clark's team leader forced him into the vehicle due to his foot injury, even though SPC Clark desperately wanted to support his fellow Soldiers. SPC Clark refused medical treatment until the platoon was back at Firebase Lane.

SPC Clark's actions on that fateful day demonstrated absolute courage under intense enemy fire. Although SPC Clark suffered a fractured bone in his foot, he continually fought throughout the engagement. SPC Clark was a beacon of hope to his fellow Soldiers during those intense moments. His valiant actions directly resulted in the destruction of more than 25 insurgent fighters and the evacuation of his fellow Soldiers. SPC Clark's actions exhibit the epitome of valor in the most extreme of combat situations.

PFC Corde M. Petry
Team Blackfoot, 1-4 Infantry
July 2007

On 25 May 2007, elements from 2nd and 3rd Platoon, Bravo Company 1-4 IN conducted a dismounted patrol in the Day Chopan District near the town of Tangay (42S xxxxx). The dismounted patrol consisted of 24 personnel, four ANA, and two interpreters. PFC Petry was assigned as 2nd Platoon's RTO for the mission. The dismounted patrol advanced just past Tangay, where the two elements split from each other to occupy different positions. 2nd Platoon's element was to travel the eastern side of the river, on the high ground once they passed through Tangay. While in a security halt past Tangay, 2nd Platoon came under extensive and massive RPG, PKM, and small arms fire. The initiation of the enemy ambush caused the element to split into two teams, each occupying cover in the nearby rocks.

Once set behind cover, both elements began initiating fire on the enemy with the M240B, M249, M4, M203, and 60mm mortar systems. PFC Petry was located with the PL and SL, attempting to call for fire with the nearby 120 mm mortar systems from FOB Baylough, all the while engaging the enemy with his M4. The firefight continued to extend, and the ammunition was running low. The M240B went black on ammo, and the only bag of ammunition left for the system was located with the other team. The badly needed ammo had to be hand carried from one covered and concealed position to the other. The route to the other team provided no cover or concealment, and was about 30 meters away. PFC Petry did not hesitate to grab the ammunition bag, and make a dash to the other team. This audacious and gallant move caused the enemy to focus all its small arms, PKM and RPG fire towards PFC Petry as he moved with the ammo towards the other team.

During the duration of his movement, the rounds were impacting all around him. PFC Petry made it to the M240B weapon system, which allowed the team to continue to suppress the enemy, eliminating their opportunity to maneuver on the element. PFC Petry then made the same audacious movement back.

PFC William K. Napier
Team Blackfoot, 1-4 Infantry
July 2007

On the morning of 23 July 2007, PFC Napier was conducting a routine mounted combat patrol in the Arghendab district of Zabul Province, Afghanistan. He was the machine gunner for the platoon leader of 3rd Platoon, Bravo Company 1-4 Infantry during the patrol to the local village of Barghantu to conduct a shura with the village elders. On the return trip back to Firebase Lane, the five-vehicle convoy came under heavy small arms, RPG, 82mm recoilless rifle and PKM machine gun fire. PFC Napier was in the UAH located in the middle of the convoy when the platoon was ambushed by a group of 50-plus insurgents no more than 100 meters away off to the right side of the vehicles. The convoy stopped as per the platoon standard operating procedures in order to return fire and achieve fire superiority. Shortly thereafter, the call was given over the radio to break contact due to the overwhelming enemy firepower. PFC Napier noticed that the lead UAH was smoking from the RPGs that impacted on the front of the vehicle. Two other up-armored UAHs passed by his UAH before PFC Napier's UAH began to move. PFC Napier noticed that 1st squad had some casualties as his vehicle passed by the damaged UAH.

Once PFC Napier's vehicle moved around to the flank of the ambush, PFC Napier could see all of the enemy fighters along the backside of the small hill. His platoon leader ordered the UAH to stop and PFC Napier immediately engaged every insurgent fighter that was located on the hill. The enemy fighters were engaging PFC Napier's UAH with such an overwhelming amount of firepower that PFC Napier was taking rounds inside his turret. With total disregard for his own life, PFC Napier continued to engage the enemy with incredible suppressive fire from his .50 caliber machine gun as rounds where whizzing by his head. He instantly eliminated three enemy fighters while they were attempting to engage the UAH with AK-47's and RPG's. PFC Napier also took off the arm of another fighter attempting to flee from the superior firepower that he was delivering with his machine gun. As the enemy were breaking contact, PFC Napier destroyed another four enemy fighters while they were running up the hill, allowing his fellow Soldiers to dismount and assist in returning fire. PFC Napier caused the enemy ambush to crumble under the awesome firepower he was delivering up on the hill.

While PFC Napier was engaging the backside of the enemy ambush, Soldiers from 1st and 2nd squads were gathering the casualties from the burning UAH and attempting to break contact to his location. PFC Napier continued to suppress the remaining enemy fighters in order to assist his fellow Soldiers in reaching his location. As soon as the remaining Soldiers made it to his location, PFC Napier learned that one of his fellow Soldiers had instantly died from the initial RPG blasts on the lead UAH. PFC Napier realized that he had to fire as much as possible in order to save the lives of the remaining Soldiers. Shortly thereafter, the decision was made to break contact to the designated air MEDEVAC site near the next village. As soon as the UAHs began moving again to the next village, the element took another barrage of overwhelming accurate enemy fire from small arms and RPGs. PFC Napier was once again taking rounds in his turret, which caused him to increase his rate of fire. PFC Napier continually exposed himself while providing suppressive firepower until the enemy broke contact completely.

PFC Napier's actions on that fateful day demonstrated absolute courage under intense enemy fire. He was a beacon of hope to his fellow Soldiers during those intense moments. The survival of his fellow Soldiers was possible through PFC Napier's engagement of the enemy. His valiant actions directly resulted in the destruction of 25 confirmed insurgent fighters and the evacuation of his fellow Soldiers. PFC Napier's actions exhibit the epitome of valor in the most extreme of combat situations.

SPC Isaiah Calloway
Team Cherokee, 1-4 Infantry
October 2006

On or about 30 October at 1100 [hours], SPC Calloway's platoon was collapsing an assembly area they had established 1000 meters west of the Marah Valley to make link up with the Afghan National Army and ODA 316 (both in battle positions on the eastern edge of the Marah Valley). They had been occupying those battle positions for 48 hours in an attempt to draw out and exploit insurgent forces in the western Day Chopan area and were about to begin movement back to FOB Lane. As SPC Calloway's platoon began to retrograde down the valley at vicinity grid 42S xxxxx SPC Calloway's platoon came under an intense complex ambush from both sides as the platoon drove down the mountainside. The ambush consisted of approximately 25 to 30 insurgents employing AK 47, PKM, and RPG fire. SPC Calloway maintained his composure and immediately returned an effective volume of fire while simultaneously ground guiding his driver as best he could down the treacherous mountainside.

On two instances, SPC Calloway had traversed his gun 180 degrees feverishly engaging insurgents from all directions. SPC Calloway's actions continued for approximately two minutes before he was fatally wounded by small arms fire. Upon consolidation and reorganization, and further examination of SPC Calloway's M240B, there was evidence of a round strike and fragmentation on the left side of the feed tray cover. SPC Calloway's wounds consisted of a gunshot wound to the right side of his forehead and fragmentation below his right eye. His wounds were consistent with the round strike on his weapon. At the instant of his death, SPC Calloway was cheek to stock engaging the enemy with effective, well-aimed fires. His actions while alive and his death are indicative of SPC Calloway's devotion to duty, comrades and country. His actions helped result in the deaths of 55 insurgents, saved the lives of many of the fellow Soldiers in his platoon, and reflect great credit upon himself, the North Atlantic Treaty Organization, and the United States Army.

SPC Brennan Brown
Team Cherokee, 1-4 Infantry
November 2008

During a combat patrol to Kandahar Air Field in support of Operation Enduring Freedom VIII, SPC Brown demonstrated his courage under fire, medical knowledge, and loyalty to his fellow Soldiers. On 28 November 2008, SPC Brown was driving the lead Mine Resistant Ambush Protected vehicle (MRAP) in a four vehicle convoy moving south on Highway 1 when the convoy came under a complex Improvised Explosive Device (IED) ambush. At approximately 1100 hours, near the village of Shari Safa, the second MRAP was hit with a one hundred pound ammonium nitrate command wire IED buried in a culvert underneath the highway. The resulting explosion completely destroyed the MRAP, cutting the vehicle in half, and seriously injured all four occupants: SGT Acosta, SPC Lesnick, PFC Parker, and SGT Alexander.

As soon as the second truck was hit, SPC Brown maneuvered his MRAP into a defensive position, retrieved his aid bag, and without any hesitation moved to help his fellow Soldiers. There were damaged 40-millimeter MK19 grenades strewn about and fuel was gushing all over the highway. With no regard to his own safety, SPC Brown reached PFC Parker and pulled him from the crew compartment. SPC Brown immediately began to assess PFC Parker's wounds and provide first aid by bracing his injured neck and spine.

After all the casualties were removed from the destroyed MRAP, Anti-Coalition forces engaged from a fortified position to the south of Highway 1 with heavy weapons and small arms fire. When the attack started, SPC Brown was behind cover tending to PFC Parker. When the IED had been detonated, SPC Lesnick had been thrown from the MRAP into a field to the south. The impact had broken both of SPC Lesnick's forearms, his femur, and his pelvis, leaving him conscious but completely exposed to enemy fire and unable to move. With ACF fire impacting all around him, SPC Brown selflessly left cover to assist SGT Ruehs and myself in dragging SPC Lesnick out of harm's way. While SPC Sumner and SGT Land laid down a heavy volume of cover fire, we dragged SPC Lesnick out of the field and up a loose gravel embankment to the safety of the destroyed MRAP's engine block. SPC Brown then returned fire with his personal weapon, providing covering fire until SGT Ruehs was able to provide a secure casualty collection point by strategically positioning his vehicle.

SPC Brown's training and experience were a vital asset in the immediate first aid given. While the MEDEVAC was enroute, SPC Brown remained calm throughout the entire incident and helped treat the other casualties by splinting SGT Acosta's broken ankle and wrist. SPC Brown then initiated the IV for PFC Parker. When the MEDEVAC helicopters arrived, SPC Brown assisted in the coordination with the in-flight medic by providing a prioritized list of casualties and descriptions of their wounds. SPC Brown then helped load each wounded Soldier onto the MEDEVAC helicopters.

In summary, Specialist Brown's valorous actions on 28 November 2008 were directly responsible for saving the lives of SPC Lesnick and PFC Parker during a complex IED ambush where the ACF had an overwhelming tactical advantage. In addition, he put the lives of his fellow Soldiers well before his own, allowing them all to be evacuated from the destroyed MRAP. There is no doubt that SPC Brown's actions on that day turned the tide of battle and saved the lives of his fellow Soldiers. SPC Brown's tactical proficiency and medical knowledge are in keeping with the finest traditions of military service and reflect great credit upon himself, Task Force Zabul, Combined Joint Task Force 101, United States CENTCOM, and the United States Army.

SPC Brian Beck
Team Blackfoot, 1-4 Infantry
May 2009

On 28 May 2009, SPC Brian Beck was on a Company mission in the Day Chopan District of Zabul Province, Afghanistan. SPC Beck was manning an observation point (OP) by the town of Vakil Kur, almost two kilometers in front of the assaulting force. Upon daylight as the Company element and two Operational Detachment Alpha teams advanced towards Vakil Kur, an IED was set off in the vicinity of Ludin which is four kilometers south of the aforementioned town. Subsequently the assaulting force was halted in the vicinity of Tangay. The IED resulted in a disabled vehicle deterring the freedom of movement for the assaulting force, thus leaving SPC Beck and his squad significantly behind enemy lines with no friendly ground forces in route.

At first daylight, SPC Beck began engaging several enemy combatants with his M249 (SAW) near the town of Vakil Kur and its outskirts. SPC Beck killed an enemy combatant as he attempted to flee Vakil Kur on horseback.

Before SPC Beck and his squad could move from their position, the enemy was able to conduct a counter-attack with multiple enemy reinforcements, whose techniques and equipment were extremely sophisticated: to include the use of smoke to conceal movement and the use of body armor and ballistic helmets. Upon the enemy's attack, SPC Beck laid down heavy suppressive fire towards the enemy who was firing at him from three different sides: from his east on the high ground, from his west just 300 meters away and from his north with recoilless rifle and RPK machine guns. Due to his accurate firing, SPC Beck had to switch positions as the rocks he was behind and in front of were peppered with enemy fire.

SPC Beck employed a Light Anti-Armor Weapon (LAAW) at a known enemy location and hit his target with precise accuracy, resulting in an enemy machine gun position being destroyed.

Through SPC Beck's courageous action, he helped his Squad, Company elements and Operational Detachment Alpha Teams avoid any further serious damage or injuries to personnel and equipment while engaging the enemy in Vakil Kur and the Tangay Valley.

PFC Wesley R. Gatewood
Team Blackfoot, 1-4 Infantry
May 2009

On 28 May 2009, PFC Wesley R. Gatewood was on a Company mission in the Day Chopan District of Zabul Province, Afghanistan. PFC Gatewood was manning an observation point (OP) by the town of Vakil Kur, almost two kilometers in front of the assaulting force. Upon day light as the Company element and two Operational Detachment Alpha teams advanced towards Vakil Kur, an IED was set off in the vicinity of Ludin which is four kilometers south of the aforementioned town. Subsequently the assaulting force was halted in the vicinity of Tangay. The IED resulted in a disabled vehicle deterring the freedom of movement for the assaulting force, thus leaving PFC Gatewood and his squad significantly behind enemy lines with no friendly ground forces in route.

At first day light, PFC Gatewood noticed enemy movement in the towns of Vakil Kur and Nowrah consisting of eight and six enemy personnel respectively. Inside the town of Vakil Kur, the enemy combatants forced civilians out of their homes. PFC Gatewood quickly alerted his team leader with an accurate description of the enemy combatants and their weapons systems, which included automatic machine guns, recoilless rifles and rocket propelled grenades (RPGs). PFC Gatewood killed an enemy combatant with his M-14 at range of 816m as he attempted to flee Vakil Kur.

PFC Gatewood's identification and fire was so accurate, effective and overwhelming, that the enemy was unable to effectively engage the rest of the Patrol for the duration of the engagement. This caused the enemy to focus all of their attention to locating and destroying his position.

Before the PFC Gatewood and his squad could move from their position, the enemy was able to conduct a counter-attack with multiple enemy reinforcements, whose techniques and equipment were extremely sophisticated: to include the use of smoke to conceal movement and the use of body armor and ballistic helmets. At one point, the enemy started engaging PFC Gatewood's position from three different sides: from his east on high ground, from his west just 300 meters away and from his north with recoilless rifle and RPK machine guns. PFC Gatewood once again identified and engaged the advancing enemy as they attempted to move towards the OP from the low ground. His superb marksmanship resulted with the enemy being thwarted and killed.

Through PFC Gatewood's courageous action, he helped his squad, Company elements and Operational Detachment Alpha Teams avoid any further serious damage or injuries to personnel and equipment while engaging the enemy in Vakil Kur and the Tangay Valley.

PFC Ryan E. Delashmit
Team Blackfoot, 1-4 Infantry
May 2009

On 28 May 2009, PFC Ryan E. Delashmit was on a Company mission in the Day Chopan District of Zabul Province, Afghanistan. PFC Delashmit was manning an observation point (OP) by the town of Vakil Kur, almost two kilometers in front of the assaulting force. Upon daylight, as the Company element and two Operational Detachment Alpha teams advanced towards Vakil Kur, an IED was set off in the vicinity of Ludin which is four kilometers south of the aforementioned town. Subsequently, the assaulting force was halted in the vicinity of Tangay. The IED resulted in a disabled vehicle deterring the freedom of movement for the assaulting force, thus leaving PFC Delashmit and his squad significantly behind enemy lines with no friendly ground forces in route.

At first daylight, PFC Delashmit started identifying enemy positions moving towards the Company and ODA's main assaulting force. PFC Delashmit quickly alerted his team leader with an accurate description of the enemy combatants and their weapons systems, which included automatic machine guns, recoilless rifles and rocket propelled grenades (RPGs). PFC Delashmit repositioned himself and his assistant gunner in order to have a better sector of fire towards the enemy. PFC Delashmit's accurate report on enemy positions deterred a surprising attack on friendly forces. PFC Delashmit killed an advancing combatant with his M240B before they could identify his position.

PFC Delashmit's fires were so accurate, effective and overwhelming, that the enemy was unable to effectively engage the rest of the Patrol for the duration of the engagement. This caused the enemy to focus all of their attention to locating and destroying his position.

Before PFC Delashmit and his squad could move from their position, the enemy was able to conduct a counter-attack with multiple enemy reinforcements, whose techniques and equipment were extremely sophisticated: to include the use of smoke to conceal movement and the use of body armor and ballistic helmets. At one point, the enemy started engaging PFC Delashmit's position from three different sides: from his east on high ground, from his west just 300 meters away and from his north with recoilless rifle and RPK machine guns. PFC Delashmit's accurate fire killed an advancing enemy as they attempted to move towards the OP from the low ground in the riverbed.

Through PFC Delashmit's courageous action, he helped his squad, Company elements and Operational Detachment Alpha Teams avoid any further serious damage or injuries to personnel and equipment while engaging the enemy in Vakil Kur and the Tangay Valley.

SSG Lucas W. Hearn
Team Blackfoot, 1-4 Infantry
May 2007

On 23 May 2007, 2nd and 3rd Platoons from Bravo Company, 1st Battalion, 4th Infantry conducted a no notice mounted quick reaction force in the Day Chopan District to destroy ACM forces in contact with a squad element from 2nd Platoon. SSG Hearn was given instructions to start his dismounted movement once the QRF reached the squad in contact. As the QRF arrived and immediately started taking fire, SSG Hearn was dispatched to start moving his squad forward. After about twenty minutes of RPG, PKM and 82mm recoilless fire, the ACM forces started their withdrawal towards the town of Davudzay. Upon reconsolidation, it was decided to pursue the fleeing Taliban. SSG Hearn's squad was given the task of securing the southern flank and moving to the high ground overlooking the town of Davudzay. (42S xxxxx) The remainder of 2nd Platoon moved four vehicles to the south to watch SSG Hearn's movement and secure the pass to Davudzay. 3rd Platoon's vehicles then moved to the north towards the town of Tangay Kalay before turning south and occupying a position four hundred meters northeast of the pass. Upon 2nd Platoon arriving at the pass, they were immediately engaged by intense small arms, RPG, and PKM fire from a free roving force of approximately 30 to 50 enemy fighters.

The mounted vehicles were receiving overwhelming fire from the southwest side of the pass on the mountain. SSG Hearn arrived, after moving approximately seven kilometers in very rugged terrain and immediately became involved in the firefight. SSG Hearn, seeing that the four vehicles and dismounts were pinned down, rallied his squad to assault up the mountain through withering fire from the enemy on top the mountain. SSG Hearn continued to press on even though he and his Soldiers were exhausted from the altitude and energy expended in assaulting up the mountain. Once on top of the mountain, SSG Hearn continued to motivate his squad to continue clearing the mountain top to the far west side (42S xxxxx) and accomplish the task of relieving pressure on the Soldiers below. SSG Hearn did not hesitate to press forward to take the high ground and influence the battle that had been raging for over an hour of intense firing. During the movement up the mountain, SSG Hearn on several instances placed himself in direct fire to cover his Soldiers and lead from the front, showing no fear for his personal safety.

On 25 May 2007 SSG Hearn again found himself engaged with the enemy on a hilltop located at 42S xxxxx. SSG Hearn's squad had been on a combat patrol when they were ambushed by an enemy force of approximately 60 personnel. SSG Hearn's squad immediately took three casualties. SSG Hearn positioned his two teams in a defensive posture and he immediately started first aid on the wounded Soldiers, one being the medic. SSG Hearn was able to hold his position for almost three hours of continuous small arms and RPG fire from the ridge above him until reinforcements could arrive and provide CASEVAC. After SSG Hearn's Soldiers were CASEVAC'd, SSG Hearn continued to fight with his degraded force along with the rest of the company.

SSG Hearn showed gallantry in the face of fanatical enemy resistance well beyond his duties as a squad leader. SSG Hearn's actions directly contributed to three enemies destroyed in the orchard and forced the withdrawal of many more by his stubbornness to give up any ground.

PFC Christian Cisneros
Team Blackfoot, 1-4 Infantry
May 2007

On 25 May 2007 elements from 2nd and 3rd Platoon, Bravo Company 1-4 IN conducted a dismounted patrol in the Day Chopan District near the town of Tangay (42S xxxxx). The dismounted patrol consisted of 24 personnel, four ANA, and two interpreters. PFC Cisneros was assigned as 1st Squad's alpha team leader for the mission. The dismounted patrol advanced just past Tangay, where the two elements split from each other to occupy different positions. 2nd Platoon's element was to travel the eastern side of the river, on the high ground once they passed through Tangay. While in a security halt past Tangay, 2nd Platoon came under extensive and massive RPG, PKM, and small arms fire. The initiation of the enemy ambush was an RPG and caused the element to split into two teams, each occupying cover in the nearby rocks. On finding out that the M240 Gunner was thrown from his position from the initial blast, PFC Cisneros quickly asked for cover fire to go retrieve the wounded Soldier and his M240. The squad laid suppressive fire for him and his recovery element while they retrieved the Soldier and his sensitive items. This audacious and gallant move caused the enemy to focus all its small firepower towards the recovery element. During the duration of this movement PKM, RPG and small arms fire were impacting all around, but PFC Cisneros was more concerned with getting the casualty out of harm's way, than he was with his own safety. Once set behind cover, both elements began initiating fire on the enemy with the M240B, M249, M4, M203, and 60mm mortar systems. PFC Cisneros was located with the separated element 30 meters away from the Squad Leader and Platoon Leader. PFC Cisneros took control of the separated element and spotted multiple ACM fighting positions for the element to fire upon. His visual scanning during the direst of circumstances effectively enabled the squad to suppress the enemy with the 60mm mortar system. Once the enemy was suppressed, PFC Cisneros was yet again indispensable in setting up northern security, with minimal weapons systems and personnel.

SPC Fredrick T. Ely
Team Blackfoot, 1-4 Infantry
May 2007

On the afternoon of the 19th of May 2007, 3rd squad with a machine gun attachment came under heavy, relentless fire in an ambush initiated by a force of some 25-30 Anti Coalition Militants. SPC Ely was the assistant gunner and MG Team Leader for a joint combat patrol. The squad, along with four ANA Soldiers, was moving dismounted in some of the most arduous terrain in the Day Chopan District. Upon cresting a rise, the squad was immediately confronted with a barrage of massive PKM machine gun fire, RPGs, and small arms. Due to the rugged mountainous terrain, the M240 machine gun was left in the rear of the squad formation.

The patrols lead elements became pinned down by the enemy and the medic and a rifleman received impacts to their front plates of body armor from the overwhelming enemy fire. Upon seeing this, SPC Ely braved the heavy and accurate enemy fire from both small arms and RPG's, and even as the enemy rounds were impacting all around him, he moved over 100 meters back to where the M240 was, and retrieved it from the new M240 gunner who was pinned down. SPC Ely then fully exposed to the enemy, moved back across the open area to the top of the hill where he took a position and began to engage the enemy targets and helped gain the much needed fire superiority.

By doing so, SPC Ely's actions helped rally the remainder of the squad that was caught in the ambush and inspired them to move to better covered positions and also put accurate fire on the enemy. SPC Ely was well aware of the consequences of his actions and knowingly placed his fellow Soldiers' lives above his own. Had SPC Ely not taken the initiative and maneuvered back to the M240 machine gunner, many of the Soldiers in contact would have undoubtedly been wounded, if not killed. SPC Ely's courage and bravery under relentless fire led to success of the mission and also in none of the Soldiers being wounded or killed.

SPC Steven Frungillo
Team Blackfoot, 1-4 Infantry
May 2007

On 25 May 2007, SPC Frungillo accompanied a mounted quick reaction force (QRF) as a .50 Cal machine gunner for one of the M1151 UAH. Elements of Bravo Company, 1st Battalion, 4th Infantry Regiment were under attack from an overwhelming enemy force. SPC Frungillo and the QRF were dispatched from FOB Baylough in order to provide assistance with the evacuation of casualties. After the casualties were evacuated, SPC Frungillo's UAH and another remained in place to provide cover for the dismounts as they began their movement down from the mountain. During the course of the movement, enemy forces counter attacked the Bravo Company elements in the valley with a large volume of small arms and RPG fire.

The friendly forces were pinned down under minimal cover on the valley floor returning fire. The enemy fire was so intense that it damaged one of the UAHs and friendly forces were unable to advance any further. Despite concentrated enemy fire in his direction, SPC Frungillo would not take cover in his turret. He continued to fire with absolute disregard for his own life in order to suppress the enemy. SPC Frungillo was receiving such effective fire from the enemy that rounds were impacting inside his turret. Although there was an incredible amount of RPG rounds exploding around his UAH, SPC Frungillo was able to locate and destroy multiple enemies firing RPGs.

Through SPC Frungillo's gallant actions, Bravo Company elements were able to fight off the enemy counter-attack and recover the damaged UAH back to the FOB. SPC Frungillo's selfless act was critical in saving the lives of his fellow Soldiers pinned down by enemy fire around the UAHs. He provided the necessary firepower to turn the tide of the battle in the favor of Bravo Company. SPC Frungillo's actions exemplify valor under the most extreme of combat conditions.

CPL David A. Kuhn
Team Dragon, 1-4 Infantry
June 2008

On the evening of 14 June 2008, 2nd Platoon departed on a joint combat patrol with Embedded Training Team (ETT), Operational Detachment Alpha (ODA), Afghan National Army (ANA), and Afghan National Police (ANP) to the Chalikor Valley, a known ACF safe haven. On the morning of 15 June 2008, at approximately 06:00 the patrol came under harassing ACF fire and began seeing spotters along the ridgeline. CPL Kuhn repositioned his vehicle with ODA and returned fire while his platoon leader was dismounted clearing the orchards with ANA, ANP, and ETT. His covering fire allowed the dismounted elements freedom of movement through the orchard and forced the ACF to break contact and reconsolidate their forces. As the platoon leader was dismounted, CPL Kuhn was forced to coordinate movement on the radio between 2nd Platoon, ETT, and ODA. His coordination ensured that all elements knew the front line trace of the dismounted element and ensured that there was no fratricide.

A few hours later, at approximately 09:00, the patrol came under extremely heavy ACF fire from 40 to 50 ACF consisting of AK-47, PKM, RPG, SPG-9, and Dragonov fire. The ACF was attacking the patrol from the North, South, and East. CPL Kuhn's vehicle was taking fire from a ridgeline to the east and he immediately returned fire with effective and accurate fire. To the north, ODA and ETT were taking extremely heavy and accurate volumes of ACF fire. CPL Kuhn's vehicle was pulled north directly into the heaviest part of the firefight.

Upon moving north, CPL Kuhn's vehicle took multiple rounds to the windshield, turret, and armor. Regardless, CPL Kuhn continued to engage and destroy multiple ACF positions. At one point, an ACF dismount attempted to break contact on a motorcycle; CPL Kuhn engaged the dismount and destroyed both him and his motorcycle. The vehicle to the west of CPL Kuhn's vehicle had their .50 Caliber machine gun go down and he was forced to cover two sectors of fire. CPL Kuhn was able to flawlessly engage ACF in both sectors of fire during the heaviest part of the fight. For close to seven hours of fighting, CPL Kuhn fired over 3,000 rounds and was forced to cross-load ammunition on multiple occasions.

Not only did CPL Kuhn serve as a gunner, but he also worked as a Radio Telephone Operator (RTO) and a Combat Life Saver (CLS) multiple times throughout the fight, to include the heaviest parts of the fight, when the Platoon Leader was dismounted. As a result, CPL Kuhn was forced to communicate via both TACSAT and FM to 2nd Platoon, ODA, and ETT. He coordinated movement, on the platoon leader's behalf, between the three different elements and was vital to developing the tactical situation. At one point, the local national interpreter in CPL Kuhn's vehicle was suffering from heat exhaustion. CPL Kuhn sent his driver to the turret so he could treat the interpreter for heat exhaustion and administer an IV, all while under fire. Immediately after, CPL Kuhn returned to the gun and continued to engage the ACF.

CPL Kuhn demonstrated immense courage, strong leadership, and calm under fire during a direct fire engagement in the Chalikor Valley on the 15th of June 2008. His ability to act as a gunner, RTO, and CLS while under direct fire was flawless. CPL Kuhn was vital to mission success and his actions saved friendly lives and destroyed ACF weapons, personnel, and equipment. CPL Kuhn is a steadfast example of dedication, loyalty, and grace under fire. His actions in combat are in keeping with the finest traditions of military service and reflect great credit upon himself, Task Force Zabul, Regional Command South, CJTF 101, and the United States Army.

SPC Seth A. Houle
Team Cherokee, 1-4 Infantry
August 2008

While serving as a dismounted team leader on a patrol to Tangay Kalay on 03 August 2008, SPC Houle displayed extraordinary heroism by pulling CPT Howell out of harm's way when he was wounded during a multiple-phased ambush by Anti-Coalition Forces (ACF). Immediately after the first engagement with ACF northeast of the village of Tangay Kalay, our four UAHs and two ANP trucks were travelling southeast of TRP 16 (42S xxxxx) towards FOB Baylough when we were again engaged by four to seven ACF armed with PKMs, AK-47s, and RPGs from the top of TRP 15 (42S xxxxx) and the base of TRP 16. We immediately began delivering suppressing fire and bounding our vehicles south. CPT Howell dismounted his vehicle to get better eyes on the location of the ACF when automatic weapons fire began impacting all around him. He attempted to take cover in a ditch, but was struck by two PKM rounds in his knee and calf.

Despite a heavy volume of accurate fire on CPT Howell's position, SPC Houle dismounted his vehicle and came to the aid of the Commander. SPC Houle then proceeded to drag CPT Howell approximately ten meters to the UAH and opened the door where he then lifted CPT Howell into the vehicle, out of danger, and began treating his wounds. Our element reconsolidated and began to exfiltrate to the east and out of the engagement area. While returning to the FOB SPC Houle helped to further treat and stabilize the wounds to CPT Howell's legs.

SPC Houle demonstrated courage and the ability to maneuver under fire. He directly aided CPT Howell and pulled him to safety despite imminent danger to his own life. His actions are in keeping with the finest traditions of military service and reflect great credit upon himself, Team Cherokee, Task Force Zabul, Regional Command South, CJTF 101, TF Anzio, CJTF-101, and the United States Army.

PFC Jacob D. Coleman
Team Blackfoot, 1-4 Infantry
May 2009

On 28 May 2009, PFC Jacob D. Coleman was on a Company mission in the Day Chopan District of Zabul Province, Afghanistan. PFC Coleman was manning an observation point (OP) by the town of Vakil Kur, almost two kilometers in front of the assaulting force. Upon daylight, as the Company element and two Operational Detachment Alpha teams advanced towards Vakil Kur, an IED was set off in the vicinity of Ludin which is four kilometers south of the aforementioned town. Subsequently, the assaulting force was halted in the vicinity of Tangay. The IED resulted in a disabled vehicle deterring the freedom of movement for the assaulting force, thus leaving PFC Coleman and his squad significantly behind enemy lines with no friendly ground forces in route.

At first daylight, PFC Coleman noticed enemy movement in the towns of Vakil Kur and Nowrah consisting of eight and six enemy personnel respectively. Inside the town of Vakil Kur, the enemy combatants forced civilians out of their homes. PFC Coleman quickly alerted his team leader with an accurate description of the enemy combatants and their weapons systems, which included automatic machine guns, recoilless rifles and rocket propelled grenades (RPGs).

PFC Coleman's identification and fire with his M4 and M203 were so accurate, effective, and overwhelming, that the enemy was unable to effectively engage the rest of the patrol for the duration of the engagement. This caused the enemy to focus all of their attention to locating and destroying his position.

Before PFC Coleman and his squad could move from their position, the enemy was able to conduct a counter-attack with multiple enemy reinforcements, whose techniques and equipment were extremely sophisticated: to include the use of smoke to conceal movement and the use of body armor and ballistic helmets. At one point, the enemy started engaging PFC Coleman's position from three different sides: from his east on high ground, from his west just 300 meters away and from his north with recoilless rifle and RPK machine guns. PFC Coleman laid down suppressive fire with his M203 in order to allow his team leader, SGT

Cisneros, and another Soldier, PFC Gatewood, to reposition themselves because they were pinned down.

Through PFC Coleman's courageous action, he helped his squad, Company elements and Operational Detachment Alpha Teams avoid any further serious damage or injuries to personnel and equipment while engaging the enemy in Vakil Kur and the Tangay Valley.

CPL Jeremy I. Davidson
Team Blackfoot, 1-4 Infantry
May 2009

On 10 May 2009, 3rd PLT, B Co, 1/4 IN REG was returning from a reconnaissance mission in the Arghasu region of the Mizan District, Zabul Province, Afghanistan. CPL Davidson, Jeremy, 3PLT's medic, had participated in the previous day's mission as part of the OP team, which had traveled a great distance over difficult terrain in an attempt to emplace an OP where the enemy would be unaware. Already 24 hours into the mission, which had begun on 09MAY, CPL Davidson and the OP team collapsed their position and conducted link-up with the vehicles. With everyone accounted for, the patrol began its return to FOB MIZAN.

At 101335LMAY2009, ANSF dismounts traveling ahead of the vehicles to mitigate the IED risk activated a PPIED vicinity 42S xxxxx. One ANP was instantly killed, while an ANA soldier sustained severe injuries to both legs. CPL Davidson immediately ran to the front of the patrol and began treating the wounded soldier, despite his rapidly worsening condition. CPL Davidson dressed the wounds, provided his PL with 9-line MEDEVAC information, and prepared the patient for transport to the emergency HLZ. The patrol established an HLZ to the west of the IED-strike, but the ANA soldier's wounds overcame him, despite CPL Davidson's best effort, before the MEDEVAC helicopter could arrive.

Leadership decided it would be necessary to dismount all available personnel for the remainder of the patrol to help negate the IED threat and to travel off-road wherever possible. However, the vehicles were currently caught in a ravine and forced to travel a seldom-used road for a short distance. In light of his exhausting efforts the previous day and his admirable attempt to save the ANA soldier, CPL Davidson was given leave to ride in his vehicle and get a proper rest.

Shortly afterward, at approximately 101435MAY2009, the sixth vehicle in the patrol, CPL Davidson's, hit a second PPIED. Everyone inside the vehicle, to include CPL Davidson, sustained injuries during the blast. Enemy forces then engaged the patrol with relentless small arms fire from the south. CPL Davidson's first thoughts were for his fellow Soldiers. With complete disregard for his safety and regardless of a broken nose, dislocated thumb, and deep lacerations all over his body, CPL Davidson immediately began treating the gunner and driver of the stricken M1151.

Without hesitation, he applied tourniquets, pressure-dressings, and bandages until he was forcefully removed from the other wounded so his own injuries could be addressed, at which point he continued to supply CLS responders with his medical expertise by instructing them from a distance. SGT Allsup treated CPL Davidson for his injuries and applied a tourniquet to his arm, which was bleeding badly. Once CLS personnel had moved on, CPL Davidson immediately reassessed the other casualties, decided they were worse off than him, and selflessly removed his tourniquet to apply it to SGT Benjamin, another Soldier injured in the explosion.

When informed the MEDEVAC helicopter was inbound, CPL Davidson, covered in his own blood, personally sought out his PL to insist he could continue and expressed his desire to remain with the patrol until everyone was safely back at base. CPL Davidson was reluctantly MEDEVAC'd a short time later.

In summary, CPL Davidson's actions on 10MAY2009 reflect the finest qualities of a combat medic. His selfless heroism, steadfast professionalism, and unshakeable courage are in keeping with the proudest traditions of military service. CPL Davidson's unflinching dedication to duty and disregard for his personal well-being reflect great credit upon himself, Blackfoot Company, Task Force Zabul, and the United States Army.

PV2 Stephen Wright
Team Blackfoot, 1-4 Infantry
February 2007

On 7 February 2007, PV2 Stephen Wright was assigned as an infantry dismount in his platoon leader's vehicle which was conducting mounted combat operations in the Mizan District of Zabul Province, Afghanistan. The coalition force of five US UAHs and one Afghan National Army pickup truck was set in an over-watch position oriented north in the vicinity of xxxxx near the town of Hamidollah Kalay. Weather on this day was clear and warm and enemy morale was high based on radio communication intercepted by the US interpreters. The location of Anti-coalition forces (ACF) was identified and the platoon leader's vehicle along with another vehicle began a flanking maneuver to the east side of the saddle located at xxxxx. When PV2 Wright's vehicle was due east of this enemy position, it began receiving heavy enemy small arms and RPG fire.

SPC Marcel Green, the M240B gunner on this vehicle began engaging the ACF that numbered approximately 10-15 at that time. SPC Green was able to get one confirmed enemy kill but was not able to gain fire superiority due to the number of enemy personnel and the large amount of enemy fire that he was receiving. One of the RPG's fired hit the vehicle just above the driver's windshield. This caused a devastating explosion which penetrated the crew compartment filling the inside with hot shrapnel and ripping the gunner's turret completely off the top. The explosion immediately ejected PFC Zaehringer, the driver, out of the vehicle. The vehicle then proceeded to roll uncontrollably down into a draw, about 50 feet, until it came to a violent stop at the bottom. The crash was almost as devastating as the round itself for the Soldiers who were still inside.

Once the Soldiers inside began to regain consciousness, 2LT Stofan and the medic PFC Murray, who was also badly injured from the shrapnel and losing a lot of blood, attempted to find cover and return fire on the enemy while the ACF continued engaging the vehicle with large amounts of small arms and RPG fire. During this time, PV2 Wright, with complete disregard for his own safety, gallantly ran to the top of the hill, exposing himself to heavy enemy fire, and pulled PFC Zaehringer, who was very badly injured, to the low ground where he was less exposed to the enemy fire. PV2 Wright then entered the badly damaged vehicle, again exposing himself to heavy enemy fire, and pulled SPC Green from the wreckage to a covered position. During the retrieval of both casualties, PV2 Wright had the situational awareness to return fire on the enemy locations which were highly advantageous to his own. His fires helped suppress the enemy and force them west over the saddle towards the other three US vehicles where the enemy suffered several more KIA and casualties.

In addition to PV2 Wright's heroic acts of pulling his fellow Soldiers to safety and returning fire on the enemy positions, he also put his combat lifesaver skills to use and began treating the wounds of SPC Green and PFC Zaehringer. He went back and forth between both casualties administering first aid while under continuous enemy fire. PV2 Wright continued providing life-saving aid to both Soldiers until qualified medics arrived on the scene.

PV2 Wright clearly acted with absolute gallantry and complete disregard for his own safety during the events that transpired on 7 February 2007. His heroic acts under the most extreme of combat conditions speak volumes for PV2 Wright's character, dedication to duty, and devotion to his fellow Soldiers.

SPC Marcel Green
Team Blackfoot, 1-4 Infantry
February 2007

On 7 February 2007, SPC Marcel Green was assigned as the M240B machine gunner on his platoon leader's vehicle, which was conducting mounted combat operations in the Mizan District of Zabul Province, Afghanistan. The coalition force of five US UAHs and one Afghan National Army pickup truck was set in an over-watch position oriented north in the vicinity of xxxxx near the town of Hamidollah Kalay. Weather on this day was clear and warm and enemy morale was high based on radio communication intercepted by the US interpreters. The location of Anti-coalition forces (ACF) was identified and the Platoon Leader's vehicle along with another vehicle began a flanking maneuver to the east side of the saddle located at xxxxx. When SPC Greene's vehicle was due east of this enemy position, it began receiving heavy enemy small arms and RPG fire.

SPC Green immediately started engaging the ACF that numbered approximately 10-15 at that time. At this time SPC Green was the only person able to engage the enemy despite the overwhelming odds he faced. With complete disregard for his own safety, SPC Green gallantly engaged the ACF with deadly accuracy. SPC Green was receiving such accurate fire from the ACF that he had bullets striking the gunners shield in front of him and all around the outside of the vehicle. SPC Green continued to engage the enemy getting one confirmed enemy kill and attempting to gain fire superiority, but the enemy numbers were too many and the volume of enemy fire was too great for him to accomplish this.

Despite SPC Green's valiant efforts the ACF were finally able to fire an RPG round that impacted five meters in front of the vehicle creating a large explosion and sending debris flying towards the vehicle and SPC Green. SPC Green did not waiver and continued to engage. The ACF fired a second RPG that impacted the vehicle just above the driver's side window, penetrated the crew compartment, and ripped SPC Green's turret completely off the top of the vehicle. SPC Green engaged the enemy until the very last seconds when his turret and gun were literally ripped away from him by the explosion of the RPG. This devastating explosion left SPC Green very badly injured. He was knocked back down into the crew compartment unconscious. SPC Green was also missing three fingers from his right hand and his thumb was barely attached. The explosion immediately ejected PFC Zaehringer, the driver, out of the vehicle. The vehicle then proceeded to roll uncontrollably down into a draw, about 50 feet, until it came to a violent stop at the bottom.

Once the Soldiers inside regained consciousness, 2LT Stofan and the medic PFC Murray, who was also badly injured from the shrapnel and losing a lot of blood, attempted to find cover and return fire on the enemy while the ACF continued engaging the vehicle with large amounts of small arms and RPG fire. During this time, PV2 Wright ran to the top of the hill and pulled PFC Zaehringer, who was very badly injured, to the low ground where he was less exposed to the enemy fire. SPC Green had found his M4 rifle and with only one good hand continued to engage the ACF from the wrecked vehicle until PV2 Wright finally reached SPC Green and removed him from the vehicle to administer first aid.

SPC Green clearly acted with absolute gallantry and complete disregard for his own safety during the events that transpired on 7 February 2007 that left six confirmed ACF dead and several wounded. His heroic acts under the most extreme of combat conditions speak volumes for SPC Green's character, dedication to duty, and devotion to his fellow Soldier.

PFC Edward Bailey
Team Blackfoot, 1-4 Infantry
February 2007

On 7 February 2007, PFC Edward Bailey was assigned as a driver for an Enhanced Tactical Trainer team vehicle, which was conducting mounted combat operations in the Mizan district of Zabul Province, Afghanistan. The coalition force of five US UAHs and one Afghan National Army pickup truck was set in an over watch position oriented north in the vicinity of xxxxx near the town of Hamidollah Kalay. Weather on this day was clear and warm and enemy morale was high based on radio communication intercepted by the US interpreters. The location of Anti-coalition forces (ACF) was identified and the Platoon Leader's vehicle along with PFC Bailey's vehicle began a flanking maneuver to the east side of the saddle located at xxxxx. When his Platoon Leader's vehicle was due east of this enemy position, it began receiving heavy enemy small arms and RPG fire.

SPC Green, the gunner, immediately started engaging the ACF that numbered approximately 10-15 at that time. SPC Green continued to engage the enemy getting one confirmed enemy kill and attempting to gain fire superiority, but the enemy numbers were too many and the volume of enemy fire was too great for him to accomplish this. Despite SPC Green's efforts the ACF were finally able to fire an RPG round that impacted five meters in front of the vehicle creating a large explosion. The ACF fired a second RPG that impacted the vehicle just above the driver's side window, penetrated the crew compartment, and ripped the gunner's turret completely off the top of the vehicle.

The explosion immediately ejected PFC Zaehringer, the driver, out of the vehicle. It also badly injured SPC Green and PFC Murray. PFC Murray received a tremendous amount of shrapnel into both arms and hands. PFC Murray was losing a lot of blood as a result of his injuries. The vehicle then proceeded to roll uncontrollably down into a draw, about 50 feet, until it came to a violent stop at the bottom. Once the Soldiers inside regained consciousness, 2LT Stofan and PFC Murray attempted to find cover and return fire on the enemy while the ACF continued engaging the vehicle with large amounts of small arms and RPG fire. During this time, PV2 Wright ran to the top of the hill and pulled PFC Zaehringer, who was very badly injured, to the low ground where he was less exposed to the enemy fire and removed SPC Green from the vehicle to administer first aid. During this time, PFC Bailey maneuvered his vehicle to his platoon leader's disabled vehicle under heavy RPG and small arms fire. Once at the location, PFC Bailey dismounted his vehicle and immediately began returning fire on enemy positions. Once he reached the location of his fellow Soldier's he began providing first aid to the SPC Green and PFC Zaehringer. PFC Bailey continued to return fire on enemy positions and provide first aid until follow on forces could reinforce his position and air MEDEVAC was able to transport SPC Green, PFC Murray, and PFC Zaehringer to the rear for treatment.

PFC Bailey clearly acted with absolute gallantry and complete disregard for his own safety during the events that transpired on 7 February 2007 that left six confirmed ACF dead and several wounded. His heroic acts under the most extreme of combat conditions speak volumes for PFC Bailey's character, dedication to duty, and devotion to his fellow Soldier.

PFC Jordan Wright
Team Blackfoot, 1-4 Infantry
March 2009

On the night of 15 March 2009, during a night river crossing in Day Chopan District, Zabul Province, Afghanistan, PFC Dispennette was swept downstream and rendered unconscious and unresponsive in waist deep, extremely cold, rushing water. SPC Wright ran along the riverbank to intercept PFC Dispennette, who was traveling quickly downstream. He entered the water with complete disregard to his personal safety ahead of PFC Dispennette and successfully secured the soldier. As they continued to drift downstream, SPC Wright moved him towards shore as two other squad members entered at the river's edge to assist him in getting the Soldier out of the water and to lifesaving aid. PFC Dispennette is alive today because of his actions.

PFC Spencer Berry
Team Blackfoot, 1-4 Infantry
May 2009

On 10 May 2009, 3rd Platoon conducted a mounted mission into the Arghasu Region of the Mizan District. 2nd Squad, two snipers, and one mortar dismounted at approximately 21:00. 2nd Squad was tasked to set up two OPs and a sniper OP. By 22:30 the same night, multiple Taliban OPs had spotted our vehicle patrol base move the opposite direction in our effort to distract the enemy.

By 05:00 the next morning our OP, while heavily concealed, was unexpectedly compromised by enemy spotters. The snipers spotted an enemy OP, but the enemy's impossible line of sight toward us indicated another enemy position must have been communicating our location to the one we were watching. The sniper team saw that the enemy OP consisted of two enemy dismounts passing binoculars between each other and hiding AK-47s. We ranged the enemy at approximately 1700 meters. SGT Marsh then took the snipers and PFC Berry, who had the 240B, 300 meters down and 400 meters closer to the enemy OP. The snipers and PFC Berry then engaged the enemy at over 1200 meters. PFC Berry shot expertly, resulting in one EKIA and one EWIA to his credit.

At 13:30 that same day, enroute to FOB Mizan and after an IED strike that killed two ANSF soldiers, a 3rd Platoon vehicle struck a second PPIED vic xxxxx. SGT Benjamin and CPL Davidson were thrown from the truck while PFC Paunescu remained injured in the turret. The patrol conducted five meter and 25-meter perimeter checks and ran to the stricken vehicle to assess the casualties. Upon realizing the Medic was wounded, PFC Berry assumed the role of primary medic without hesitation. He ran to the downed vehicle with his CLS bag to begin treating the casualties. PFC Berry and SGT Marsh assessed and treated SGT Benjamin for multiple leg wounds. Shortly after, enemy dismounts began shooting at the patrol. With no regard for his personal safety, PFC Berry began dragging SGT Benjamin behind cover, exposing himself to enemy fire, but ensuring the wounded Soldier's safety. Once the medic was treated and could perform his duties, PFC Berry and CPL Davidson applied a tourniquet and a splint to SGT Benjamin's leg. PFC Berry, despite never experiencing such a stressful combat situation, maintained his composure and calmly executed his CLS duties. He performed admirably, using CLS skills he learned in a brief, one-week class to assess, treat, and prep wounded soldiers for MEDEVAC. Once SGT Benjamin was stabilized, he and CPL Davidson moved to another wounded soldier, who PFC Berry gave an IV.

Despite the exhausting climb, the OP, the IEDs, and the treatment of casualties, PFC Berry continued to dismount in front of the vehicles for another 9 hours. Though extremely fatigued and risking heat exhaustion, he stayed out front to provide a heavy weapon capable of maneuvering in terrain the vehicles could not.

In summary, PFC Berry's professionalism and devotion to his wounded comrades exhibits the most admirable qualities of the United States Army Infantryman. Even with little time and experience in the military, he conducted himself with honor, loyalty, and personal courage during a highly dangerous and extremely stressful situation. His unwavering resolve during the engagement with the enemy OP, selfless treatment and protection of wounded soldiers, and courage under fire, showed despite his limited experience, he is capable of reacting as a seasoned, proficient soldier worthy of recognition.

On the 14th and 15th of June, 2nd Platoon was on a joint combat patrol to the southern end of the Chalikor Valley with Embedded Transition Team (ETT), Operational Detachment Alpha (ODA), Afghan National Army (ANA), and Afghan National Police (ANP). The patrol came under harassing Anti-Coalition Forces (ACF) fire on the morning of the 15th at approximately 06:00. At the time, SGT Rubio was gunning for ETT and he was vital in returning fire on multiple ACF positions. At 09:00, the patrol was engaged by 40 to 50 ACF in a complex attack with AK-47, PKM, SPG-9, RPG, and Dragonov fire. SGT Rubio was still gunning for ETT and his vehicle immediately drove into the attack under a hail of ACF fire and he flawlessly returned fire from his turret. SGT Rubio's turret was hit multiple times with ACF fire, but he showed no signs of fear and continued to engage the enemy. After about ten minutes of fighting, SGT Rubio's .50 Caliber machine gun went down and the Platoon Leader's vehicle was forced to cover both sectors and fire. Without being told, SGT Rubio immediately dismounted and began cross loading ammunition from the ETT vehicle to the platoon leader's gunner, CPL Kuhn, allowing him to engage multiple ACF positions. He then began returning fire with his M4 and M203 effectively suppressing the ACF in an orchard to the north of his position. Between ETT, SGT Rubio, and CPL Kuhn multiple ACF personnel and positions were both suppressed and destroyed.

During the heaviest parts of the fight, ACF had an overwhelming fire superiority and tactical advantage. To make matters worse, the platoon leader, 1LT Swintek, lost communications with the ODA team leader, CPT xxxxx, greatly jeopardizing command and control. The decision was made that 1LT Swintek would have to run to CPT xxxxx's vehicle in order to establish face-to-face communications. SGT Rubio volunteered to run with the Platoon Leader, with no regard to his own personnel safety, close to 200 meters through open terrain and no cover to CPT xxxxx's vehicle. While running, SGT Rubio returned fire, effectively covering the platoon leader's movement. Upon arriving, SGT Rubio noticed that one of the ODA team members, SFC xxxxx, was close to the point of heat exhaustion due to the fact that he had been running a 60mm mortar tube for close to twenty minutes on his own. SGT Rubio immediately assisted SFC xxxxx with a 60mm mortar tube. He carried ammunition and hung rounds for

SFC xxxxx, allowing him to catch his breath, but still suppress the ACF. SGT Rubio and SFC xxxxx effectively laid indirect fire on multiple ACF positions and as a result, the mortar tube was so hot from the volume of fire that they were forced to use bottled water to cool the tube off. While cooling off the tube, they received extremely accurate and heavy fire from the Northeast. Both individuals were forced to drop to the ground in order to avoid being shot. Regardless of the danger, they continued to fire the 60mm mortar tube, but were forced to low crawl while firing due to the heavy ACF fire. ACF rounds were impacting within inches of both SGT Rubio and SFC xxxxx, but they continued to fire the mortar tube until they ran out of ammunition. They then low crawled away from the tube in order to avoid being shot by ACF.

Once the mortar tube position ran out of ammunition, SGT Rubio low-crawled to 1LT Swintek's position to see if he could be of further assistance. At the time, 1LT Swintek was developing a new course of action with the ODA Team Leader. The ODA Team Leader and 1LT Swintek began receiving heavy and accurate fire from the east. 1LT Swintek began returning fire with his M4 and as a result could not hear SGT Rubio yelling for him to take cover because the volume of ACF fire was so heavy and accurate. SGT Rubio reached up and pulled him to the ground. Moments later, PKM rounds flew directly where the Platoon Leader had been standing, thus saving 1LT Swintek's life. Once the ODA Team Leader and 1LT Swintek came up with a plan, SGT Rubio and his platoon leader once again ran close to 200 meters back to their vehicle in order to begin maneuvering on the enemy. Upon arriving, SGT Rubio noticed that CPL Kuhn, the Platoon Leader's gunner, was trying to hold his ammunition while simultaneously firing his .50 Caliber machine gun because his ammunition can had been knocked lose by an ACF round. SGT Rubio put his own personnel safety aside, and climbed on the hood of the vehicle while under heavy fire and held the ammunition for CPL Kuhn allowing him to effectively engage and kill multiple ACF combatants. Rounds impacted on the windshield of vehicle, inches from SGT Rubio's leg. Regardless, he continued to hold the ammunition and eventually was able to fix the ammunition can. During that time, CPL Kuhn's accurate fire forced the ACF to begin breaking contact and he engaged and destroyed multiple ACF and a motorcycle as they were attempting to break contact. CPL Kuhn was almost black on ammunition so SGT Rubio began cross loading ammunition from both the ETT vehicle and other 2nd platoon vehicles, allowing CPL Kuhn to never cease his heavy and accurate fire on the ACF.

In summary, Sergeant Rubio's valorous actions on 15 June 2008 allowed coalition forces to establish fire superiority and gain a tactical advantage over ACF in an extremely complex attack. At times, the situation was dire and ACF appeared to be winning the battle, but SGT Rubio's courage inspired his subordinates, peers, and superiors to drive on in the face of the enemy. His actions while under heavy fire saved the life of his platoon leader and allowed coalition forces to sustain combat operations during a seven-hour firefight. There is no doubt that SGT Rubio's actions on that day were responsible for multiple enemy KIAs and WIAs and not only turned the tide of battle, but also prevented both injuries and possibly death to the members of 2nd Platoon. SGT Rubio's leadership, courage, and actions are in keeping with the finest traditions of military service and reflect great credit upon himself, Task Force Zabul, Regional Command South, CJTF 101, and the United States Army.

SGT Jamie Rubio
Team Dragon, 1-4 Infantry
June 2008

On the afternoon of 09 June 2008, while conducting a joint patrol with Afghan National Security Forces (ANSF) and Embedded Transition Team (ETT) in the northeast sector of the Arghendab District, 2nd Platoon came under a complex ambush from an estimated 8 to 10 anti-coalition forces (ACF). The platoon was attempting to maneuver through a choke point along the Arghendab River when the ACF initiated contact. The ambush was initiated with a SPG-9 recoilless rifle [round] that impacted approximately 10 meters from SGT Rubio and followed immediately with small arms fire. At the time, SGT Rubio was dismounted near the edge of the river attempting to survey how deep the fording site was. SGT Rubio dropped to the ground in order to avoid any shrapnel from the recoilless rifle fire, after which he maneuvered under direct fire back to his vehicle. During this time, the platoon began taking contact from both the North and West in the form of an 'L' shaped ambush. There were heavy volumes of PKM, AK-47, and recoilless rifle fire. The ACF transmissions on the iCOM indicated that the ACF were foreign fighters, which was evident because they were taking well-aimed shots and using complex battle drills in order to isolate our movement.

The Afghan National Security Forces (ANSF) vehicle was taking heavy volumes of fire that forced the ANSF to move away from their vehicle and seek cover in a nearby orchard. ACF had a superior tactical advantage due to an overwhelming presence on the high ground. M2 fire could not create any ACF casualties due to the terrain and an explosive weapon was needed. The platoon's MK19 and 60mm mortar tube were engaging the forces to the NE. The Platoon Leader, 1LT Swintek, told SGT Rubio to contact the ANSF via iCOM and direct them to move to their vehicle and engage the ACF position to the north with their RPGs. Due to the high volume of ACF fire, the ANSF were unable to move to their vehicle. Seeing this, SGT Rubio decided to take action himself and ran approximately 100 meters in the open and under direct fire from his vehicle to the ANSF vehicle. While he was running, there were PKM rounds impacting within two feet of his position, forcing him to return fire while running to the vehicle. When he got to the ANSF vehicle, he picked up an RPG, and fired two rockets at the ACF positions. While firing the RPGs, he was being heavily engaged by the ACF with PKM rounds impacting within six inches of his boots. Immediately after the impact of the second RPG, the ACF broke contact.

After firing the RPGs, SGT Rubio ran back to his vehicle and he was directed, by his Platoon Leader, to reposition his vehicle north, across the river, in order to cut off the ACF's retreat. While attempting to cross the river, his vehicle hit a drop off and was submerged up to the turret in the river with water rushing in. SGT Rubio quickly evacuated his entire team from the vehicle before leaving the vehicle himself, ensuring the safety of his Soldiers over his own personal safety. Before climbing out of the vehicle, SGT Rubio removed all sensitive items from his vehicle. He also assisted the platoon leader in swimming under the truck in order to attach a tow strap. SGT Rubio then climbed back into the submerged vehicle in order to put the vehicle into neutral, allowing it to be recovered.

In summary, Sergeant Rubio's valorous actions on 09 June 2008 forced the ACF to break contact during a complex ambush where the ACF had an overwhelming tactical advantage. In addition, he put the lives of his team well before his own, allowing them all to be safely evacuated from his vehicle while it was flooding. There is no doubt that SGT Rubio's actions on that day turned the tide of battle and saved the lives of members of his platoon. SGT Rubio's leadership, courage, and actions are in keeping with the finest traditions of military service and reflect great credit upon himself, Task Force Zabul, Regional Command South, CJTF 101, and the United States Army.

SGT Nolan Thomasee
Team Dragon, 1-4 Infantry
August 2005

On 29 August 2005, SGT Nolan F. Thomasee was returning from a reconnaissance patrol of MSR Crimson. The platoon had halted to conduct a communication check with Dragon Base. Upon establishing contact with the TOC, the patrol was informed of a possible I.E.D. attack along route Crimson. After a short maintenance halt, the Squad Leaders, along with the Platoon Sergeant and Platoon Leader, performed a map reconnaissance to identify possible choke points and ambush areas. After completing the maintenance halt, SGT Thomasee along with the rest of the Platoon, continued on to Camp Phoenix. Approximately two kilometers east from the maintenance halt, the Platoon drove into an ambush, initiated by an RPG and followed by small arms fire. As the second vehicle in the order of movement was attacked with the initial RPG strike, SGT Thomasee immediately jumped up in the turret with the M240 gunner, SPC Travis Stockdale. Immediately understanding the importance of his position by being the rear vehicle and the sectors of fire his vehicle was responsible for, SGT Thomasee did not hesitate to assume a critical secondary position within the turret. At this time, SPC Stockdale was engaging the enemy to the south of the convoy. Upon getting in the turret, SGT Thomasee immediately started scanning the northern flank of the patrol when he noticed another RPG being fired at his vehicle. SGT Thomasee immediately grabbed SPC Stockdale without hesitation and pulled him down inside the vehicle to brace for impact, placing his body between SPC Stockdale and the impending RPG. After a near miss, SGT Thomasee and his gunner commenced to engage targets in their respective sectors, successfully covering the platoon's vulnerable flanks and allowing the patrol to safely leave the engagement area. Through SGT Thomasee's courageous action, he helped the platoon to escape an enemy ambush without any serious damage or injuries to personnel or equipment.

On 29 August 2005, SFC Weiskittel was a key leader of a route reconnaissance patrol along MSR Crimson. Before beginning the return trip to Camp Phoenix, SFC Weiskittel received an intelligence report indicating a likely IED strike along MSR Crimson. SFC Weiskittel immediately disseminated the information effectively and quickly to all members of the platoon. After insuring that all soldiers were aware of the threat, SFC Weiskittel's planning allowed the patrol's squad and team leaders to prepare their respective vehicles for contact. When contact was made at one of the two predicted locations, the patrol was prepared to deal with the threat, as the attack did not come as a complete surprise; SFC Weiskittel's planning directly impacted the readiness and performance of the platoon's reaction to contact.

Upon receiving the first RPG strike, SFC Weiskittel immediately took control of the platoon radio net and alerted the entire patrol of the contact. SFC Weiskittel commenced to guide the platoon's fires calmly and accurately while directing firepower to enemy positions all around the patrol's perimeter. SFC Weiskittel's cool demeanor under fire inspired the entire platoon to maintain discipline. Squad and team leaders were able to look to SFC Weiskittel as an example in order to rally their ambushed soldiers to gain and maintain fire superiority over the enemy. SFC Weiskittel's direction and leadership allowed the platoon to overwhelm the enemy with devastating firepower and prevented further casualties due to the lack of accurate opposition fires.

During the middle of the firefight, SFC Weiskittel quickly planned and implemented a reconsolidation plan. Calmly and accurately describing the rally point, SFC Weiskittel was able to lead the platoon a safe distance away while receiving personnel and equipment reports from squad and team leaders. SFC Weiskittel's quick thinking allowed the platoon to effectively reconsolidate at a distant location from the ambush site, accurately report to higher casualty reports, and safely move the patrol out of harm's way.

After personally inspecting the platoon's sole casualty, SFC Weiskittel took the lead vehicle position and safely guided the patrol to Camp Phoenix. SFC Weiskittel successfully coordinated medical efforts with

Camp Phoenix enroute, allowing the casualty to quickly seek medical attention. SFC Weiskittel's actions directly impacted the success of the patrol, the failure of the enemy ambush, and saved the lives of soldiers within the platoon. Without SFC Weiskittel's personal example, courage, calm under fire, and planning abilities, the platoon would have been rendered combat ineffective.

SSG Matthew Ritenour
Team Apache, 1-4 Infantry
September 2007

On 4 September 2007 at 05:00 local FOB Baylough, in the Day Chopan district, Zabul Province, Afghanistan, was attacked by an enemy force estimated at over 180 fighters. The attack included 82mm mortar fire, 82mm recoilless rifle, RPGs, heavy machine guns, and small arms with at least four snipers. This attack was following an attack the previous night with mortar, RPGs and small arms that lasted over two hours.

SSG Ritenour's squad was responsible for our northern sector at the most vulnerable point in our defensive perimeter. This position is referred to as the Rock Guard.

As the FOB was hit, SSG Ritenour's squad got into position under direct and indirect fires, bounding across 150 meters of mainly open terrain to get into place. An enemy sniper and machine gun team emplaced themselves 300 meters away from rock guard with direct line of sight to the position. SSG Ritenour's squad was effectively fixed and was not able to return fire. The enemy continued to infiltrate more infantry into the cover and concealment of the orchard and river bed directly north of SSG Ritenour's squad position. During the initial exchange of automatic weapons fire, SPC Hargus was wounded with a graze on his neck, PFC Kanewske was wounded when a bullet entered his right wrist, and PFC Simms was wounded as a bullet entered his right hand. SSG Ritenour pulled all three of the Soldiers to safety under direct machine gun fire. PFC Byrd, the medic, and CLS-qualified Soldiers at the position administered initial care to these wounded Soldiers but could not move them the rest of the way to the aid station because of the enemy fire.

As SSG Ritenour was moving to another area within the position to maintain contact with the enemy, he was shot in the ACH by sniper fire. The bullet penetrated the helmet and continued into his skull. PFC Byrd assessed him, but left SSG Ritenour's helmet on because of the heavy fire. SSG Ritenour maintained consciousness and reported the situation to the TOC as well as the injuries, including his own. SSG Ritenour's injury left him without the ability to move the right side of his body.

Although badly wounded, he kept his squad on the position and focused on the task at hand: keep the enemy out of the wire. SSG Ritenour ensured his squad was ready when the enemy stopped firing long enough for his squad to return fire and allow the wounded to be removed. The squad was able to do this and the two most severely wounded were extracted, but SSG Ritenour remained at his position leading his squad and adjusting indirect fire onto the enemy less than 300 meters north of his location. The information he provided allowed the Platoon Sergeant to get indirect fires, 500 pound bombs, and AH-64 direct fires on enemy positions throughout the northern sector of the FOB, killing and wounding over twelve enemy fighters, forcing their retreat.

As the second wave of the attack slowed and the enemy began to withdraw from their positions, SSG Ritenour had been wounded for over an hour. SSG Ritenour was finally removed from the Rock Guard and brought to the aid station by stretcher. He still asked about his squad and their condition as he was placed on the MEDEVAC helicopter.

SSG Ritenour displayed the highest degree of selflessness and bravery by pulling injured Soldiers to safety while under direct machine gun fire and by his insistence to stay in the fight after being wounded. SSG Ritenour's calm and professionalism while severely wounded inspired his squad to hold steady and successfully defend the most vulnerable point of the walls during a crucial fight to keep the enemy from overrunning FOB Baylough.

SPC Silas W. Betten
May 2010

SPC Silas W. Betten was the M2 .50 cal gunner for SSG Wade's M1151 HMMWV on the afternoon of 06 May 2010 when the Quick Reaction Force was requested to over watch an IED that was found earlier in the morning. Shortly after the IED was found, a storm moved into the Tangay Valley and heavy rain began to fall. At that time, the platoon leader, 1LT Meegan requested a mounted QRF to move to the IED site in order to allow the over watch element to be protected from the elements. SSG Wade maneuvered his M1151 into position to maintain a cordon around the IED, while the other two M1151s were placed on a hill directly west of the IED in order to maintain security on high-speed avenues of approach.

Once the storm passed through the valley, the enemy realized that there were three M1151s just outside the orchards where the IED was located. The enemy amassed forces and prepared to attack the over-watch element. As an Explosive Ordinance Disposal team and dismounted QRF approached the mounted element, enemy forces initiated contact against the over-watch and QRF elements with PKM, 82mm mortars, RPG and AK-47's, from the north and west of the over-watch position. With his truck commander dismounted and awaiting EOD's arrival, SPC Betten took control of his vehicle and immediately returned accurate fire against the enemy which was maneuvering toward his vehicle. The enemy continued to engage accurately with PKM and attempted to airburst RPGs over the gun truck's turret occupied by SPC Betten. With the enemy's morale high and the number of fighters estimated between 50 and 60, SPC Betten continued to engage enemy forces that closed within 100 meters of his vehicle while accurately reporting enemy locations to 1LT Meegan at great risk to himself. With the QRF and over-watch elements in contact, the Taliban sensed Combat Outpost Baylough's vulnerability and initiated an assault with RPGs, PKM and DshK fire.

After defeating the initial attack, the QRF maneuvered into a support by fire position to assist the COP which was still in contact. The Air Weapons Team, soon after coming on station, notified the ground commander that they had limited time to provide cover due to incoming weather. 1LT Meegan briefed EOD on the plan for the reduction of the IED. SSG Wade loaded the EOD personnel into his M1151 and maneuvered towards the IED. SPC Betten provided close over-watch for the EOD personnel as they blew the IED in place and conducted site exploitation. Once EOD operations were complete, all elements returned to COP Baylough.

SPC Betten's actions on 06 May 2010 resulted in all elements sustaining zero casualties and assisted in increasing the overall security of the Day Chopan District, Zabul Province, Afghanistan.

CPT Cleland
October 2007

On 25 October 2007, during the second day of the ISAF and ANSF advance into the Davudzay Valley in the Deh Chopan area, ETT elements from 2-205 BDE in the town of Davudzay reported finding an IED vicinity grid 42S xxxxx. CPT Cleland was located in a support by fire position on the southern side of the valley near xxxxx in order to provide elements of the ANA KANDAK and ETT with over watch. With limited combat power available as an escort, CPT Cleland had his vehicle accompany the Navy Explosive Ordnance Disposal Team UAH from the mouth of the valley in the east into the town, which is only accessible via a narrow one-lane road. CPT Cleland and his Navy EOD reached the IED site, linking up with ETT and ANA on site and established security for the EOD. After exploiting and destroying the IED. CPT Cleland received a call from the Venom ETT element stating they had found a cache of recoilless rifle rounds approximately 500 meters to the west of the IED site. Accompanied by Navy EODC xxxxx and Navy EODC xxxxx, Navy EOD & CPT Cleland requested and were escorted by an ANA squad up to the cache point, which was on a hill mass on the north edge of the Davudzay bowl, approximately one kilometer to the west of the large ridgeline near the villages of Barlagho and Abdollah Kalay that was the objective for the day's attack.

As CPT Cleland and his dismounted element approached the hill, ACM fighters began engaging the ANA ETT elements who were using the hill with RPG and PKM fire from the objective area. The volume of fire was heavy enough to suppress the elements on the hilltop, who were under cover when CPT Cleland arrived. CPT Cleland linked up with MAJ Harmon of 2-205 BDE ETT at the peak of the hill, who was with the ANA KANDAK Commander. MAJ Harmon informed CPT Cleland that the assault had stalled under the enemy fusillade of PKM machine gun and RPG rockets. CPT Cleland immediately suggested the use of A Company 1-4 IN indirect fire support in the form of 120mm mortars. Knowing that ANA and ETT elements were danger close to the enemy attack and any subsequent friendly indirect fire support, CPT Cleland worked up a series of polar fire missions, delivering mortar fire into the rear of the enemy and then walking the indirect tire forward over the enemy locations towards his friendly front line trace while minimizing the risk of short rounds.

Because of radio difficulties, CPT Cleland had to relay the fire commands through Navy EODC xxxxx who was positioned with the cache approximately 15 meters behind CPT Cleland. Due to the restrictive terrain and dead space near CPT Cleland's position, many of the mortar fire corrections had to be done with CPT Cleland exposing himself to the enemy. Braving enemy AK assault rifle and PKM machine gun fire, on multiple occasions CPT Cleland observed the impact of 120mm mortar rounds and made the subsequent adjustments onto various enemy attack by fire positions and pockets of armed resistance. His efforts opened the way for the ANA to gain a foothold on the enemy ridgeline.

Despite the initial success of ANA and ETT, CPT Cleland's position was still receiving PKM and RPG fire from the more northern portions of the ridge, as the ENY was arranged in a generally north-south defensive line on the ridge. CPT Cleland again began making small adjustments and repeating the fire for effect up the ridge from south to north. After approximately six iterations of firing for effect the enemy had been driven off the backside of the ridgeline and was attempting to reposition to the north and make for a small pass in the northwest corner of the valley. In an effort to seal the enemy in the Davudzay Valley and complete their destruction with ANA forces, CPT Cleland adjusted fire to block their escape and was informed by the ETT that the enemy had begun moving south instead, towards Barlagho and Abdullah Kalay.

It was evident in the Task Force Zabul TOC from the Predator UAV feed, that the 120mm mortar tire was having an adverse effect on the enemy's ability to occupy their ABFs. Groups of enemy fighters started to displace and regroup at a rock pile at the base of their ABF positions to reorganize their attack or conduct a hasty defense. CPT Cleland's mortars continued to target the enemy ABFs, forcing no less than 15 to20 Taliban to move to their ORP near the rock pile. At this point CPT Cleland began receiving recoilless rifle fire from the southern end of the valley near the crews of A/1-4 IN and ETT UAHs had also received recoilless rifle and some small arms fire back at the IED site. CPT Cleland, with the ETT Joint Fires Officer and subsequently the JTAC & CPT Piluek at TF Zabul, targeted the enemy with a pair of 500lb bombs dropped on the rock pile. It was estimated that over 20 Taliban were killed with the air strike. The close air support ultimately broke the enemy's will to fight. CPT Cleland's heroic actions not only resulted in saving the lives or our ANSF allies, but allowed them to seize enemy terrain, and subsequently killing them.

SGT Ruehs
November 2008

SGT Ruehs was driving the Hemmit Wrecker as the third vehicle in a four-vehicle convoy moving south along Highway 1 towards Kandahar Air Field on 28 November 2008 when the convoy was hit with a complex Improvised Explosive Device ambush. At approximately 11:00, near the village of Shari Safa, the ambush was initiated with a one-hundred-pound ammonium nitrate command wire IED detonated in a culvert as the second vehicle passed. The resulting explosion completely destroyed the Mine Resistant Ambush Protected vehicle, severed the engine from the crew compartment, and critically injured the four occupants: SGT Acosta, SPC Lesnick, PFC Parker, and SGT Alexander.

As soon as the IED was detonated, SGT Ruehs responded without hesitation to help secure the area and began pulling the wounded Soldiers from the destroyed MRAP. Fuel was gushing from the MRAP, and there were damaged 40-millimeter Mark 19 grenades scattered all over the area. With no regard to his own safety, SGT Ruehs reached SGT Alexander first who was unconscious, bleeding, and draped across the top of the crew compartment. With the assistance of SSG Weaver, SGT Ruehs pulled SGT Alexander from the MRAP and began to assess his wounds and render first aid. SGT Alexander's wound to his buttock was bleeding profusely, and SGT Ruehs applied direct pressure and bandaged the wound with a hemorrhage control bandage.

A few minutes after SGT Ruehs and the other truck commanders in the convoy dismounted to help the casualties, they were engaged by Anti-Coalition Forces from the south of Highway One with heavy weapons and small arms fire. When the small arms fire started, SGT Ruehs was behind cover treating SGT Alexander's wounds. The IED ejected SPC Lesnick from the MRAP and threw him into an open field to the south. The impact broke SPC Lesnick's femur, pelvis, and both forearms, leaving him conscious but incapacitated and completely exposed to enemy fire. With Anti-Coalition Forces fire impacting all around him, SGT Ruehs, with the help of SPC Brown, selflessly left cover, secured SPC Lesnick by his body armor, and dragged him out of direct Anti-Coalition Forces fire. SGT Ruehs dragged SPC Lesnick out of the field and up a loose gravel embankment to safety behind the destroyed engine block while SPC Sumner and SGT Land laid down heavy volumes of cover fire. As soon as all of the casualties were behind cover, SGT Ruehs returned fire with his personal weapon and returned to his Hemmit Wrecker. SGT Ruehs then moved the wrecker up to establish a more secure casualty collection point by strategically positioning his vehicle to provide cover.

Once the Anti-Coalition Forces broke contact and the area was secured, SGT Ruehs then returned to the casualty collection point to continue to provide first aid. SGT Ruehs splinted SPC Lesnick's broken forearms, finished bandaging SGT Alexander's multiple lacerations, and initiated the IV for SGT Alexander. Throughout the entire incident, SGT Ruehs remained calm and professional and constantly reassured the wounded Soldiers until the medevac helicopters arrived.

In summary, SGT Ruehs's valorous actions on 28 November 2008 were directly responsible for saving the lives of SPC Lesnick and SGT Alexander during a complex IED ambush throughout which the Anti-Coalition Forces had an overwhelming tactical advantage. In addition, he put the lives of his fellow Soldiers well before his own preventing any further injury from the direct fire engagement. There is no doubt that SGT Ruehs' actions on that day turned the tide of battle and saved the lives of his fellow Soldiers.

SGT Sturgeon
May 2010

On the morning of 09 May 2010, SGT Sturgeon was conducting a dismounted combat patrol, west of COP Baylough, to TRP 5. While moving towards TRP 5 the patrol began receiving ICOM chatter that the Taliban was tracking the patrol through the village, and wanted to attack. At that time, SGT Sturgeon and his team were moved to the northern rock spur of TRP 2, where they could provide over watch as the patrol moved through the village of Basyan. Once the patrol was through the village, Alpha Team fell in behind the patrol. As 2nd Squad continued to move west through Basyan ICOM chatter increased and Taliban began talking about attacking the patrol. The patrol continued to push to the west clearing a footpath through the orchards.

Just west of Basyan while still in the orchards, the patrol was engaged in a close complex ambush from the south by multiple Taliban armed with PKM's and AK-47's, and from the west by a Taliban mortar team. Despite the enemy's high morale and almost equal numbers SGT Sturgeon immediately began to engage the enemy with M4 and M203 fire despite PKM, and AK-47 rounds impacting within a foot of himself and his team, along with 82MM mortar fire landing within 80 meters. He encouraged his men to do the same, all at great personal risk to himself. Once the ambush had been defeated, SGT Sturgeon led his men through the orchards in order to clear the area of enemy forces so the patrol could continue on to TRP 5.

While clearing the orchards after the ambush, SGT Sturgeon's team began receiving accurate sniper fire. SGT Sturgeon led his team to cover while under accurate enemy fire from a determined enemy and assisted in calling for fire against the sniper. After mortars were called against the sniper, SGT Sturgeon finished clearing the orchard with his team. He then pushed his team up onto TRP 5 to provide covering fire, while the rest of the patrol secured TRP 5. After establishing his team in a support by fire position, he continued to engage Taliban numbering 20 – 25 to the west of TRP 5.

An hour into the battle an Air Weapons Team (AWT) came on station to support the patrol and due to the enemy's high morale began receiving RPG fire from a rock formation near the entrance to the town of Davudzay. AWT and the patrol then fired on the rock formation finally causing Taliban to break contact and flee west. At 1625 [hours] the elements broke down off of TRP 5 and started heading east back towards COP Baylough using the AWT as cover for the exfil. At approximately 1808 hours, all elements arrived back at Baylough.

SGT Summers
July 2007

On the morning of 23 July 2007, SGT Summers was conducting a routine mounted combat patrol in the Arghendab district of Zabul Province, Afghanistan. He was the mechanic of 3rd Platoon, Bravo Company, 1-4 Infantry during the patrol to the local village of Barghantu to conduct a shura with the village elders. On the return trip back to Firebase Lane, the five-vehicle convoy came under heavy small arms, RPG, 82mm recoilless rifle and PKM machine gun fire. SGT Summers was in the HMMWV located in the middle of the convoy when the platoon was ambushed by a group of 50-plus insurgents no more than 100 meters away off to the right side of the vehicles. The convoy stopped as per the platoon standard operating procedures in order to return fire and achieve fire superiority. Shortly thereafter, the call was given over the radio to break contact due to the overwhelming enemy firepower. SGT Summers noticed that the lead HMMWV was smoking from the RPG's that impacted on the front of the vehicle. Two other up-armored HMMWV's passed by his HMMWV before SGT Summers' HMMWV began to move. SGT Summers noticed that 1st Squad had some casualties as his vehicle passed by the damaged HMMWV.

SGT Summers' vehicle drove around to the flank of the enemy ambush before it stopped. Once the backside of the enemy ambush was exposed to SGT Summers' HMMWV, he dismounted in order to return fire. With complete disregard for his own life, SGT Summers exited the HMMWV under a hail of enemy gunfire that was ricocheting off the hood and top of his vehicle. He returned fire towards the enemy insurgents who were now running straight for his vehicle and engaging with AK-47s and RPGs. SGT Summers could see at least two dozen of the enemy fighters and he began to engage them at close range, causing the enemy to break contact. SGT Summers would pick up his rate of fire every time his gunner was reloading, suppressing the enemy long enough for the machine gunner to return fire. SGT Summers completely exposed himself to very accurate and effective enemy fire in order to launch an AT-4. He launched the AT-4 while rounds whizzed by his head, destroying three enemy fighters trying to maneuver on their position.

While SGT Summers was engaging the backside of the enemy ambush, Soldiers from 1st and 2nd Squads were gathering the casualties from the burning HMMWV and attempting to break contact to his location. SGT Summers continued to suppress the remaining enemy fighters in order to assist his fellow Soldiers in reaching his location. As soon as the remaining Soldiers made it to his location, SGT Summers learned that one of his fellow Soldiers had instantly died from the initial RPG blasts on the lead HMMWV. SGT Summers realized that he had to continue fighting in order to save the lives of his fellow Soldiers. Shortly thereafter, the decision was made to break contact to the designated air MEDEVAC site near the next village. As soon as the HMMWVs began moving again to the next village, the element took another barrage of overwhelming accurate enemy fire from small arms and RPGs. SGT Summers was among the dismounted Soldiers who were walking along side the HMMWV's as they moved out of the ambush area. SGT Summers continued to return fire, suppressing the enemy even though many rounds were ricocheting of the HMMWVs next to him. The enemy finally broke contact once the element reached the MEDEVAC site.

SGT Summers' actions on that fateful day demonstrated absolute courage under intense enemy fire. He was a beacon of hope to his fellow Soldiers during those intense movements. The survival of his fellow Soldiers was possible through SGT Summers' ability to motivate them through action. His valiant actions directly resulted in the destruction of more than 25 insurgent fighters and the evacuation of his fellow Soldiers. SGT Summers' actions exhibit the epitome of valor in the most extreme of combat situations.

FINAL SALUTES

As the book itself crawls to a close, the lives of the Warriors we have lost continue on through the men who served alongside them, their families, and you the reader. This is not by any means a final salute to our Warriors, but a humbled act of honor towards their memory. In the spirit of that, I offer the following poem inspired by the style of *In Flanders Fields* by John McCrae, a veteran of the First World War.

In Afghan Lands our Soldiers go,
Among the mountains, high and low,
They'd guard that place; and not ask why
Their brothers bravely fighting, die
For better life to bloom and grow

They are now dead. Few years ago
They lived and breathed, and as we know
Watched and watched over us in life
Eternally

Take up their story for us to know
To them on bended knee we go
In awe; to continue with their life
To share their burdens and their strife
They have not died, as memories show
Within our minds

Fallen Warriors

CPL Isaiah Calloway, *d. 30 October 2006,*
Arghendab District

CPL Conor B. Masterson, *d. 08 April 2007,*
Arghendab District

CPL Zachary R. Endsley, *d. 23 July 2007,*
Arghendab District

PFC Tan Ngo, *d. 27 August 2008,*
Mizan District

MAJ Brian M. Mescall, *d. 09 January 2009,*
Tarnak Wa Jaldak District

SGT Jason R. Parsons, *d. 09 January 2009,*
Tarnak Wa Jaldak District

CPL Joseph M. Hernandez, *d. 09 January 2009,*
Tarnak Wa Jaldak District

CPT Mark A. Garner, *d. 06 July 2009,*
Den Chopan District

SSG Marc A. Arizmendez, *d. 06 July 2010,*
Qalat District

SPC Roger Lee, *d. 06 July 2010,*
Qalat District

PFC Michael S. Pridham, d. *06 July 2010,*
Qalat District

CPL Isaiah Calloway

CPL Isaiah Calloway was born on the 8th of September 1983. He grew up in up in Jackson, Florida and entered the Army on the 1st of October 2003. CPL Calloway attended his basic training and AIT at Fort Benning, Georgia, becoming an Infantryman. Upon completion of AIT, CPL Calloway left Fort Benning to his first duty station at the Joint Multinational Readiness Center, Hohenfels, Germany.

CPL Calloway assigned to the Scout Section in C Company, 1st Battalion, 4th Infantry Regiment. His outstanding work effort and dedication to duty resulted in CPL Calloway being promoted to Specialist within a year. He was later assigned to 2nd PLT, Charlie Company from which he deployed to Afghanistan in July.

CPL Calloway was a great Soldier and we knew him as a Soldier. Isaiah Calloway was also known as "Daddy". CPL Isaiah Calloway is survived by his wife Alecia Denee, his daughters Alexius Michelle (4 yrs. Old), Aleiah Savannah (3 yrs. Old) and son Isaiah Jr.(2 yr. old)

CPL Calloway's awards and decorations include the Purple Heart, National Defense Service Medal, Afghanistan Campaign Medal, Global War on Terrorism Service Medal, NATO Medal, Expert Infantrymen's Badge, Combat Infantrymen's Badge, and Driver and Mechanic's Badge. CPL Calloway was a true professional and lived up to the Warrior Ethos. All Soldiers looked to and followed his example. CPL Calloway was a superb Soldier and will be missed by everyone that knew and worked with him.

CPL Conor B. Masterson

CPL Conor Gerard Masterson was born on 22 March, 1986. He was a native of Woodbury, Minnesota where he entered the Army on 28 February 2005. CPL Masterson entered Basic Training at Fort Knox, Kentucky, on 3 March 2005 and continued to Advanced Individual Training at Fort Sam Houston, Texas, on 12 May 2005. Upon completion of AIT, CPL Masterson left Fort Sam Houston for his first duty station at the Joint Multinational Readiness Center, Hohenfels, Germany.

CPL Masterson has served as an ambulance driver while attached to Alpha Company, 1-4 Infantry then later served as a forward line medic for Bravo Company where he ultimately deployed to Afghanistan in support of Operation Enduring Freedom under the command of the International Security Assistance Force (ISAF).

CPL Masterson, known by friends as "Dougy", was well thought of by his peers and showed a great desire to excel in his chosen field. *"He was always so excited as he learned each new (medical) procedure and helped somebody,"* his mother said. She continued to say, *"He was really proud, and we were really proud of him."*

CPL Masterson had been married less than a year to his wife, Lorena, and planned to attend college to study medicine.

CPL Masterson's awards and decorations include the Purple Heart, Bronze Star Medal w/ "V" device, National Defense Service Medal, Global War on Terrorism Expeditionary Medal, Global War on Terrorism Service Medal, Army Service Ribbon, and the Overseas Ribbon. CPL Masterson was a true professional and lived up to the Warrior Ethos. He will be missed by everyone that knew him.

CPL Zachary R. Endsley

We gather today to pay tribute to and honor Corporal Zachary Endsley who died tragically just one week ago while engaged in combat with the enemy in Afghanistan. While we recognize that little can be said to ease the impact of his loss, on his family, and on this unit and community, this memorial and our conscious effort today to reflect on Corporal Endsley and his sacrifice is part of the healing process.

Corporal Endsley epitomized the greatest characteristics and values of our Army. By his exceptional performance day to day, compassion for his buddies, positive personality, and passion for Soldiering, Zachary reflected the traits that set him apart and made him shine as a Soldier and friend in the battalion.

Zachary distinguished himself by his selfless dedication to duty, the mission and his unit. His commander, Captain Edwards, remembers Corporal Endsley as fearless, a trait that no doubt gave courage and confidence to his battle buddies during this past five months of combat.

Respected by all, Corporal Endsley was remembered by his team leader, Sergeant Thompson, as that unique Soldier who approached every task with a smile. His sense of professionalism, evident even in such a young Soldier of 21, was clear to all who served with him.

What all have shared, to a man, is that Zachary Endsley possessed an infectiously positive personality, ingrained with integrity and a tremendous sense of humor that buoyed his buddies' spirits and the company even in the hardest of times. Well known for his talent with the guitar, Zachary drew a crowd every time he brought out the instrument to lighten the mood or ease the stress through a funny song.

Corporal Endsley will be remembered for his dedication, caring and compassion. As Sam Edwards remembered, Zachary demonstrated his love and dedication to his friends to the last.

On behalf of the Battalion and Corporal Endsley's family, I thank you all for honoring his sacrifice and remembering this young man so dedicated to duty and his company mates. Remembering Zachary Endsley, honoring his sacrifice and continuing his example of selfless dedication now becomes our sacred charge and the Warriors of 1st Battalion, 4th Infantry Regiment collectively endeavor to preserve his legacy as we continue the mission – as Zachary would have expected.

PFC Tan Ngo

PFC Tan Q. Ngo was born on June 23, 1988. He grew up in Beaverton, Oregon and entered the Army on October 10, 2007 as an Infantryman. PFC Ngo attended Basic Training and AIT at Fort Benning, Georgia. Upon completion of AIT, PFC Ngo left Fort Benning for his first duty assignment at the 1st Battalion, 4th Infantry Regiment at the Joint Multinational Readiness Center, Hohenfels, Germany, where he was assigned to 1st Platoon, Cherokee Company. His outstanding work ethic and dedication to duty resulted in Tan's selection as an M240 Machine Gunner. He deployed to Afghanistan in June of 2008 with Team Cherokee.

PFC Ngo was a great Soldier, dedicated to the accomplishment of the mission and his fellow Soldiers. Tan Ngo was known to his fellow 1st Platoon Soldiers as "No Go," and could always be depended upon for a good laugh. PFC Tan Ngo is survived by his mother Binh T. Sam, his father Ut Q. Ngo, and a younger brother, Tien Q. Ngo.

PFC Ngo's awards and decorations include the Bronze Star Medal, the Purple Heart, the National Defense Service Medal, the Afghanistan Campaign Medal with Campaign Star, the Global War on Terrorism Service Medal, the Army Service Ribbon, the NATO Medal and the Combat Infantryman's Badge.

PFC Tan Ngo was a true professional who lived the Warrior Ethos. His fellow Soldiers looked to and followed his example. PFC Ngo was a superb Warrior and will be missed by everyone who knew him.

MAJ Brian M. Mescall

MAJ Brian Michael Mescall was born on 18 April 1975, in Teaneck, NJ. He attended The Citadel, the Military College of South Carolina, where he majored in History, receiving his commission on 17 May 1997.

MAJ Mescall's assignments included Tank and Scout Platoon Leader, 1-72 AR; Company Executive Officer, A CO 120th AG Reception BN; Troop Executive Officer, A Troop, 4-7 Cavalry; Assistant Regimental S-3, Squadron Logistics Officer, and Ghost Troop Commander with 2nd Armored Cavalry Regiment; Battalion Maneuver Advisor, MiTT 342; Company Team Observer/Controller Timberwolves O/C Team, and Battalion Operations Officer in the 1st Battalion, 4th Infantry Regiment. He served overseas for two years in the Republic of Korea, two years in Iraq, two years in Germany, and for the past seven months in Afghanistan as Task Force Zabul's Chief of Staff.

His Awards include the Bronze Star (3OLC), the Meritorious Service Medal, the Army Commendation Medal (3 OLC), the Air Force Achievement Medal, the Iraqi Campaign Medal (four star devices), the Presidential Unit Citation, the Joint Meritorious Unit Award, the National Defense Service Medal, the Afghan Campaign Medal, the Global War on Terrorism Expeditionary Medal, the Global War on Terrorism Service Medal, the Korean Defense Service Medal, the Army Service Ribbon, the Army Overseas Ribbon (with numeral 3) and the Combat Action Badge.

He is survived by his son Nathan, his parents John and Margaret, his brother John, and his two sisters Jamie and Stacey.

SGT Jason R. Parsons

SGT Jason Ray Parsons was born 31 October 1984 in North Carolina. On 11 December 2003, SGT Parsons entered into the Army and began his Infantry OSUT Basic Training at FT. Benning, GA. SGT Parsons completed his Infantry OSUT Training and was assigned to Headquarters and Headquarters Company, 1st Battalion, 4th Infantry Regiment, Joint Multinational Readiness Center, Hohenfels on 20 February 2004 as a M113 driver and rifleman. SGT Parsons served with Headquarters and Headquarters Company for four years when he volunteered to join Cherokee Company, 1st Battalion, 4th Infantry Regiment, already deployed to Zabul Province, Afghanistan in support of Operation Enduring Freedom VIII. Upon arriving to Afghanistan, SGT Parsons was assigned to the Personnel Security Detachment for Headquarters Platoon at Forward Operating Base Lagman, Zabul Province, Afghanistan. SGT Parsons's motivation and dedication led him to be assigned as a UAH Driver for the PSD. His attention to detail and hard work was a great asset for the PSD element. SGT Parsons was a great Soldier and was essential to securing freedom for Afghanistan.

SGT Parsons's awards and decorations include the Bronze Star Medal, Purple Heart, National Defense Service Medal, Afghanistan Campaign Service Medal, Global War on Terrorism Service Medal, Army Service Medal, Overseas Service Medal, Army Achievement Medal, Combat Infantryman's Badge, Good Conduct Medal, the Combat Infantryman's Badge and a NATO Medal.

SGT Parsons was a true professional and lived up to the Warrior Ethos. His fellow Soldiers looked up to him and followed his example. SGT Parsons was a superb Warrior and will be missed by everyone who knew and worked with him.

SGT Parsons is survived by his wife, Elvira, his stepsons, Manuel and Daniel and his stepdaughter, Jasmin

CPL Joseph M. Hernandez

CPL Joseph Michael Hernandez was born 26 February 1984, in Hammond IN. On 28 April 2005, two years after completing high school, he entered the Army at the Indianapolis MEPS station. After completing Basic Infantry OSUT training at FT. Benning, GA, he was assigned to A Company, 1-3 IN at Fort McNair from 11 October 2005 to 17 October 2007. After serving with 1-3 Infantry at Fort McNair, CPL Hernandez was assigned to A Company 1st Battalion, 4th Infantry Regiment, Joint Multinational Readiness Center, Hohenfels, Germany as an automatic rifleman, and later assigned to Headquarters and Headquarters Company, 1st Battalion, 4th Infantry Regiment. In December 2008, CPL Hernandez volunteered to serve with Cherokee Company 1st Battalion, 4th Infantry Regiment, already deployed to Zabul Province, Afghanistan in support of Operation Enduring Freedom VIII. Upon arriving to support Team Cherokee, CPL Hernandez was assigned to Headquarters Platoon as a Gunner for the Personnel Security Detachment. His outstanding work ethic resulted in CPL Hernandez's becoming a MK 19 and M240B machine gunner for the PSD. CPL Hernandez was a great Soldier who was dedicated to the accomplishment of the mission and to his fellow Soldiers.

CPL Hernandez's awards and decorations include the Bronze Star Medal, Purple Heart, Army Commendation Medal, Army Achievement Medal, National Defense Service Ribbon, Afghanistan Campaign Service Medal, Global War on Terrorism Service Medal, Army Service Ribbon, Good Conduct Medal, and NATO Medal and the Combat Infantryman's Badge.

CPL Hernandez was a true professional and lived up to the Warrior Ethos. His fellow Soldiers looked up to him and followed his example. CPL Hernandez was a superb Warrior and will be missed by everyone who knew and worked with him.

CPL Hernandez is survived by his wife Alison Yvonne and his two sons Jacob and Noah.

CPT Mark A. Garner

CPT Mark Andess Garner was born on 17 March 1979 in Elkin, NC. He graduated from the United States Military Academy at West Point in 2002 with a Bachelor of Science in Engineering Management. Upon graduation from the military academy, he was commissioned as a 2nd Lieutenant.

Upon completion of the Infantry Officer's Basic Course and Ranger School, CPT Garner was assigned to the 3rd Battalion, 325th Airborne Infantry Regiment as well as the 2nd Battalion, 508th Infantry Regiment, Fort Bragg, NC. He served as a Rifle Platoon Leader, Company Executive Officer, Battalion S-1, and completed two combat tours in Iraq. He completed the Infantry Captains' Career course in December 2006, and was assigned to the 1-4 Infantry Regiment in Hohenfels, Germany serving as Battalion S-4 and Company Commander for B CO 1-4 Infantry.

CPT Garner was known by his peers to be an approachable leader who no matter how stressful the environment always had a smile on his face. CPT Garner loved to be involved in every aspect of his company, from individual Soldiers to the mission at hand.

CPT Garner's awards and decorations include the Ranger Tab, Combat Infantryman's Badge, Parachutist Badge, Army Commendation Medal (1 Oak Leaf Cluster), Army Achievement Medal (1 Oak Leaf Cluster), Bronze Star Medal and the Purple Heart Medal.

CPT Garner is survived by his wife, Nikayla Myers of Jonesville, NC, his mother and father Don and Beth Garner and as he put it, his "two adorable fuzzy kitty cats, Buzz and Lily". CPT Garner will be truly missed by all and well-remembered by all who know him.

SSG Marc A. Arizmendez

Staff Sergeant Arizmendez was born on 31 March 1980, in Anaheim, CA. He enlisted in the Army 21 Jan 1999. He completed Basic and Advanced Individual Training at FT. Lee VA. SSG Arizmendez's duty assignments include: 1st Battalion, 33rd Field Artillery at Warner Barracks, GM from 20 September 1999 to 11 October 2001, 1st Battalion, 9th Calvary Regiment at FT Hood, TX from 12 October 2001 to 10 February 2002, Headquarters and Headquarters Company, 2-2 Infantry Regiment at Vilseck, GM, Headquarters and Headquarters Company 1-4 Infantry Regiment at Hohenfels, GM from 01 September 2005 to 12 June 2008, 501st CSF Co in FT. Bliss, TX from 11 June 2009 to 11 June 2009. SSG Arizmendez deployed to Iraq as a member of the 2-2 IN in support of Operation Iraqi Freedom. On 01 March 2010 SSG Arizmendez deployed with Team Dragon serving as Chief Mechanic to 2nd Platoon in Zabul Province Afghanistan in support of Operation Enduring Freedom.

SSG Arizmendez's awards and decorations include the Bronze Star Medal, Purple Heart, Meritorious Service Medal, Army Commendation Medal, Army Achievement Medal, Good Conduct Medal, National Defense Service Medal, Afghanistan Campaign Medal, Iraq Campaign Medal, Global War on Terrorism Service Medal, NATO Medal, Combat Action Badge and Driver Mechanic Badge.

SSG Arizmendez was a Non-Commissioned Officer with an unequaled character. He is survived by his wife Barbara, his daughter Jennifer and son Justin.

SPC Roger Lee

Specialist Lee was born on 2 February 1984, in Monterey, California. On 19 November 2007, he entered the Army as an 11B Infantryman. After completing one station unit training at Fort Benning, Georgia, he was assigned to Charlie Company, 1st Battalion, 4th Infantry Regiment in Hohenfels, Germany from 3 March 2008 to 7 October 2009. On 20 June 2008, SPC Lee deployed to with C Company as a Rifleman at Forward Operating Base Lane in the Arghandab District of Zabul Province. On 8 October 2009, SPC Lee was assigned to Delta Company as rifleman. On 29 October 2009, SPC Lee deployed with Team Dragon to Romania and participated in a field training exercise with Romanian Forces. On 1 March 2010, SPC Lee deployed with Team Dragon to Forward Operating Base Bullard, Zabul Province, Afghanistan in support of NATO's International Security Assistance Force.

SPC Lee's awards and decorations include the Bronze Star Medal, Purple Heart Medal, Army Commendation Medal, National Defense Service Medal, Afghanistan Campaign Medal, Global War on Terrorism Service Medal, NATO Medal, and the Combat Infantryman's Badge.

SPC Lee was a quiet professional who lived the Warrior Ethos. His peers looked up to him and followed his example. He was one of those few special people that would always put everyone ahead of themselves. SPC Lee was a superb Warrior and will be missed by everyone who knew and worked with him. He is survived by his wife Elvina, and his daughter Jazmyne.

PFC Michael S. Pridham

(Courtesy of Keri Pridham, mother)

Micheal Shane Pridham served with 1st Battalion, 4th Infantry Regiment Hohenfels, Germany, with tenacity and excellence. He died July 6th in Qalat, Afghanistan; he was just six weeks from returning home when he died from wounds he suffered when insurgents attached his vehicle with an improvised explosive device. He died while serving during Operation Enduring Freedom.

The military saved my son's life and provided him a better path then the one he was on. After he returned from basic training he was more mature and much more laid back and was focused on building a life. He was much more mature at age 19 then most grown men I know.

ACKNOWLEDGEMENTS

I wish to offer a personal debt of gratitude to the following individuals for supporting this project. Your support made all of this possible.

*****SUPPORTERS
Clayton Blackwell
Mark Mount
Sidney (Sid) Tambunga
Stephen Hamilton
Steven Price

****SUPPORTERS
Adam Mancini
Alexander Moeckler
Barbara Arizmendez
Boyd Johansen
Cassidy Dauby
Dave Starnes
David Kuhn
Eric London
Gampiero Scattalon
Jason Cunningham
John Slander
Jose Lambarena
Lee Turner-Douglas
Phillip Myers
Robert Mueller
Scott Frederiksen
Tim Albin
Timothy Ostrand

***SUPPORTERS
Christopher Shane
Gary Dauby
Jackie and Tom Tellefsen
Joshua Beetle
Kyle Aldrich
Nicholas Bye-Carnes
Robbie Langdon
Tim Murphy

**SUPPORTERS
Andrea Strausbaugh
Bryan Hammond
David Schwartz
Dennis Davis
Jeffery Trammell
Nancy and Mike Aldrich
Tom Ambrosetti
Tyler Hollingshead
William Savage
Yev Meister

*SUPPORTERS
Heather Madell
Jesse Roos
Max Copello

CLOSING THOUGHTS

After nearly two years of work, this book project has come to a "finish". However, for some, this is just the beginning of being able to share their experiences with audiences that may not have known about the effects of war on those involved. I want to once again express my extreme gratitude for the patience, understanding, and willingness of all those who helped contribute to and support this book project. What started out as a simple recommendation for just another book blossomed into a project that I will hold near and dear to me for years to come.

While I have made every effort to provide a voice to those who needed it, some parts of this book require censorship in order to protect information and individuals. For instance, we still have interpreters who live in Afghanistan and the protection of their lives is a paramount concern. I've attempted to use editing only to increase readability and understanding. My desire throughout this project has been to keep the individual voices of the contributors as authentic as possible.

And finally, this project opened my eyes and ears to a generation of heroes that hopefully the world will come to know and be proud of. To borrow again from literature, I believe that Shakespeare surmises my thoughts most accurately:

From this day to the ending of the world,
But we in it shall be remembered—
We few, we happy few, we band of brothers;
For he to-day that sheds his blood with me
Shall be my brother

(Excerpt from Shakespeare's play *Henry V*)

It has been an honor and a privilege from battlefield to book to serve alongside some of the greatest men I will ever know. To their families, take pride in their actions. To the Afghan people, perhaps one day we will be able to meet again on simpler and safer terms. To the reader, I hope that I have enlightened your understanding of the realities of war.

PERSONAL PROFILE

Steven London is a retired United States Army veteran and Purple Heart recipient. Following nearly ten years of military service and multiple overseas deployments with 1st Battalion, 4th Infantry Regiment, he returned to academia as both a student and an instructor. He remains actively passionate in his engagement of International Relations and Diplomacy. He enjoys writing, traveling, and philosophy. He currently resides in a cozy mountain city with his fiancée, Viktoria and their two parakeets.

Connect with Steven
Twitter: @Steven_L_London
Instagram: the_journeys_end_
Facebook: Steven London
Email: stevenlondon1@hotmail.com

Thank you for taking the time to read this book. Taking a moment to add an honest review on Amazon or other online sites will help shape future projects and provide valuable feedback.

Made in the USA
Middletown, DE
10 April 2019